3rd International Conference on Intelligent Computing and Cognitive Informatics (ICICCI 2018)

ITM Web of Conferences Volume 25 (2019)

Mexico City, Mexico
19-21 December 2018

Editors:

Garry Lee

ISBN: 978-1-5108-8066-5

Printed from e-media with permission by:

Curran Associates, Inc.
57 Morehouse Lane
Red Hook, NY 12571

Some format issues inherent in the e-media version may also appear in this print version.

No changes have been made to the content of these proceedings. There may be changes to pagination and minor adjustments for aesthetics.

Printed with permission by Curran Associates, Inc. (2020)

For additional information, please contact EDP Sciences – Web of Conferences at the address below.

EDP Sciences – Web of Conferences
17, Avenue du Hoggar
Parc d'Activité de Courtabœuf
BP 112
F-91944 Les Ulis Cedex A
France

Phone: +33 (0) 1 69 18 75 75
Fax: +33 (0) 1 69 28 84 91

contact-edps@webofconferences.org

Additional copies of this publication are available from:

Curran Associates, Inc.
57 Morehouse Lane
Red Hook, NY 12571 USA
Phone: 845-758-0400
Fax: 845-758-2633
Email: curran@proceedings.com
Web: www.proceedings.com

TABLE OF CONTENTS

Preface

2018 3rd International Conference on Intelligent Computing and Cognitive Informatics (ICICCI 2018) will be held on December 19-21, 2018, Mexico City, Mexico. ICICCI 2018 is co-sponsored by Information Engineering Research Institute, USA and Singapore Management and Sports Science Institute, Singapore. ICICCI 2018 is also technically co-sponsored by University of Otago, New Zealand, University of Birmingham, UK, and Technical University of Berlin, Germany.

The purpose of ICICCI 2018 is to bring together the researchers from academia and industry as well as practitioners to share ideas, problems and solutions relating to the multifaceted aspects of Intelligent Computing and Cognitive Informatics.

ICICCI 2018 received 114 submissions. All full paper submissions were peer reviewed and evaluated based on originality, technical and research content depth, correctness, relevance to conference, contributions, and readability. Submissions were chosen based on technical merit, interest, applicability, and how well they fitted a coherent and balanced technical program. Finally, only 39 best papers were selected as regular papers with the acceptance rate at about 34.2%. iThenticate Software was also used for plagiarism detection to ensure the originality of ICICCI 2018 proceedings.

All accepted papers of ICICCI 2018 will be published by ITM Web of Conferences (ISSN: 2271-2097). ICICCI 2018 covered the topics as follows:
1) Intelligent Computing;
2) Information Systems;
3) Data Analysis and Application;
4) Computer Aided Instruction.

Finally, we would like to express our sincere thanks to all staff without whose help we can't carry out the important steps during the process of conference preparation. In addition, thanks for your support and participation.

Sincerely

ICICCI 2018International Organizing Committee

Statement of Peer review

In submitting conference proceedings to *Web of Conferences*, the editors of the proceedings certify to the Publisher that

1. They adhere to its **Policy on Publishing Integrity** in order to safeguard good scientific practice in publishing.
2. All articles have been subjected to peer review administered by the proceedings editors.
3. Reviews have been conducted by expert referees, who have been requested to provide unbiased and constructive comments aimed, whenever possible, at improving the work.
4. Proceedings editors have taken all reasonable steps to ensure the quality of the materials they publish and their decision to accept or reject a paper for publication has been based only on the merits of the work and the relevance to the journal.

Title, date and place of the conference

2018 3rd International Conference on Intelligent Computing and Cognitive Informatics (ICICCI 2018)
December 19-21, 2018, Mexico City, Mexico

Proceedings editor(s):

Garry Lee, Information Engineering Research Institute, USA

Date and editor's signature 2019. 01. 02

Research on Network Drop Truck Scheduling Based on Dijkstra Algorithm

Yang Li[1], Luhua Zhao[1,a], Entong Wang[1]

[1]*Shandong University of Science and Technology, Qingdao, 266590*

Abstract. In view of the important link of vehicle dispatching under the network-type trailer-drop transport strategy of vehicle sharing, this paper uses JAVA to implement the Dijkstra algorithm for the transportation route based on the distance between stations and the demand of freight transportation, so as to find the shortest path, and then through the model of trailer-drop transport, an example is given. The advantages of this vehicle scheduling are analyzed.

1 Introduction

As an advanced organizational mode of hung-and-drop transport, the innovation of its organizational mode is very important. The original "one line, two points" and "circulation mode" can not meet the requirements of today's "smart logistics". In order to pursue higher economic benefits, achieve more efficient hung-and-drop transport mode, network-type hung-and-drop transport mode. As the times require, it is the product of the development of the hang-and-drop transport to a certain stage. On the basis of "one line, two points", it gradually expands the circular hang-and-drop and develops to the network type of hang-and-drop transport mode. Network drop off is a nationwide joint operation cooperation mode.

First of all, it is necessary to divide the distribution tasks of a single yard, integrate the transport functions of different enterprises, and integrate all kinds of logistics resources (including vehicles, personnel, warehousing, etc.), so that the transportation network can realize the saving, high efficiency, rationalization of distribution, and improve the utilization rate of vehicles. Combined with the different characteristics of duty stations, the distribution cluster is formed to simplify the complex distribution problem. In order to realize the reasonable dispatching of goods and the allocation of stations and yards, and to meet the needs of informationization, GPS dispatching management system should be adopted, combined with GPS distribution orders, tractors and trailers should be rationally arranged, and the best driving route should be calculated by Dijkstra algorithm to make a good dispatching plan.

2 Network type drop and pull transport model

2.1 Problem analysis

From the development experience of foreign countries and the current situation in China, the drop-and-hang transport is not the innovation of single enterprise transport mode, but the transformation of the whole industry transport mode. The transport forms, advantages and disadvantages of different drop-and-hang transport modes are different, and their applicable fields are also different. In the process of the development of hung-and-drop transport, we need to pay attention to the inter-regional cooperation between different enterprises, from the single line operation within the enterprise to the inter-regional circulation operation mode and then to the inter-regional network operation, the road freight transport industry in China is constantly innovating the new organization mode of hung-and-drop transport, giving play to different types of hung-and-drop transport. The advantages of transportation mode and its combination characteristics form a new mode of network drop and pull transport. The network-type hung-and-drop transport mode integrates special lines, establishes different station centers according to the distribution of lines and goods, realizes intensive allocation of freight sources of special lines in the same direction, realizes hung-and-drop operation of different stations and lines in the network, makes full use of the economic benefits of the network and reduces the overall transportation cost. On the other hand, the network-type hang-and-drop transport mode needs to strengthen communication with Shipper enterprises, from a single temporary employment relationship to a long-term cooperative partnership, to ensure stable hang-and-drop operation, adequate supply of goods, and through efficient organization to improve the quality of service. This mode is consistent with the requirements of drop and hang transport mode, and is an important manifestation of logistics network. Through the

[a] Corresponding author: Luhua Zhao, Email: luhuazhao@163.com

intensive arrangement in each yard, the tractor can be dispatched reasonably according to the need in the operation network besides ensuring a stable supply of goods. There are many yards in the network-type trailer-and-drop transportation. The tractor trailer operates between the nodes. If necessary, the branch line can cooperate with the small truck to transport, so as to reduce the logistics cost as much as possible and improve the transport efficiency.

The common layout of network-type hang-and-drop transport mode is that there are S distribution centers in a certain place, and each distribution center area forms a distribution area. Set up S distribution center with K tractors, each tractor maximum load, distribution center I to j transport distance.

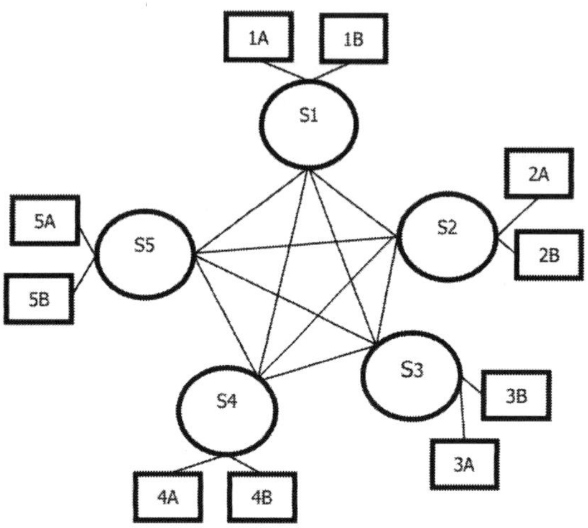

Figure 1. Network-type hang-and-drop transport diagram

The network transportation scheduling problem can be described as starting from several distribution centers and using multiple tractors to send goods to other distribution centers. It is assumed that the location of each distribution center and the quantity of goods required by customers are predetermined, the number of tractors in the distribution center and the number of tractors in each distribution center are determined. The number of trailers can meet the maximum demand for freight transportation. The goal is to make the total cost smaller and larger. The total cost here consists mainly of the following two parts: (1) Travel cost, which is related to the distance of transportation and the fuel consumption per unit distance. (2) Fixed costs, mainly including vehicle depreciation fee, insurance fee, annual inspection fee, vehicle maintenance fee, artificial salary and so on.

2.2 Basic assumptions

1. Distribution centers have sufficient supply of goods, regardless of the transfer of goods or other supplementary supply between the distribution centers.

2. The number of trailers reserved by the distribution center is sufficient, and the transportation cost is only related to the transportation distance, without considering other specific transportation details.

3. Does not consider the storage cost of goods in distribution centers.

4. Each trailer is loaded with cargo and will not be empty, not full load.

5. The capacity of each yard can meet the demand of freight forwarding and temporary storage, and charge a fixed management fee.

2.3 Variables and symbols

Q_a: Fuel consumption per 100 km

d_{ij}: The distance between task nodes i and j

C_2: Unit Trailer price of truck trailers

W_a: Tractor loading condition

q_k: The load of the k tractor

Q_{ij}: Yard i transport to station j freight volume

2.4 Establishment of models

1. According to the mode of transportation, the target value of the model is considered as two parts: the least cost and the maximum benefit.

It has been assumed that the running cost of the trailer is only related to the driving distance and fuel consumption of the K vehicle. It is easy to write down the running cost of a trailer for transporting goods at one time without considering the non-full load state of the trailer $\sum_{s=0}^{a}\sum_{i=0}^{i}\sum_{j=1}^{j}\sum_{k=1}^{k} Q_a d_{ij} x_{sk}(i,j)$, that is, the K tractor of Distribution S will be the cost of travelling from i trailers to j. And in the actual transportation process, not only the driving cost, but also the vehicle depreciation fee, toll, labor wages, maintenance costs, management costs and so on, these fixed costs are analyzed, Then select the appropriate coefficient C1 to express comprehensively, $\sum_{k=1}^{k}\sum_{i=0}^{i}\sum_{j=1}^{j} C_1 x_k(i,j)$, The K vehicle runs from task node i to task node j. In summary, the model with the lowest cost is $\sum_{a=0}^{a}\sum_{i=0}^{i}\sum_{j=1}^{j}\sum_{k=1}^{k} Q_a d_{ij} x_{sk}(i,j) + \sum_{k=1}^{k}\sum_{i=0}^{i}\sum_{j=1}^{j} C_1 x_k(i,j)$.

2. In the process of trailer-drop transportation dispatching, there are certain constraints for distribution centers and trailer-drop vehicles. The number of tractors from all stations does not exceed the total number of tractors reserved in the station yard $\sum_{s=1}^{s}\sum_{k=1}^{k}\sum_{j=1}^{j} x_{sk}(0,j) \le k$, the number of tractors from all stations does not exceed the total number of tractors reserved in the station yard $W_a \le C_w$, tractor trailer capacity limitation $\sum_{s=1}^{s}\sum_{k=1}^{k} q_k x_{sk}(i,j) = Q_{ij}$

The sum of all tractor loads traveling from any station to complete a task equals the total freight demand for the task.

3. Design of network drop and pull transport

algorithm

$$r_1\sum_{i\in V}\sum_{j\in V}\sum_{k\in K}C_{ij}X_{ijk}+r_2\sum_{i\in V}\sum_{j\in V}\sum_{k\in K}r_2c_{ij}x_{ijk}+\sum_{j\in V}F_jz_j+P(t_{ik})$$

r_1 : Loading cost coefficient

Tractor fuel consumption on Trailer laden semitrailer on Section (i,j)

r_2 : Empty car running coefficient

Fuel consumption of tractor when traveling alone on Road (i,j)

$X_{ijk}=1, x_{ijk}=0$: Tractor k Trailer laden semitraile r driving

$X_{ijk}=0, x_{ijk}=1$: Tractor k no load driving

F_j : Fixed costs of j freight stations

$z_j = 1$ (Freight station selected);

0(Other)

4. The penalty cost of tractor k arriving at the starting point of i.

$P(t_{ik})=a(s_1-t_{ik}), t_{ik}<s_1$; Waiting cost

$0,\ s_1\le t_{ik}\le s_2$;

$b(t_{ik}-s_2), t_{ik}>s_2$ Late cost

3 Design of network drop and pull transport algorithm

1. According to the model of network-type hung-and-drop transportation, the cost is closely related to the transportation distance in the process of hung-and-drop dispatching, so the shortest route should be chosen as far as possible, and then the lowest cost of hung-and-drop transportation should be considered comprehensively to adjust, which becomes the shortest path problem. The shortest path problem is usually abstracted as a network problem in the sense of graph theory. The core of the problem becomes the shortest path problem in network graph (the implementation of fast Dijkstra shortest path optimization algorithm). According to the freight demand of each service point, it is connected into a directed graph, and then the information of the graph is stored by matrix.

2. Algorithm steps:

Step 1: initialize, update the freight demand of each service point and the number of trailers and tractors.

Step 2: Connect the service points into a directed graph in matrix form, and the distance between the service points is the transportation distance.

Step 3: mark the v[0], vis[0] = 1 (VIS initialize 0 at the beginning);

Step 4: Find the nearest point v [k] adjacent to V [0], record the V [k] point, and mark the distance between V [k] and V [0] as min.

Step 5: mark v[k], vis[k]=1;

Step 6: Compare dis [j] with min + W [k] [j] to determine whether the direct V [0] connection V [j] is shorter or the connection V [j] through V [k] is shorter, that is, dis [j] = MIN (dis [j], min + W [k] [j]);

Step 7: continue to repeat steps three and five.

The JAVA implementation code is as follows:

```
public class Dijkstra {
static int MAX=10000;
public static void main(String[] args) {
  String l=null;
  Conutil con=new Conutil();
   l=con.getConnection();
  System.out.println(l);
  int[][] weight = {
      {0,210,80,45,90,170,220,65,120,135},
      {210,0,135,155,200,75,90,55,270,50},
      {80,135,0,85,110,40,200,280,95,115},
      {45,155,85,0,240,270,70,120,75,100},
      {90,200,110,240,0,130,50,85,30,95},
      {170,75,40,270,130,0,110,90,100,180},
      {220,90,200,70,50,110,0,40,45,100},
      {65,55,280,120,85,90,40,0,160,200},
      {120,270,95,75,30,100,45,160,0,70},
      {135,50,115,100,95,180,100,200,70,0}
  };
  int start=0;
  int[] shortPath = Dijsktra(weight,start);
  for(int i = 0;i < shortPath.length;i++)
  {
    System.out.println("The shortest distance from"+start+"to"+i+"is:"+shortPath[i]);
  }
}
public static int[] Dijsktra(int[][] weight,int start){

  int n = weight.length;
  int[] shortPath = new int[n];
     String[] path=new String[n];
  for(int i=0;i<n;i++)
  {
    path[i] = start + "-->" + i;
      }
     int[] visited = new int[n];
  shortPath[start] = 0;
  visited[start] = 1;
  for(int count = 1;count <= n - 1;count++)
  {
    int k = -1;
    int dmin = Integer.MAX_VALUE;
    for(int i = 0;i < n;i++)
    {
      if(visited[i] == 0 && weight[start][i] < dmin)
      {
        dmin = weight[start][i];
        k = i;
      }
    }
    shortPath[k] = dmin;
    visited[k] = 1;
    for(int i = 0;i < n;i++)
    {
      if(visited[i] == 0 && weight[start][k] + weight[k][i] < weight[start][i])
      {
        weight[start][i] = weight[start][k] + weight[k][i];
        path[i]=path[k]+"-->"+i;
      }
    }
```

```
    }
    for(int i=0;i<n;i++)
    {
      System.out.println("The shortest path from"+start+"to"+i+"is:"+path[i]);
    }
System.out.println("=========================================");
    return shortPath;
  }
}
```

4 Example analysis

To simplify the calculation, it is assumed that the management cost of the station is the same; the transport speed of the trailer is 60 km/h; the cost of the tractor is 0.8 yuan/km with a load and 0.45 yuan/km with no load; the driver's salary is determined by the working time and the environment; and the maximum working time is 24 hours per day, the traditional transport party will be provided. The formula is calculated with Dijkstra algorithm and the result is compared.

Table 1. Distance between stations in network transportation (unit: km)

	0	2	3	4	5	6	7	8	9
0	0	80	45	90	170	220	65	120	135
1	210	135	155	200	75	90	55	270	50
2	80	0	85	110	40	200	280	95	115
3	45	85	0	240	270	70	120	75	100
4	90	110	240	0	130	50	85	30	95
5	170	40	270	130	0	110	90	100	180
6	220	200	70	50	110	0	40	45	100
7	65	280	120	85	90	40	0	160	200
8	120	95	75	30	100	45	160	0	70
9	135	115	100	95	180	100	200	70	0

The above table describes the distances between the stations. For example, the second row in the first column indicates that the distance between the No. 1 and No. 0 stations is 210 km, and the distance between the station and the station itself is 0.

The demand for goods between each station is shown in the following table:

Table 2. Transport demand between stations (unit: Trailer)

	0	1	2	3	4	5	6	7	8	9
0	0	2	0	0	0	0	0	0	0	0
1	0	0	0	1	0	0	0	0	0	0
2	0	0	0	1	0	0	0	0	0	0
3	0	0	2	0	0	0	0	0	0	0
4	0	0	0	0	0	0	3	0	0	0
5	0	0	0	0	0	0	2	0	0	0
6	0	0	0	0	0	0	0	0	4	0
7	0	0	1	0	0	0	0	0	0	0
8	0	0	0	0	0	0	0	0	0	0
9	0	0	0	0	0	0	0	0	1	0

The above table forms a transport demand relationship table according to the demand for goods between stations. For example, the fourth row in the second column indicates that two trailers need to be transported from station 1 to station 2.

Traditional path of hanging and hanging transportation:

$0 \longrightarrow 1 \longrightarrow 3 \longrightarrow 2$

$7 \longrightarrow 2$

$4 \longrightarrow 6$

$5 \longrightarrow 6 \longrightarrow 8$

$9 \longrightarrow 8$

The Dijkstra algorithm is calculated by JAVA, and the best transport path is obtained, as shown in the following figure.

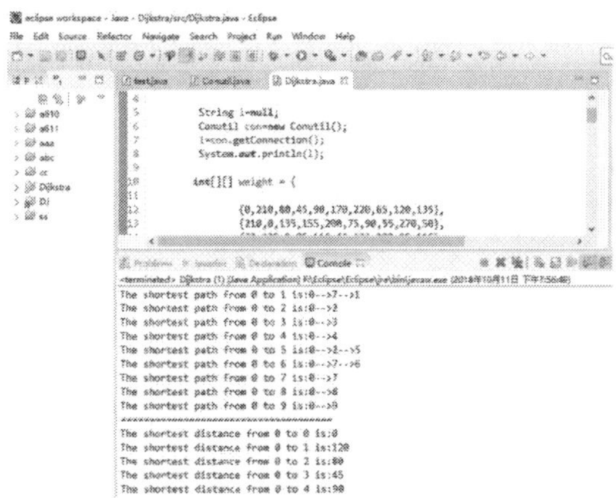

Figure 2. Dijkstra algorithm

Dijkstra algorithm is used to adjust the transport path to:

The shortest path from 0 to 1 is 0-->7-->1, and the shortest distance is 120.

The shortest path from 1 to 3 is 1-->9-->3, and the shortest distance is 150.

The shortest path from 3 to 2 is 3-->2, and the shortest distance is 85.

The shortest path from 7 to 2 is 7-->5-->2, and the shortest distance is 130.

The shortest path from 4 to 6 is 4-->6, and the shortest distance is 50.

The shortest path from 5 to 6 is 5-->6, and the shortest distance is 110.

The shortest path from 6 to 8 is 6-->8, and the shortest distance is 45.

The shortest path from 9 to 8 is 9-->8, and the shortest distance is 70.

0——→7——→1——→9——→3——→2

7——→5——→2

4——→6

5——→6——→8

9——→8

Table 2. Comparison of results

	Stroke (load)	Journey (no load)	Total travel	Cost
Traditional hanging transport	1005km	100km	1050km	1149
Dijkstra algorithm for drop and pull transport	760km	100km	860km	953

5 Conclusion

As an efficient transportation mode, the drop-and-drop transportation has been widely used at home and abroad. Using Dijkstra to study the vehicle scheduling problem can better reduce the logistics cost, promote energy conservation and emission reduction, and improve economic efficiency. In this paper, a preliminary study on the network-type trailer-and-drop transport mode is carried out, and it is necessary to continue to study the multi-trailer and dynamic situation of a vehicle.

Fund projects

Shandong University of Science and Technology Teaching Top Talent Project (BJRC20170505).

References

1. Li Xinya, Liu Yao. Dropping and Hanging Transport Model and Its Standardization [J]. Logistics Engineering and Management, 2018, 40(08): 88-90.
2. Xiao Liekun, Li Gonglili, He Jiao, Jiang Jiamin, Xu Qingqing. Sichuan Province Throw Transport Alliance Network Layout Problem and Optimization Strategy [J]. Management observation, 2018(18) :33 -34 +43.
3. Huang Yong, Yi Yongsong, Qiu Qi. Optimization of container tractor scheduling under circular throwing transportation network[J]. Journal of the East China Jiaotong University, 2018, 35(03): 62-68.
4. Miao Xindeng. S Company's implementation plan design and benefit evaluation of the Bohai Bay throwing transportation [D]. Shandong University, 2018.
5. Liangshibin, Hu Jingfu. Optimization analysis of transportation organization based on the lowest cost [J]. Inner Mongolia Highway and Transport, 2018 (04): 53-56.
6. Sheng Yukui, Xiong Binhui. On hanging transport organization model [J]. Highway and motor transport, 2018(01): 57-59.
7. Liu Xudong, Liu Xiaorong, Xie Tai, Liu Wenbao. Jiyudijiesitela's algorithm for the search and rescue route optimization software design and implementation [J]. Medical and health equipment, 2016, 37(04): 9-12.
8. Pu Zaiyi, Ren Jianjun. Dijiesite algorithm for realizing the single-source shortest path problem using the tag method [J]. Journal of Sichuan Normal University (Natural Science Edition), 2003(01): 122-126 + 131.

Research of the Channel Estimation in Wireless Communication Systems

Lili Zhao[a], Peng Zhang, Qicai Dong, Xiangyang Huang, Jianhua Zhao and Zeyu Su

No.12 Fan Gongting south street, Shandong, China

Abstract. Wireless communication technology has been developed rapidly after entering the 21st century. Data transfer rate increased significantly as well as the bandwidth became wider and wider from 2G to 4G in wireless communication systems. Channel estimation is an import part of any communication systems; its accuracy determines the quality of the whole communication. Channel estimation methods of typical wireless communication systems such as UWB, 2G and 3G have been researched.

1 Introduction

According to the Federal Communications Commission, a signal with a relative bandwidth of more than 20% at -10dB or an absolute bandwidth exceeding 500MHz is called ultra-wideband. It is defined as follows:

Relative bandwidth:

$$B = \frac{(f_h - f_l)}{\frac{(f_h + f_l)}{2}} \times 100\% = \frac{2(f_h - f_l)}{(f_h + f_l)} \times 100\% > 20\% \quad (1)$$

Or absolute bandwidth: $B = (f_h - f_l) \geq 500MHZ$.

In the formula, f_h, f_l is the maximum limiting frequency and the minimum frequency corresponding to the power spectral density of the signal at -10dB. (fh+fl)/2 is the central frequency. In ultra-wideband applications, FCC prescribes that the band of 3.1GHZ-10.6GHZ allows access to the civilian sector. FCC also specifies UWB radiation power to avoid interference with other systems.

Ultra-wideband (UWB) systems are divided into two types: UWB based on pulse form using direct sequence spread spectrum technology, that is DS-UWB; and UWB based on traditional OFDM technology, namely MB-OFDM-UWB. MB-OFDM-UWB system is studied in this paper.

The ultra-wideband (UWB) system uses extremely short narrow-band pulses to transmit data, has high bandwidth in the frequency domain, and enables high-speed data transmission for short-range wireless communication. UWB system also has other characteristics, such as low power consumption, low power spectrum density and good ability to resist multipath interference. UWB system is widely used in many fields. It is suitable for indoor wireless communication, ranging, short-range accurate positioning and so on.

UWB systems can achieve very high transmission rates (above 100Mbps). When UWB operates in high-rate mode, its transmission distance is relatively close, generally between 10-20 meters; when operating in lower-rate mode, the transmission distance will become longer. The UWB system also has the function of locating, and the UWB in the form of pulse has strong perspective ability, and can communicate or locate through the thick walls of several layers.

2 Introduction to Compressed Sensing Technology

In a communication system, if the receiving end wants to recover the signal of the transmitting end without distortion, the receiving end must satisfy the Nyquist sampling theorem when sampling, that is, the sampling rate of the analog signal cannot be less than twice the signal bandwidth. In the past half century, the Nyquist sampling theorem has been used for the acquisition, processing, transmission, and storage of all images and signals.

The frequency of ultra bandwidth system is above GHz, according to the sampling theorem, the receiver is required to have a very high sampling rate, which will produce a huge amount of data. In order to reduce the cost of transmission or storage, only a small amount of important data can be retained. This results in a serious waste of sampling resources.

Donoho, Candes and Taoundefineds new theory of Compressed Sensing (CS) can solve this problem well. The core idea of the theory of compressed sensing: according to the sparsity of the signal, the high-dimensional signal is projected into the low-dimensional space by using a specific matrix, and the original signal is restored by a linear or nonlinear reconstruction algorithm. Simply put, if the signal is sparse (or sparse through a certain transform), then the sparse signal can be reduced

[a] Corresponding author: 147490292@qq.com

https://doi.org/10.1051/itmconf/20192501002

by an uncorrelated measurement matrix, and then the original signal is recovered by the reduced dimension data. Compressed sensing theory consists of three parts:

(1) Sparse representation of the signal: The so-called "sparse" means that the signal itself has few non-zero elements or a small value that is mostly approximately zero after the transformation, with only a small number of elements being larger.

(2) The design of the observation matrix: Find a matrix that is uncorrelated with orthogonal bases, which is capable of converting a high-dimensional signal to a low-dimensional representation, that is, a process that obtains fewer observations.

(3) Signal reconstruction algorithm: Designing high-quality reconstruction algorithms to accurately recover the original signal from fewer observations is also a key technology in compressed sensing.

3 Ultra-wideband channel estimation method

Ultra-wideband systems are limited by FCC power, resulting in a very short transmission distance (only 0 to 10 m). Most of the literature studies the ultra-wideband indoor channel model. The UWB channel model is divided into a path loss model and a multipath channel model. This paper uses a multipath channel model.

Among the many channel models, the models that can well represent the characteristics of the ultra-wideband channel are *Δ-K* model, *S-V* model and IEEE802.15.3a channel model. Among them, IEEE802.15.3a is improved on the basis of *S-V*. This channel model fits the measured data well, and it is closer to the measured value in terms of RMS extended delay and average extended delay.

The UWB channel model studied in this paper is released by the IEEE802.15.3a working group. There are four UWB channel types of CM1-CM4. The description of each channel is shown in Table 1. The research and simulation in this paper is carried out under the CM1 channel. Figure 1 shows the impulse response of the CM1 channel model.

Table 1. UWB channel parameter statistics table

Channel model	CM 1	CM 2	CM 3	CM 4
NSEC	5.05	10.38	14.18	
NSEC	5.28	8.03	14.28	20
Λ (1/nsec)	0.0233	0.4	0.0667	0.0667
λ (1/nsec)	3.75	1	3	3
r	7.1	5.2	14.93	17
γ	4.37	6.5067	7.03	12
σ (dB)	4.8	4.8	4.8	4.8
Environment	LOS (0-4m)	NLOS (0-4m)	NLOS (4-10m)	Extreme NLOS

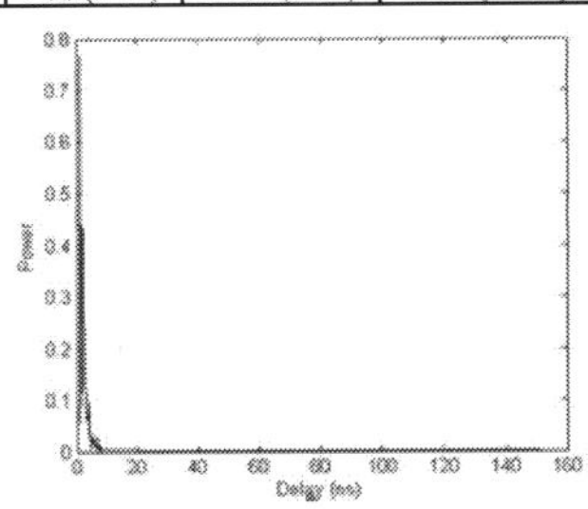

Figure 1. Channel impulse response of the CM1 channel model

3.1 Traditional UWB channel estimation method

The UWB system utilizes a training sequence known at the receiving end, according to the following formula:

$$Y = XH + Z \quad (2)$$

Figure 2 shows the baseband system model of UWB on the MATLAB platform.

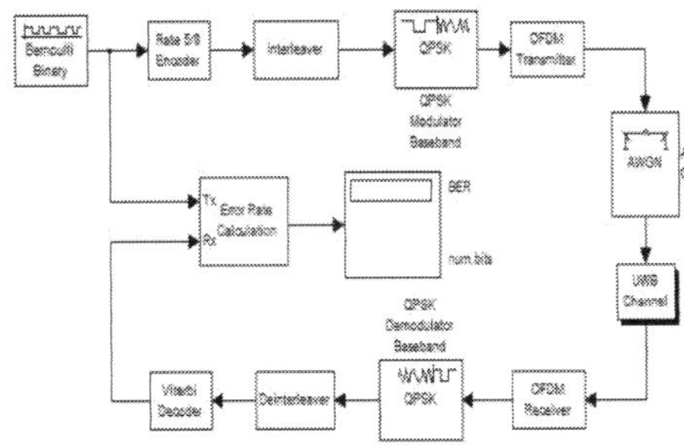

Figure 2. MATLAB platform UWB system diagram

The transmitter of the UWB system inserts six training sequences into each symbol of the OFDM for channel estimation. In frequency domain, after estimating the position of the training sequence, the average value is taken as the frequency domain response of a frame of OFDM symbols.

3.2 Application of Compressed Sensing in UWB

This method uses compressed sensing in time domain to receive the information received by the receiver:

$$r = x * h + n = Ah + n \quad (3)$$

Where h is the channel time domain impulse response and n is the noise.

$$A = \begin{bmatrix} x_0 & L & 0 \\ x_1 & O & M \\ M & O & x_0 \\ x_{N-1} & O & x_1 \end{bmatrix} \quad (4)$$

If there is an M-dimensional observation matrix, A is reduced from N to M, where M<<N:

$$y = \Phi Ah = \Theta h \quad (5)$$

If $\Theta = \Phi A$ satisfies the constrained equidistant side (RIP) and h is sparse, then compression sensing can be used to reconstruct h.

The matrix A is a Topplitz matrix, and a new matrix consisting of a number of rows spaced from the tops of the Topplitz matrix is called a quasi-topplez matrix. The form is as follows, the Topplitz matrix on the left and the quasi-topplez matrix on the right.

$$A=\begin{pmatrix} x_1 & L & & 0 \\ x_2 & x_1 & & \\ x_3 & x_2 & x_1 & \\ M & O & O & O \\ x_p & & x_3\ x_2 & x_1 \\ & x_p & & x_3\ x_2 \\ & & O & x_3 \\ & & x_p & M \\ 0 & L & & x_p \end{pmatrix} \Rightarrow \begin{pmatrix} x_1 & L & & 0 \\ x_3 & x_2 & x_1 & \\ M & M & M & M \\ x_p & & x_3\ x_2 & x_1 \\ & & & x_3 \\ 0 & & & x_p \end{pmatrix} \quad (6)$$

Reference [6] pointed out that if the elements in the topology are obeying a normal distribution with a mean of 0, then the quasi-top Pritz matrix constructed by this topology can also be used for compressed sensing.

The training sequence needs to follow a normal distribution of zero mean. Figure 4 shows the channel estimation and equalization portion of the receiver.

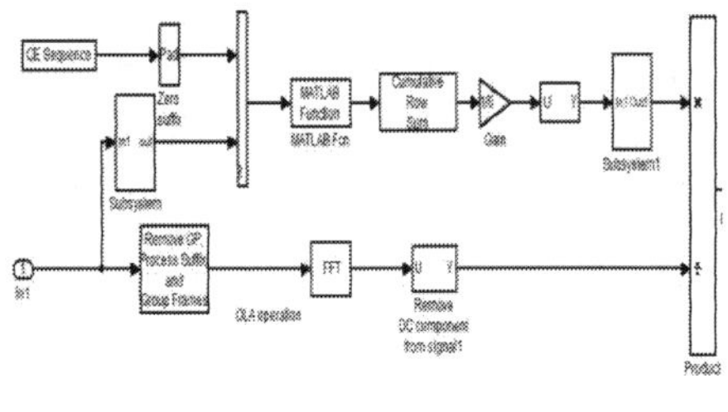

Figure 4. UWB channel estimation equalization part

The CE Sequence module in Figure 4 is a training sequence added by the sender in the time domain. The following module extracts the training sequence of the receiver. The Matlab Function module is an OMP reconstruction algorithm in which channel estimation is performed. The latter module averages the channel estimates and then equalizes the received signals. Figure 5 shows the curve of BER changing with signal-to-noise ratio (SNR) obtained by simulation. It can be seen from the simulation diagram that the BER of the system decreases gradually with the increase of signal-to-noise ratio (SNR). When the BER of SNR= 6 reaches 10 ~ (-6), it shows that this method can estimate the impulse response of the channel well.

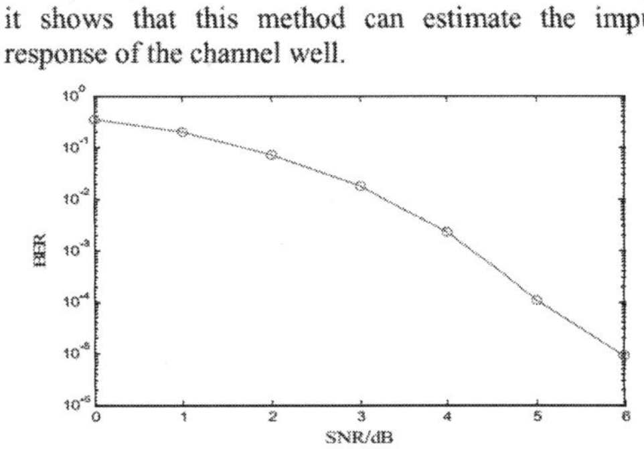

Figure 5. Bit Error Rate Graph

Figure 6 is a contrast diagram of the reconstructed channel and the original channel at snr=6. As can be seen from this graph, the reconstructed channel is very close to the original channel, which also shows that the method can estimate the impact response of the channel Well.

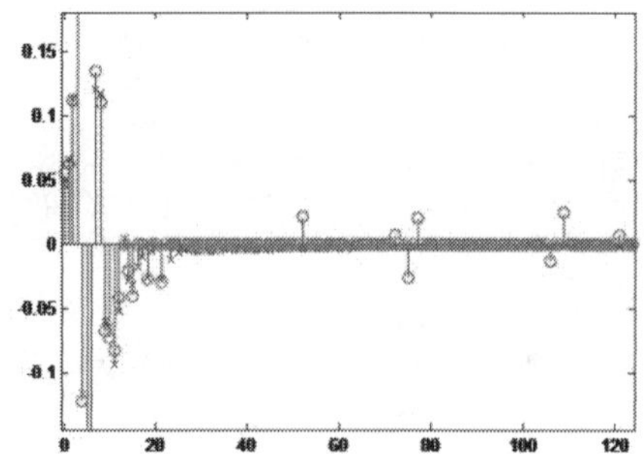

Figure 6. Comparison of reconstructed channel and original channel

It can be seen from the simulation diagram that the method of compressive sensing in the time domain can well estimate the frequency domain response of the channel.

4 Conclusion

This paper introduces the application of the theory of compression perception in Ultra-wideband channel estimation, is a time domain using known training sequence, Time-domain Channel estimation method in the time domain, need to add to the transmitter to meet the known conditions of the training sequence. Because the time domain method needs to join the known training sequence, it needs to change the system structure, and the system has been stipulated in the standard, the disadvantage of this method is to add a training sequence which conforms to the known condition in the time domain, and the implementation is more Complicated. In the future study, we try to use 6 training sequence symbols in the frequency domain for channel Estimation.

References

1. Yang L, Giannakis G B. Ultra-wideband communications: an idea whose time has come [J]. Signal Processing Magazine, IEEE, 2004, 21(6): 26-54.
2. Donoho D L. Compressed sensing [J]. Information Theory, IEEE Transactions on, 2006, 52(4): 1289-1306.
3. Bajwa W U, Haupt J, Sayeed A M, et al. Compressed channel sensing: A new approach to estimating sparse multipath channels [J]. Proceedings of the IEEE, 2010, 98(6): 1058-1076.
4. Tropp J A, Gilbert A C. Signal recovery from random measurements via orthogonal matching pursuit [J]. Information Theory, IEEE Transactions on, 2007, 53(12): 4655-4666.
5. Molisch A F, Balakrishnan K, Chong C C, et al. IEEE 802.15. 4a channel model-final report [J]. IEEE P802, 2004, 15(04): 0662.
6. Li Shutao, Weidan. A review of compression sensing [J]. Journal of automation, 2009, 35 (11): 1369-1377.

Analysing Big Social Graphs Using a List-based Graph Folding Algorithm

Eugenia Muntyan[1], Nikolay Sergeev[1], and Alexey Tselykh[2,a]

[1]*Southern Federal University, Department of Computer Engineering, Taganrog, Russia*
[2]*Southern Federal University, Department of Information Security Systems, Taganrog, Russia*

Abstract. In this paper, we explore the ways to represent big social graphs using adjacency lists and edge lists. Furthermore, we describe a list-based algorithm for graph folding that makes possible to analyze conditionally infinite social graphs on resource constrained mobile devices. The steps of the algorithm are (a) to partition, in a certain way, the graph into clusters of different levels, (b) to represent each cluster of the graph as an edge list, and (c) to absorb the current cluster by the cluster of the next level. The proposed algorithm is illustrated by the example of a sparse social graph.

1 Introduction

Currently, there is a growing interest in modeling and analyzing interrelationships between professional, religious, ethnic, and other types of social groups [1-4]. The knowledge underlying these models comprises both the knowledge of personality psychology and social psychology of interpersonal relationships as well as anthropology, sociology, theology, ethnography, conflict theory, and history.

The basic unit of modeling here is either an actor (human person or group) or, in Actor-Network Theory (ANT) [5], an output of actor's activity – a material artefact. Both are collectively called actants.

In terms of graph-hypergraph paradigm [6], an entity (actor or actant) can be represented by a vertex in a graph or by a hyperedge in a hypergraph. In second case, a set of vertices forming a hyperedge can be associated with certain characteristics of an entity: situation awareness, evaluation of event, communication or individual activities.

The two most common representations of a social graph are an adjacency matrix (sociomatrix) and an incidence matrix [7]. Both are memory-intensive, especially for sparse high-dimensional graphs, when most of the elements of the matrix have 0 value.

In this paper, we use a list data structure [8, 9] to represent and analyze sparse social graphs. Furthermore, we describe a list-based algorithm for graph folding that eventually makes possible to analyze conditionally infinite social graphs on resource constrained mobile devices.

Using a list data structure to analyze social graphs was previously considered in [10-13].

2 Research methodology

2.1 List representations of a graph

There are two ways to represent a graph as a list. Adjacency list describes the set of neighbors of a vertex in the graph; its main data structure is an array of linked lists, one linked list for each vertex. Edge list is a list of node pairs (edges).

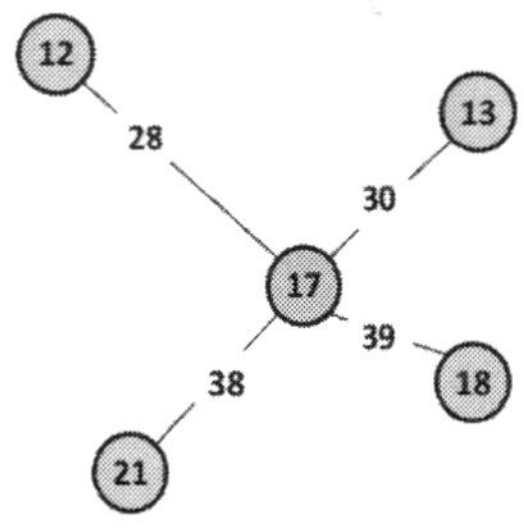

Figure 1. Undirected graph

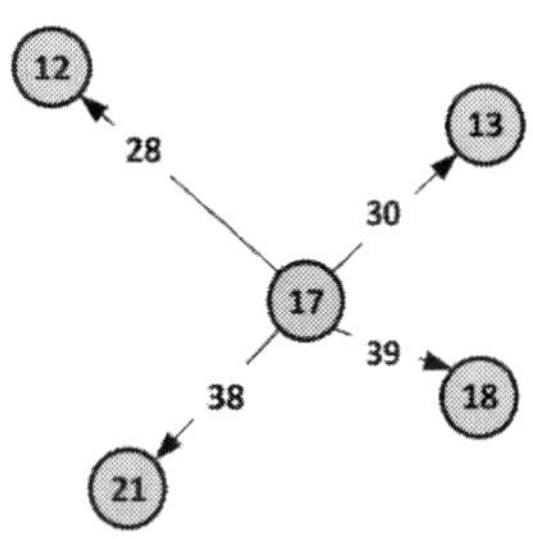

Figure 2. Directed graph

---

[a] Corresponding author: tselykh@sfedu.ru

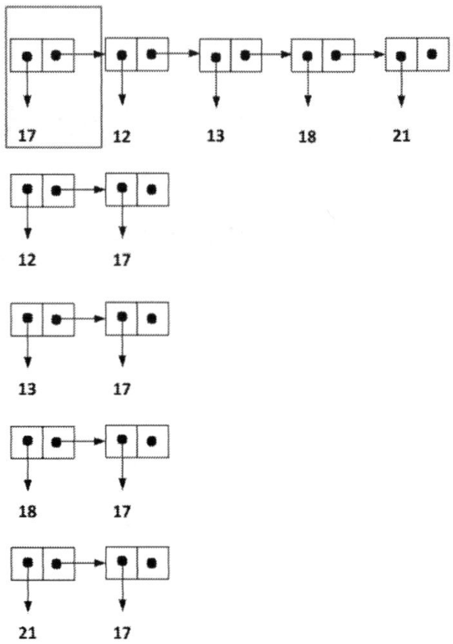

Figure 3. Adjacency list

As an example, consider an undirected graph G_U in Fig. 1 and an appropriate directed graph G_D in Fig. 2.

The adjacency list of a graph is an *n*-element array of linked lists, one for each vertex, where the i_{th} element points to a linked list of edges for vertex *i*. This linked list represents the edges by the vertices adjacent to vertex *i*. Every element (node) of the list consists of two fields. The left field is a pointer to the vertex index, e.g. 17, while the right field is a pointer to the next node as shown in Fig 3.

Adjacency list of the graph G_U is X_c = (17, 12, 13, 18, 21), (12, 17), (13, 17), (18, 17), (21, 17) as shown in Fig. 3.

Adjacency list for an appropriate directed graph G_D is X_c = (17, 12, 13, 18, 21).

The edge list of the graph is a list, or array, of edges. When representing undirected graph with an edge list, all the edges are repeated in reverse order.

Edge list for graph in Fig. 1 is X_p = (17, 12), (17, 13), (17, 18), (17, 21), (12, 17), (13, 17), (18, 17), (21, 17) as shown in Fig. 4. In the above example, the graph has 4 edges, so the edge list consists of 8 pairs.

Edge list for an appropriate directed graph in Fig. 2 is X_p = (17, 12), (17, 13), (17, 18), (17, 21). Graphical representation of X_p corresponds to the left part of the edge list in Fig. 4.

2.2 Operations on the lists

In this section, we consider split and join operations on the lists. Appropriate functions were described in [8].

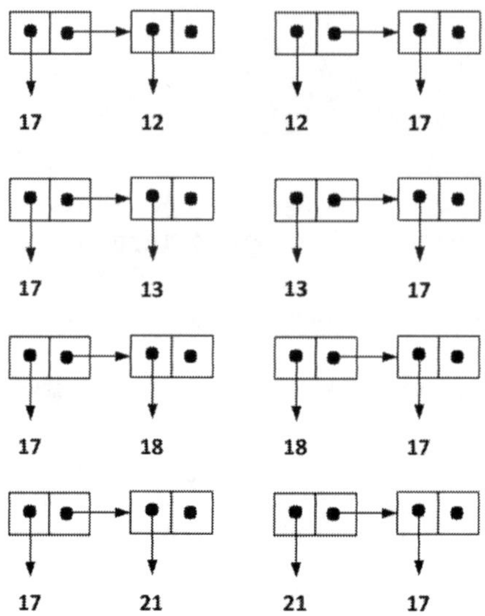

Figure 4. Edge list

To split the list, we use functions *hd* (*x*) and *tl* (*x*). These functions get the head (the first element) and tail (all but the first element) of a list, respectively.

Given the list *x* = (17, 12, 13, 18, 21), the following values are returned: *hd* (*x*) = (17) and *tl* (*x*) = (12, 13, 18, 21). If we take *tl* (*x*) as a new list x_1 = (12, 13, 18, 21), then *hd* (x_1) = (12), and *tl* (x_1) = (13, 18, 21). Similarly, we construct lists x_2 and x_3. Summarizing the example, list *x* can be represented as follows:

hd (*x*), *hd* (*tl* (*x*)), *hd* (*tl* (*tl* (*x*))), *hd* (*tl* (*tl* (*tl* (*x*)))), …

To join lists, we use function *cons*. Given *a* – an element or a list and *b* – a list, the function *cons* (*a, b*) is a new node in the list.

In our case, if *a* = 17 and *b* = (12, 13, 18, 21), then the following value is returned: *cons* (*a, b*) = (17, 12, 13, 18, 21).

List $z = (z_1, z_2, z_3, z_4, \ldots, z_n)$ is constructed using a formula

cons (z_1, *cons* (z_2, *cons* (z_3, *cons* (z_4, …, *cons* (z_n) …)))).

We can make a conclusion that operators *hd (x)* and *tl (x)* are inversely related to *cons*: *hd* (*cons* (*a, b*)) = *a*, *tl* (*cons* (*a, b*)) = *b*. The reverse rule is not always true. *cons* (*hd* (*x*), *tl* (*x*)) returns a new element, that contains the same pointers as the source element *x*. Function *cons* (*hd* (*x*), *tl* (*x*)) returns a copy of the cell *x*, but not the cell *x* itself.

The concept of a doubly linked list is given in [9]. It can be conceptualized as two singly linked lists formed from the same data items, but in opposite sequential orders. Each node of a doubly linked list contains three fields: an integer value (*key*), the link to the next node (*next*), and the link to the previous node (*prev*) as shown in Fig. 5.

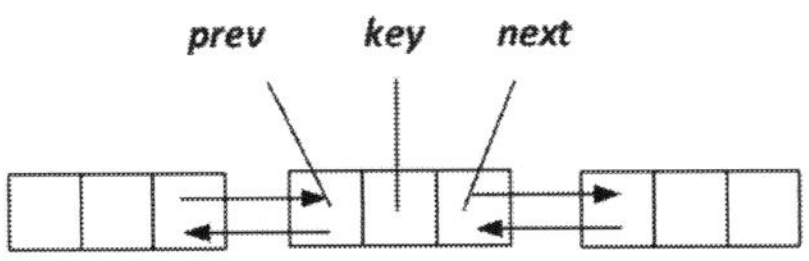

Figure 5. The structure of an element of a doubly linked list

Consider a doubly linked list $x = (x_1, x_2, x_3, x_4, \ldots, x_n)$. Given a node x_i, *next* (x_i) refers to the next node, and *prev* (x_i) refers to the previous node. If *prev* (x_i) = NIL, then x_i is the entry point called the head of the list *hd* (x). If *next* (x_i) = NIL, then x_i is the last node in the list called the tail of the list *tl* (x).

There are 2-element and 5-element lists among the adjacency lists considered earlier. The 5-element list x = (17, 12, 13, 18, 21) implies that we can get from node 17 to nodes 12, 13, 18 and 21. Meanwhile, there's no other way to get from node 12 to node 13, but through the node 17.

Eventually we end up with the edge lists discussed earlier. From this we can conclude that it is reasonable to represent graphs as lists of edges.

3 Graph folding algorithm

Let G_1 and G_2 be graphs and f: $G_1 \rightarrow G_2$ be a continuous function. Then f is called a graph map, if

(i) For each vertex $v \in V(G_1)$, $f(v)$ is a vertex in $V(G_2)$.

(ii) For each edge $e \in E(G_1)$, $\dim(f(e)) \leqslant \dim(e)$.

A graph map f: $G_1 \rightarrow G_2$ is called a graph folding if f maps vertices to vertices and edges to edges, i.e., for each vertex $v \in V(G_1)$, $f(v)$ is a vertex in $V(G_2)$ and for each edge $e \in E(G_1)$, $f(e)$is an edge in $E(G_2)$. [14]

In this section, we describe a list-based algorithm for graph folding in a sequence of steps (1) to (8).

First, we introduce the following notations:

Nodes = {1…(*n*-1)} – the vertex set of a social graph;

Node$_j$ – the j_{th} vertex in the graph;

cNode – the source vertex in the graph;

Cluster$_i$ – the cluster at the i_{th} layer;

Neighbors (*cNode*) – the set of neighboring (adjacent) vertices for *cNode*;

C – the number of neighboring vertices.

The basic steps of the algorithm are:

1)Define the level of the cluster, i=0;

2)Define the source vertex (*cNode* = *Node*$_j$);

3)Perform the search function to discover neighboring vertices for *cNode*, *C* = *get Neighbors* (*cNode*);

4)If $C \neq 0$, then $i = i + 1$;

5)Define the cluster of the i_{th} level as an aggregated set of source vertex *cNode* and its neighbors *Neighbors* (*cNode*), herewith the cluster is a list *Cluster*$_i$ = *cons* (*cNode*, *Neighbors* (*cNode*)), where *hd* (*Cluster*$_i$) = cNode, *tl* (*Cluster*$_i$) = *Neighbors* (*cNode*);

6)Fold the vertices of the cluster at the i_{th} level into a new source vertex *cNode*, *cNode* = *Cluster*$_i$;

7)return to step (4);

8)if C=0 then terminate.

We explain algorithm using the example in Fig. 6. The initial graph has n vertices numbered from 1 to 42. They are connected by edges numbered from 1 to 73. The size of incidence matrix is 42x73. The size of adjacency matrix is 42x42. Both matrices are sparse.

We designate vertex 17 as a source vertex *cNode*. Vertex 17 has neighboring vertices 12, 13, 18, and 21.

According to algorithm, the cluster of the i_{th} level *Cluster*$_i$ (i=1) contains a source vertex *cNode* = 17 and its *Neighbors* (*cNode*) = 12, 13, 18, and 21. They can be represented with an edge list *Cluster*$_{1\text{-}4}$ = (17, 12), (17, 13), (17, 18), (17, 21). Using an algorithm, we fold the cluster at the 1st level into a new vertex and assign it the next available index *cNode* = 43.

For source vertex *cNode* = 43 in the cluster of the 2nd level, *Neighbors* (*cNode*) = 3, 9, 7, 10, 19, 27, 16. The edge list is *Cluster*$_{2\text{-}8}$ = (43, 3), (43, 7), (43, 9), (43, 10), (43, 19), (43, 16), (43, 27), (9, 10).

We emphasize the fact that some merging vertices are connected by multiple edges, e.g. in the list (43, 9) the vertices are connected by three edges: 16, 17 and 18.

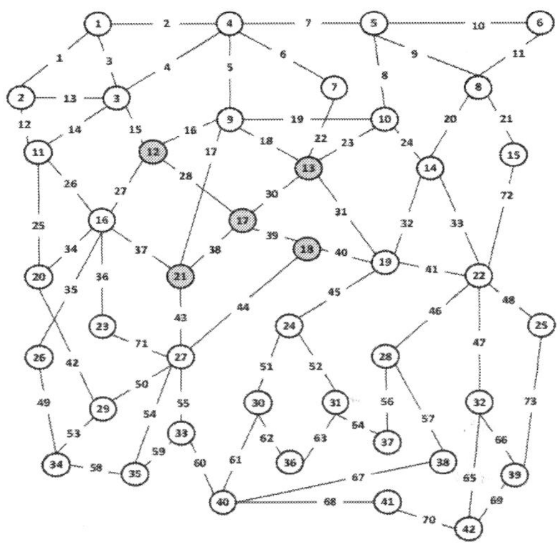

Figure 6. Graph with a highlighted cluster at the 1st level

We note the case when two or more merging vertices are linked not only to the source vertex but are interconnected to each other. For appropriate mapping of merged vertices, we add list (9, 10).

We proceed with designating *cNode* = 44 as a source vertex with *Neighbors* (*cNode*) = 1, 2, 4, 5, 11, 14, 20, 22, 23, 24, 26, 29, 33, and 35.

Edge lists with merging vertices in the cluster of the 3rd level are produced accordingly: *Cluster*$_{3\text{-}22}$ = (44, 1), (44, 2), (44, 4), (44, 5), (44, 11), (44, 14), (44, 20), (44, 22), (44, 23), (44, 24), (44, 26), (44, 29), (44, 33), (44, 35), (2, 11), (2, 1), (1,4), (4,5), (14, 22), (11, 20), (20, 29), (33, 35).

In Fig. 7, it is shown an example of merging vertices in the cluster of the 4th level into a new vertex *cNode* = 45. *Neighbors* (*cNode*) = 6, 8, 15, 25, 32, 28, 31, 30, 40, 34. *Cluster*$_{4\text{-}13}$ = (45, 6), (45, 8), (45, 15), (45, 25), (45, (45, 30), (45, 31), (45, 32), (45, 34), (45, 40), (8, 6), (8, 28), 15), (40, 30).

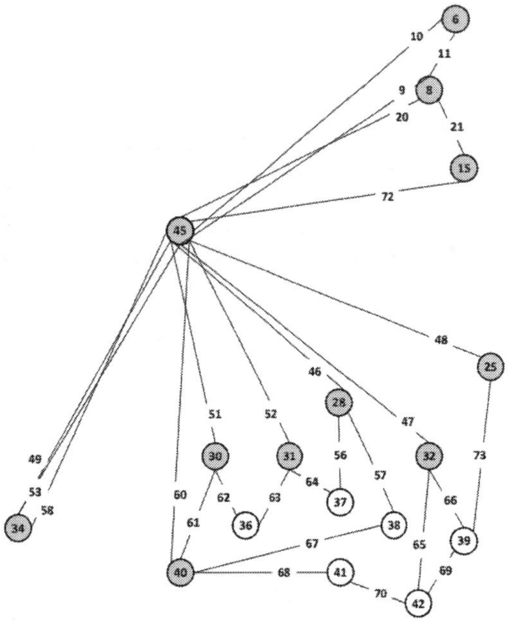

Figure 7. Folded graph with a highlighted cluster at the 4th level

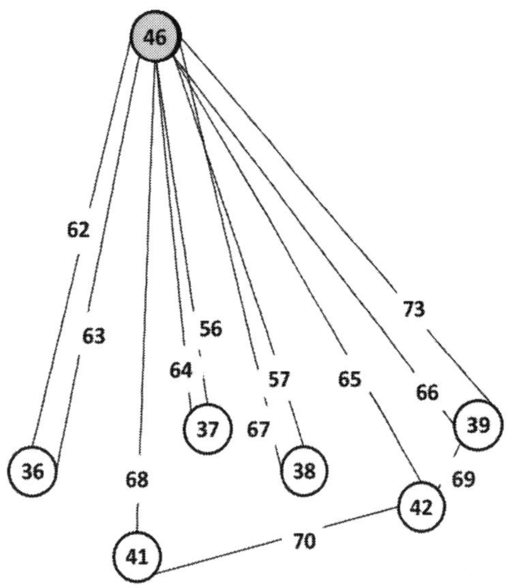

Figure 8. Folded graph with a highlighted cluster at the 5th level

The resulting graph contains vertex 46 and its *Neghbors* (*cNode*) = 36, 41, 37, 38, 42, 39 (Fig. 8). The edge lists for the cluster of the 5th level is the following: $Clusters_{5\text{-}8}$ = (46, 36), (46, 37), (46, 39), (46, 38), (46, 41), (46, 42), (42, 41), (42, 39).

4 Conclusion

In this paper, we described a list-based algorithm for graph folding. According to the results of experiments, by reducing calculation redundancy, the above algorithm is 30% less memory-intensive and 20-30% faster, depending on the density of the graph, in comparison to algorithms using adjacency/incidence matrices and iteration over vertices. In our case it was the only possible algorithm for analyzing conditionally infinite graphs on resource constrained mobile devices.

5 Acknowledgements

This work was supported by the grant of Southern Federal University, research project No. 07/2017-28 and by the grant of Russian Foundation for Basic Research, project No. 17-01-00243.

References

1. R.A. Grier, B. Skarin, A. Lubyansky and L. Wolpert, *In 2nd Intl. Conf. on Computational Cultural Dynamics* (2008).
2. C.C. James and Ö. ÖZdamar, Foreign Policy Analysis, **5**, 17-36 (2009).
3. J. Kopecky, N. Bos and A. Greenberg, *In 19th Annual Conf. on Behavior Representation in Modeling and Simulation* (136-143, 2010).
4. G.M. Levchuk, F. Yu, T. Haiying, K.R. Pattipati, Y. Levchuk and E. Entin, *In 12th Intl. Command and Control Research and Technology Symposium* (2007).
5. B. Latour, *Reassembling the Social: An Introduction to Actor-Network-Theory* (Oxford University Press, 2007).
6. N. Sergeev, A.A. Tselykh and A.N. Tselykh, *In 4th Intl. Conf. on Security of Information and Networks* (2013).
7. S. Wasserman and K. Faust, *Social Network Analysis: Methods and Applications* (Cambridge University Press, 1994).
8. J.M. Foster, *List Processing* (Macdonald, London, 1968).
9. T.H. Cormen, C.E. Leiserson, R.L. Rivest and C. Stein, *Introduction to Algorithms* (MIT Press, 2009).
10. F. Hildorsson, *Scalable Solutions for Social Network Analysis* (Diva portal, 2009).
11. C. Wickramaarachchi, A. Kumbhare, M. Frincu, C. Chelmis, and V.K. Prasanna, *In IEEE/ACM 15th Intl. Symposium on Cluster, Cloud, and Grid Computing* (829-834, 2015).
12. F. Claude and G. Navarro. *In Algorithms and Applications* (77-91, Springer-Verlag, 2010)
13. P. Liakos, K. Papakonstantinopoulou and A. Delis, *In ACM 25th Intl. Conf. Inf. Knowl. Manag.* (2317-2322, 2016).
14. E.M. El-Kholy and H.A. Mohamed, Journal of Applied and Computational Mathematics, **7**(1) (2017).

ITM Web of Conferences **25**, 01004 (2019) https://doi.org/10.1051/itmconf/20192501004
ICICCI 2018

Analysis and Development Forecast of O2C Model

Wenrong Jiang

The School of Computer and Information, Shanghai polytechnic University, Shanghai, China
wrjiang@sspu.edu.com

Abstract. O2C English can name office to the customer can be interpreted as enterprise customers on hand for customized services. At the same time O2C English can also be full name online configuration, translation online configuration mode of electronic business affairs, its meaning is the customized products from the store moved to the Internet, by app or web online platform to implement the product sales configuration, such as cabinets, wardrobe and other furniture products. This paper mainly introduces the burning van Persie, good cook this two big Chinese custom platform, and this platform is a typical analysis of the A class of O2C platforms is currently in the environment and new direction.

1 Introduction

O2C mode is in foreign countries has been very popular, but in China is still in the continuous exploration of new e-commerce model. In good cook, cooking rice, etc. all the O2C catering customization platform, herding behavior of Chinese people on online shopping started signs, the industry to meet the a good momentum of development, but although the O2C mode is popular, but generate profits is relatively low, so many companies can not accept such consumption patterns. Especially logistics problems, to food products not easy to implement, so the industry still exist many problems still need to industry leaders and successor not Exploration and practice.

2 Two platform's profile

"Cook the meal" is Recommended outsourcing the earliest cooking rice of "life" is somewhat complex, which the parent company the Lord do app development and operation service started, once for KFC, pizza hut, UNIQLO development and operations over the official app. After the second transition to do the shopping platform "good things" and found that the color is not in the beginning of the end of the third transformation, "cooking rice" is the third "toss" product. Cooking meal service is only limited to the Shanghai area, the daily orders more than 200, the peak 300 single. Signing the chef, was still in the training, a single daily cooks after 2 single, belonging to a still in the continuous development of beauty.

Van Persie home cook smashing cast is to rely on to survive but in October 13, home cooks "cooking rice" users received from its founder Zhang Zhijian of a letter of farewell letter, once billed to start the fourth kind of meal pattern "cooking rice in the 11 months after declared closed transformation. Some people say o2o start-up companies in the initial stage of burn to the development, many companies because did not survive the winter capital closed their doors, but Lei Junlian 3 out of o2o" cooking rice "is not short of money. In the burning van Persie founder to the user of a letter, said Zhang Zhijian: very sorry, after 11 months of effort, we do not have the ability to burn Become a profit model is clear, and can scale expansion of the business.

Figure 1. Cook Rice Online application

Good cook app launched in June 2014, get road capital 500 million yuan Angel round of financing in October 2014, 2015 in February at the speed of light an Zhen completed on 8 good cook a round of $500 million investment.2015 chef home platform good cook announced that has completed 100 million RMB B round of funding, led by Cowin investment. According to the good cook CEO Xu Zhiyan: B round of financing in fact before the last month has been completed, the company of the current round of financing to expand the size of the market, and in 2015 opened dozens of second tier cities, expansion while continuing to services standardization, continue on the line More categories, more personalized packages to meet consumer demand.

A good cook to his first defined as a service company, do is service and quality, then an Internet company, combine is the use of the Internet to the traditional service quantitative. Good cook said, to cook in the next step will come up with a large amount of subsidies to encourage outstanding chef, and ultimately more pay for more work, the chef's overall service can continue to improve.

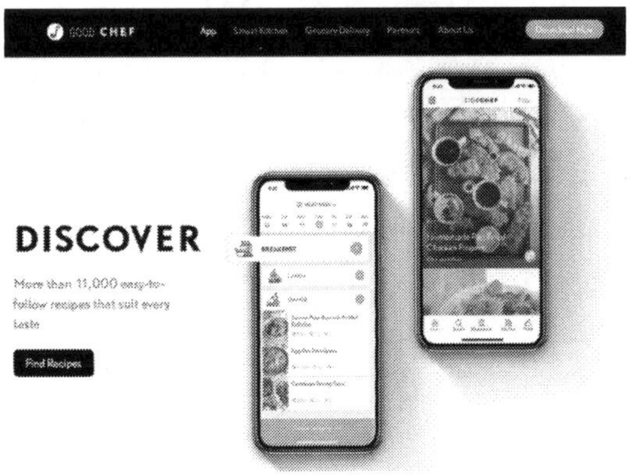

Figure 2. Good Cook Online application

3 Business model of the two platforms

Good cuisine and Sichuan cuisine chef of entrepreneurship, and in fact, from the beginning of this year to provide private kitchen, "the direction of entrepreneurial people up, gambling is people's future life will leave on door-to-door service can let oneself from the kitchen liberated chefs. And the two companies" good cook "," cooking rice "is one of the leaders, they provide is the booking door-to-door service products. Open the app, users can according to their own want to choose to be a chef, such as you are more preference, and the Hunan cuisine, the cuisine, Shandong cuisine, and so on. Selected, the user can according to the category to show cook dishes, and ultimately selected chefs. And then make an appointment to the time of a chef's door service, need to do a number of dishes and whether or not to buy food.

when each point can provide the standard of service, the future of this platform is possible, will not happen in the scale of the quality of the control is not good, causing negative events such as users.

Out front as far as possible to train in order to let the chef to stick to the user, the above mentioned "good cook" will be through the establishment of a line of chef, chef service standards, then cook to how the service can let users on the platform have a favorable impression? Generally speaking, these cooks at home when it has systemic dress well in the door (first impressions), and in half an hour to put all the dishes prepared and swing disc (similar to the hotel to the pendulum disk), and back to the user. When the user to prepare a good meal, a chef will prepare good Bonus gift (such as imported ice cream, etc.), to the user a surprise. When these processes are After the completion, the chef will leave, and then the platform will be a certain way to ask the user for the evaluation of the service.

Little chef at chef cooperation will the cooks in the preparation process and user communication, if the user home for the elderly or children, the chef who will design nutritious meals to meet these particular populations. The platform model and working chefs, cooks, and users of the docking platform, do a good job in the user's service and control. In addition to the healthy card, working chefs and other necessary barriers to entry management, cooking rice platform settled before and after each stage, will cook training. The cooking rice platform for 30 years or so, generally 10 years Chef experience. Males accounted for 90%, the professional feature is apparent, the words within the majority. it is characteristic of such professional groups with training meal burn control, can achieve the quality of service guarantee.

4 Profit model

In finished them into the bulk of the charges are good cooks present on the user's four dishes and one soup, 79 yuan, six dishes and one soup 99 yuan, if is a full-time chef, they will take the income of all attributable to cook, and if is a part-time chef, each person will smoke into 9 yuan. But the service fees and not their expected future earnings, the chef is a user's home in the "entrance", the future more imagination space. For example, now with a meal giveaway of imported ice cream, there are many users will ask is what brand, where to buy? So the future with a meal of goods and services have the opportunity to follow the cook together into the user's home.

"Good cook" team in September this year, was formally established, currently covers only the Shanghai area, existing IOS application. We reported before "love Chef" product form and a good cook is similar, but in the front end and back end are different, such as product level at present love chef has been able to see user comments and reply, the embryonic form of the community, and good chef app active is little, also backend love chef tend to platform, but the good cook will be heavier.

And "cooking the meal," the payment mode is also very interesting. It allows the user to a single purchase, but were more likely to in the user to the cook formed good impression after allowing users to purchase a membership to recharge, and single dispersed users into long-term users. Before the fact, I in the trial of this service obviously feel the less demand, if the user needs of its frequency is not high, may for a long period of time, they will happen again the second purchase, the membership I think should be the good way.

5 Two platform competitive Strength

Eat, is definitely a priority for the Chinese people, all users have to Aunt home cooking with strong demand, but domestic companies definitely meet they do not. The

 https://doi.org/10.1051/itmconf/20192501004

two platform first found not a chef home enterprises, they took the lead in the first on-line account for the pit, so days later when investors take the relatively smooth, set up the team. The advantage is in July to get the first round of financing, at present, service users have more than 140000, the members are stored value is in three thousand and opened in Beijing, Shanghai, Hangzhou, now cooperation cook for thousands of people. In less than a year of time, completed the fourth round of financing.

While cooking rice network in December 2014 obtained by IDG capital and Lei [microblogging]'s shun a capital investment of $150 million C round, three rounds of financing amounted to $833 million. 11 months operation of products, condensed the love of more than 20 million users with more than 700 professional chef and more than 30 entrepreneurial small partners sweat. The two companies undoubtedly in the capital operation first prize.

6 Two platform's Weakness

For this type of platform is the biggest problem is not to find a clear profit and scale expansion of the business model. From the point of view of "cooking rice, mature clear commercial pattern is decided the door key to the success or failure of the o2o. Home cuisine CEO SUN Hao said:" industry does not want to see the prisoner's dilemma situation, resources should not be wasted in guessing each other and fear of competing products strategy. "SUN Hao stressed that the duopoly is catering o2o industry evolution of optimal shape, industry to the venture full opportunity to come to the fore, and really good service, is done in a healthy competitive environment evolution.

No difference, no user loyalty, the industry will not leave a real asset. The next step is to adhere to the path of differentiation, focus on details, adhere to the early heart, good service, to provide users with better dining scene services. For large kitchen door how to break out of the problem, the industry has said that in the back of the game should also have more differences.

Each burn out Zhang Zhijian thinks, now most of the collapse of o2o business company a is a common problem in the burn burned the wrong place. "Cooking rice" is the same, the money to burn in the superficial, and did not use the money to build their own core competitiveness, for their own long-term development of the road. As the saying goes, good steel should be used in the blade, although o2o industry in burn money, but the money spent on where also determines the road can go far. To find the real pain, find strong demand, is the home of o2o first to clear direction. But for pain points is not easy Zhang Zhijian said: "the door to burn rice is actually a little pain, but also there is a demand, but the pain and Users can not let the pain, the demand is not strong enough to let users rely on. Find the user's real pain point, strong demand to find their core business, to find their own to coordinate the part of the resources, the industry chain to have control and power to form a scalable model.

Easy 'occupy the home o2o to want to survive, we need from the existing users find their real users, the difference in service to increase user stickiness. Period, a large number of subsidies in the form of market business model is the fundamental for entrepreneurs. "Cook rice' closed transformation after the taste buds' in order to survive, to the real users do more precise targeting of services. After all, to live long, length ratio were on the verge of important." find a little pain, but let the pain becomes profitable difficult. Lock which resources, grasping what demand, mode quicker is fundamental. If the pattern began to pack a lot, but not bad.

7 Two platform's opportunity

A report from the China Cuisine Association shows that in 2014 the national food industry revenue was 2.786 yuan, is expected in 2015 will reach 3000000000000 yuan.2014 (including takeaway door, buy coupons, home cooking, etc.) market size increased by 51.8% to 951 yuan, 2014 catering O2O online users grew by 38.5%, significantly higher than the national food and beverage revenue growth is expected in 2015 O2O market size and online users will be more than 30% to 1300 yuan and 2.2 people.

Xu Zhiyan for the demand in general, this industry there are three opportunities. One is from consumers and ordinary family every day to eat, and seize the consumer preferences share characteristics; second is from the chef, chef industry income level is relatively low, the daily workload, and a good cook cooks provides a best platform. According to CEO, said to the current orders, cook every day to pick up three single, noon, evening two single day do 18 dish of income can be maintained in the 8000 yuan, easily earn than the original or even more times income; the third is the social influence, private kitchen door for consumers to provide a kind of new Way of life, and do not lose in the home to eat a warm feeling, more than one stroke.

8 Two platform's Threat

The rice cooking design business model, CEO Zhang Zhijian firmly choose the "Taobao" platform mode, he thinks "Jingdong" self mode in the home cook o2o project is not sustainable. "We do not employ any full-time chef, because when one day, at the date of the order up to 1 million, to maintain high efficiency, a chef processing a single, need to recruit million people, which for a start-up company is not economical and unreasonable." Zhang Zhijian also said, "full-time chef and our employment relationship is working attitude. Part-time cook is different, their own in the use of burning van Persie platform business, dynamic the home cooking service to do a good job, establish a good reputation. We hold the attitude of open platform, the chef can be as free as the Uber driver "

Insiders said that with mobile payment scenarios of expanding, life service of o2o is constantly infiltration and transformation of various types of segments of life service market. "Entrepreneurial minority only see home situation o2o fiery unwilling to remain out of the limelight." the source said from early to call to order

 https://doi.org/10.1051/itmconf/20192501004

takeout, and later the PC, mobile terminal, takeaway has high frequency, but before o2o D-Will, chef home cooking has not been the norm.

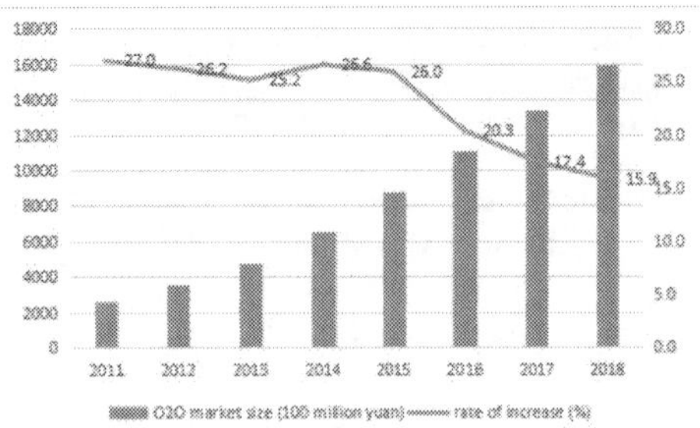

Figure 3. o2o market analysis in China

Chef of the door to door service o2o ends of supply and demand is not balanced, for example, when dinner need a chef of the door to door service, often need a lot of chef. This is often hotel is the most busy time, cooks very difficult to go to do a part-time job. This makes no sufficient number of chefs to meet user demand, resulting in both supply and demand is out of balance. From the concrete operational level, the chef also need equipment and tools, part of the hotel chef is not suitable for in home to do the ordinary food.

Chef of the door to door service o2o another obstacle is, meal also belongs to non standardized products, for example, a dish 9 people say the food is delicious, but also has a person that can not say. Eventually, the chef of the door to door service o2o also face difficult to cater for all tastes of embarrassment. In this series of factors, put aside "Internet +, o2o shared economic, drops of food industry" the fetters of the normal thinking buzzword, back to the pioneering early heart is to settle down in this.

9 Future development forecast of Chinese custom platform

This field service in o2o concept after the rise of certain trendency hot door, a variety of services industry scramble to catch the express door-to-door service. Because the market is hot, "service + home" situation is appropriate is ultimately not awake for a couple of people see, as long as the concept of blowing good, the investor's money will soon hand, with subsidies and other means to gradually stop, the market will eventually return to calm. When the door service sector will usher in a stormy baptism, can foresee future mortality of door-to-door service categories will be more and more, this is the choice of the market, and consumer choice. After the ebb tide, left is the real For the genes of the Internet service industry, those who try to ride the, playing the subversion of service industry finally fear or gods reparations bale.

Good cook, cook rice, chef home o2o project of the better known Xianfeng Huaxing and Gao Rong, Datai of millions of dollars in investment projects in Beijing love chef.O2O entrepreneurial hot rise, similar to the "good service" business like a rising wind and scudding clouds, but the feelings of feelings and business students meaning. Venture will eventually return to the business nature of: profit oriented, clearly scale profit model. For the catering business, central kitchen, a single product explosion models, much food distribution, raw and semi-finished products distribution, is catering o2o future direction.

10 Acknowledgement

This work is supported by the Key Disciplines of Computer Science and Technology of Shanghai Polytechnic University under Grant No. XXKZD1604.

References

1. Wenrong Jiang, Yingyan Liu. Analysis of the double 11 ouyeel business promotion effectiveness [C]. 2016 ISSGBM International Conference on Information, Communication and Social Sciences (ISSGBM-ICS 2016), Dubai, United Arab Emirates, Singapore Management and Sports Science Institute, October 8, 2016, 49-55. WOS:000391774900010.
2. Zhu Huabing, Gong Jianghong. Analysis of the impact of the financial crisis on the foreign trade of Zhejiang [J]. Commercial era, 2010(7): P129-131.
3. Wenrong Jiang. Analysis and Research on Failure Reasons of NOKIA [J]. Lecture Notes in Management Scient. Vol.94. 2018 6th International Conference on Physical Education and Society Management (ICPESM 2018), London, UK, Singapore Management and Sports Science Institure. July 22-24, 2018, 290-295.
4. Wenrong Jiang, Shiwei Li. Analysis of Xiaomi Tech's E-commerce model [J]. 2nd International conference on E-commerce and Contemporary Economic Development (ECED 2015), Nanjing, China, December 5-6, 2015, DEStech Publications, Inc. 196-200. WOS:000380277700040.
5. Wenrong Jiang, Jian Chen. Traditional Enterprises Transformation and Strategy to Deal with E-Commerce [J]. 2015 4th International Conference on Physical Education and Society Management (ICPESM 2015), Singapore, December 6-7, 2015, Lecture Notes in Management Science, 2015 (12), Vol 47, 301-306. IDS No.: BF3BX.
6. Wenrong Jiang. Analysis the O2O marketing model about old network website [J]. The Second International Conference on Economic and Business Management (FEBM2017), Shanghai, China, ATLANTIS Press. October 21-23, 2017, 507-512.

Research of Digital Based on Network Model in the Fingerprint of Traditional Chinese Medicines (TCM)

Qinglian Yu[1,a], Tao Qi[2]

[1] *Modern Education Technology Center, Qiqihar Medical University, Qiqihar, China*
[2] *Qiqihar No. 6 Middle School, Qiqihar, China*

Abstract. In this paper, a network model is used to simulate the fingerprint of TCM, the fingerprint is digitized, it is easy to store and display by simplifying the data processed. Application of digital processing technology and pattern recognition technology sets up the standard fingerprint. According to the standard fingerprint of TCM, Identify the quality and authenticity of the medicines, especially with the lack of medicines. It can realize medicinal materials testing in comprehensive evaluation of internal quality and overall control of the whole matter, according to the fingerprint of TCM. Improve the overall level of the TCM industry and promote the early development of the Chinese medicine industry to the world.
Keywords. Network model; Fingerprint of TCM; Digital pattern recognition

1 The introduction

With the development of the times and the development of medical technology, the research craze of TCM is on the rise. Compared with chemical drugs, Chinese medicine has the advantages of low toxicity side effects and remarkable clinical efficacy, more and more countries and regions have begun to pay attention to the unique diagnosis and treatment methods of Chinese medicine. With the increasing use of Chinese medicine, the quality supervision of TCM has become a popular research direction and the international medical research hotspot[1-2].

Because of the composition of Chinese medicine is complex, quality testing and analysis are difficult. The efficacy of Chinese medicine is restricted, growing environment, territory, collection time, collection site, processing method, storage method, for example[3]. The quality of Chinese medicine must be determined and controlled to ensure the safety and effectiveness of Chinese medicine. By analyzing the ingredients of medicinal materials, it is an effective method to determine the quality of Chinese medicine. The fingerprint of TCM has become an effective means to control the quality of various medicines[4-5].

2 Computer information processing in the fingerprint of TCM

The fingerprint of TCM is an effective method to detect medicine quality. The components of medicinal materials are monitored and evaluated by a variety of disciplines and comprehensive techniques. With the maturity of various research theories, the integration of various technologies, the importance of applying computer data processing technology to the research of the fingerprint of TCM is gradually noticed[6]. The composition of is complex, the factors affecting the pharmacodynamic effect are more, so the accuracy of artificial fingerprint is open to discussion. It is imperative to combine the fingerprint of TCM with computer data analysis and pattern recognition technology.

With the use of fingerprint in the field of medicine detection and quality control, how to control the pharmacological information of pharmacological substances by fingerprint, Gradually turning into a mathematical method involving a large number of calculations to analyze and process data[7-10]. The common computer processing methods of medicine information data have regression analysis, cluster analysis, artificial neural network, and so on [11-17].

3 Network model and digital expression in the fingerprint of TCM

The fingerprint of TCM is a kind of map that can show the common peaks of certain medicine characteristics. It has the characteristics of overall similarity and individual ambiguity. At present, the application of TCM fingerprint technology is very wide. The digital information processing method urgently needs to be integrated into the fingerprint data processing. In order to explore the deep data relation of fingerprint map and improve the identification method of fingerprint map. At present, the application of signal and digital information processing technology to fingerprint is more and more. Some

[a] Corresponding author: yuqinglian@qmu.edu.cn

mathematical methods are also gradually applied to the analysis of the fingerprint map. But, some of these methods affect the integrity of the data, complicated, the retention value of chromatographic peak is unstable. These factors add to the difficulty of the analysis of the fingerprint. To resolve these issues, this paper proposes a new method to extract TCM fingerprint based on network diagram theory, the characteristics of fingerprint are simulated by using the graph of network. This kind of research method is clear and easy to understand. The unity of data integrity and fuzziness can be guaranteed.

3.1 Network model in the fingerprint of TCM

With the proliferation of modern analytical instruments, in particular, computer application technology and instrument analysis data fuse together. The data presented in this mode is intelligent and automated. The information on medicinal materials is huge, researchers have been unable to identify the relevant characteristics and internal rules of medicines with their subjective professional experience.

The simple pattern recognition has been unable to obtain the inherent law of data and valuable information. In this paper, the digital expression of medicine data is carried out using the network diagram structure. The data feature selection of pattern recognition field is combined with digital display. This fusion technique is used to analyze the original data set of TCM fingerprint. The information map can reflect the chemical characteristics of the medicine. This kind of digitized reticular structure is used to visually identify and evaluate the quality of medicine. The network model acquisition process of TCM fingerprint is shown below.

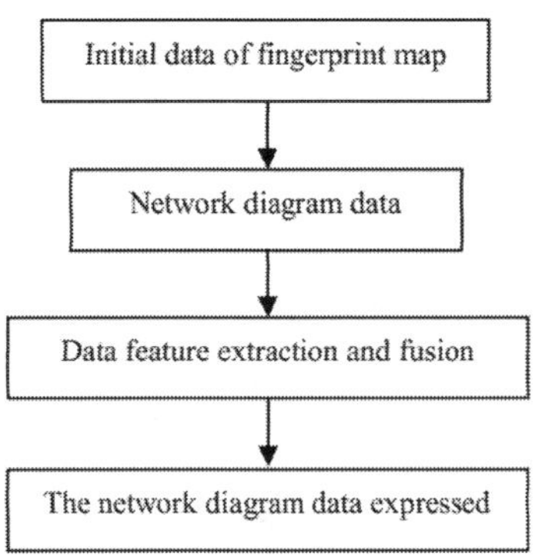

Figure 1. Flow Chart

3.2 Digital expression in the fingerprint of TCM

The data of fingerprint is presented, it is usually based on the integral result or the retention value data as the basis of data statistics. In the processing of data, first, the raw data is analyzed, ignore the external influence of the analysis system. Then a peak of the fingerprint was selected as the reference peak, compare the other peak data to it, based on the relative value obtained compare the fingerprint patterns.

The basic principle of the digital chromatographic fingerprint is to determine a chromatographic peak as the reference standard in the chromatographic map of all the samples participating in the identification. This determined reference chromatographic peak exists in each sample to be identified. Use it to calculate the relative retention value of each peak. The relative retention value is relatively stable compared with that of the chromatographic peak retention value, the systematic error in the analysis data is eliminated, the drift of the retained value is reduced, in this way, the location of chromatographic peak is ensured. The fingerprint of TCM, which is based on relative retention value, is the digital fingerprint.

Select the peaks that are common to each sample, and the peak time in the residence as the reference peak, the calculation formula of relative retention value is follow, $\alpha = tRi/\ tRs$.

tRi is the peak time of each group.

tRs is the peak time of reference peak.

The fingerprint of TCM is transformed into easy-to-display data by means of information, by digitizing the fingerprint map, it makes the quality identification of medicine more convenient and more objective. Digital processing of massive data samples is carried out, fuzzy individual characteristics, it can get a more reliable standard fingerprint. In reality, it is difficult to determine the standard material, but the standard fingerprint map that is determined by technical means is relatively easy. According to the standard fingerprint map, able to identify the quality of medicinal materials.

4 Example analysis

his paper is based on the network diagram representation principle, the species of ginseng was studied by using near-infrared spectroscopy. The fingerprint map was extracted using the network diagram, ensure the integrity and the objectivity of the data. It is an effective research method.

The number of peaks detected when different wave body width is selected from the data of various experimental samples. The data table is as follows. The process flow diagram is as follows.

The peak detection procedure is applied to the peak detection of all sample data. Select the first eight crest characteristics, the characteristic mean of the sample data is used as the characteristic mode of the class. Draw the network diagram of all kinds of samples. The initial data set is composed of all the crest in the spectral curve, when it comes to the fusion of characteristics. The characteristic fusion method is using network diagram, parameter is setting 3 layers, characteristic optimization techniques adopt improved genetic algorithm strategy. The results are as follows.

The results of the experiment can be seen, the method presented in this paper has obtained relatively higher identification accuracy.

Table1. The number of spectral peaks detected of Ginsengs

Data sample \ Crest parameter	4	8	12	16	20	24	28
Salvia	140	98	43	17	12	10	8
Mountain ginseng	97	78	35	11	8	7	6
Adenophora verticillata	142	112	50	18	8	7	5
Radix pseudostellariae	147	115	44	15	9	6	5

Table 2. The error rate of the recognition experiment

Characteristic presentation method	Linear classifier	Bayes classifier	k nearest neighbor classifier
The original characteristics of standardization(data)	0.1070	0.0925	0.1072
Principal component characteristics of the original data(data+PCA)	0.1362	0.0933	0.1202
The characteristics of the wave crest detected(fengdata4)	0.0402	0.0444	0.0522
Fengdata4+PCA	0.0814	0.0605	0.0496
Presentation in this paper	**0.0102**	**0.0004**	**0.0035**

5 Conclusion

In this paper, the data characteristics of TCM fingerprint are analyzed by using the network graph structure. By building network model, extraction data, digital analysis, calculating relative retention value, determine the standard fingerprint map. It provides a new way of thinking and means for the quality, monitoring and evaluation of medicine.

Acknowledgement

This work was supported by science and technology research project of education department of Heilongjiang Province under grant No. 12531785 and guidance project of the science and technology bureau of Qiqihar, Heilongjiang Province under grant No.GYZD-2017010.

References

1. Xiaohe, Xiao; Luqi, Huang; Xiaojun, Ma.On the new connotation and significance of the modernization of Chinese medicine and traditional Chinese medicine.China Journal of Chinese Materia Medica, 28(3):282-286, 2003.
2. Liping, Yang. The thought and exploration of Chinese medicine modernization .New Journal of Traditional Chinese Medicine, 36(9):3-4, 2004.
3. Huaizhou, Zhao; Ying, Jia; Shanghua, Zhao, etc.The development of Chinese medicine qi and theory .China Journal of Chinese Materia Medic, 30(24):1898-1901, 2005.
4. National pharmacopoeia commission.Pharmacopoeia of the People's Republic of China (2005 edition) .Beijing: Chemical Industry Press, 2005.
5. Bo, Hong; Wenjing, Li; Shumin, Liu; Jicheng, Liu. HPLC Fingerprinting and Cluster Analysis of Diterpenoids Constituents in Euphorbia fischerian. Natural drug research and development, 27:617-620, 2015.
6. Xiayan, Wang. The application of modern analytical techniques in the study of traditional Chinese medicine fingerprint. Chinese Traditional and Herbal Drugs, 35(7):127-130, 2004.
7. Weiwei, Su; Zhong, Wu; Jian, Quan.Construction of traditional Chinese medicine fingerprint and computer analysis. Journal of Chinese Medicinal Materials, 24(4):295-298, 2001.
8. Libo, Yan; Bingren, Xiang. The molecular similarity method is used for the study of the relationship between pharmacological antiphase chromatogram.Chinese Journal of Chromatography, 19(5):427-432, 2001.
9. A. Rahman, D.V. Smith, B. Little, A.B. Ingham, P.L. Greenwood, and G.J. Bishop-Hurley, Cattle behaviour classification from collar, halter, and ear tag sensors. Information Processing in Agriculture 5(1), 124-133, 2018.
10. N.P. Seeram, and B. Burton-Freeman, The seventh biennial berry health benefits symposium. Food & Function 9(1), 20-21, 2018.
11. R. Hu, Y. Zhang, Y. Chen, and G. Lin, Dynamic metabolic profiling in vegetable soybean seed development. Emirates Journal of Food and Agriculture 30(2), 90-98, 2018.
12. M. Cruz Campas, A.G. Villalba Villalba, and R. Ramirez Leal, Editorial. Revista Internacional De Contaminacion Ambiental 33(SI), I-I, 2017.
13. M. Duan, Z. Liu, D. Yan, W. Peng, and A. Baghban, Application of lssvm algorithm for estimating higher heating value of biomass based on ultimate analysis.

https://doi.org/10.1051/itmconf/20192501005

Energy Sources Part a-Recovery Utilization and Environmental Effects 40(6), 709-715, 2018.

14. Z. Liu, Economic analysis of energy production from coal/biomass upgrading; Part 1: hydrogen production. Energy Sources Part B-Economics Planning and Policy 13(2), 132-136, 2018.

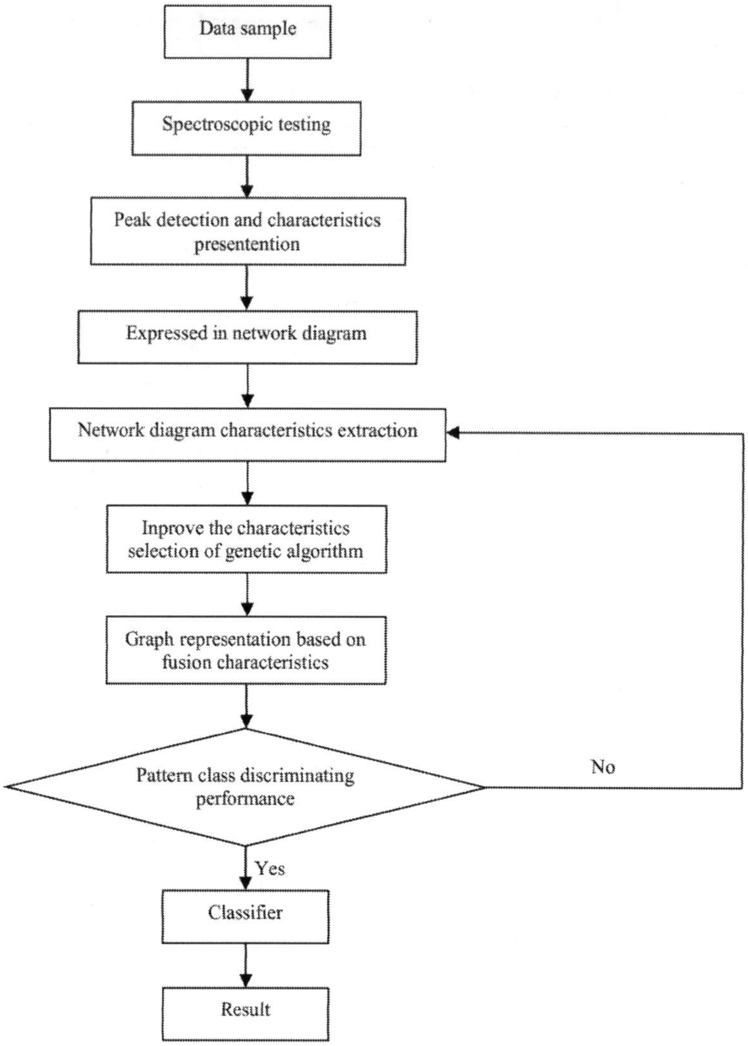

Figure 2. The process flow diagram

Exploration on Campus Network Construction Mechanism and Application Mode

Zhongbao Chen

Jilin Institute of Chemical Technology

Abstract: In recent years, accelerating the process of educational informationization and comprehensively promoting the informatization level and connotative development of educational institutions have been put forward in the National Medium and Long Term Plan for Education Reform and Development (2010-2020). Based on extensive research and repeated argumentation, this paper aims to provide corresponding solutions to the problems existing in the current network structure. On the basis of present situation, this paper puts forward the construction objectives and key contents according to the guideline, that is, overall planning and step-by-step implementation. In order to achieve the expected goals and get satisfied results, the construction mainly includes six parts -- the construction of basic hardware platform, application software service platform, high-quality education and teaching resources, security system, operation and maintenance system and information-based team.

1 The current status and problems of the Internet

1.1 Existing network infrastructure

There is a school information center in our school taking responsibility for the construction of school information which began in 2007.The main nodes of the campus network are connected by Gigabit fiber and are converged to the network center of school. There are more than 1800 information points and nearly 800 computers being connected to the network. The network center server provides services including WWW service, DNS service, FTP service, DHCP service, and external network export certification to the entire network users.

The network topology is shown as follows:

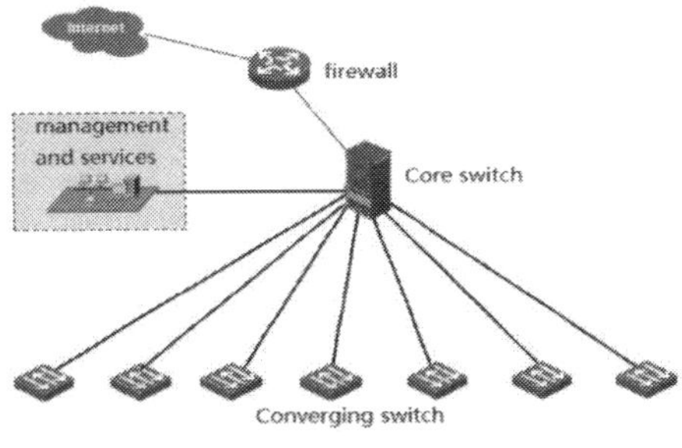

1.2 The existing problems

Though the school has a good foundation in the construction of digital campus, there is still some distance between the goal of the "three links and two platforms" (Establishing broadband network in each school, providing high-quality resources for each class, making everyone have network learning space, building a public educational resource service platform and an educational management service platform) proposed by the Ministry of Education.

(1) Failure to achieve full network coverage in the whole campus

At present, the school has finished the fiber-optic laying of the campus backbone network, but the network integrated wiring has not covered all classes, laboratories and training places. Thus, it needs to be improved.

(2) Failure to satisfy the system software operation requirements with current hardware configuration

Our school is the first batch of construction schools. According to the specific requirements of the three ministries and commissions (Ministry of Finance, Propaganda Department, Ministry of Education) of the state on the construction of digital campus, current hardware and equipment configuration of the school network center can no longer meet the requirements of the system software operation of the digital campus. As a result, the digital teaching resources that are under construction cannot be used normally, which affects the normal development of educational informationization. And this has become a serious obstacle and bottleneck factor restricting the construction and development of school information. Therefore, in light of the actual needs of digital campus construction for campus network, it is not only the urgent needs of the model school construction, but also the basic needs of the school informatization construction. All in all, it is of great significance to improve the hardware conditions of the campus network appropriately on the basis of the original campus network.

(3) Limitations of the campus information management service platform

There is no mature educational management software, network teaching platform software, and automated office system software, which affects the normal use of digital teaching resources and affects the normal development of educational informationization. The construction of digital educational resources needs to be strengthened.

2 Construction goals

Based on the construction of information infrastructure, focusing on the information supporting environment and connotative construction, through the construction of “three links and two platforms”, we aim to enrich the information management tools, improve the resource co-construction and sharing mechanism, improve the application ability of information technology in teaching, and promote both teachers and students’ information application competencies and skills.

We strive to complete the construction of educational management information system platform and education and teaching resources platform in recent 2 years, and realize the construction goals of establishing broadband network in each school, providing high-quality resources for each class, making everyone have network learning space, building a public educational resource service platform and an educational management service platform so that schools can become informationalize in education, teaching and administrative management, and finally reach digital campus construction standards, becoming a fully functional digital campus, and play a demonstration and leading role in the school information construction and application fields.

3 Research on the content of construction

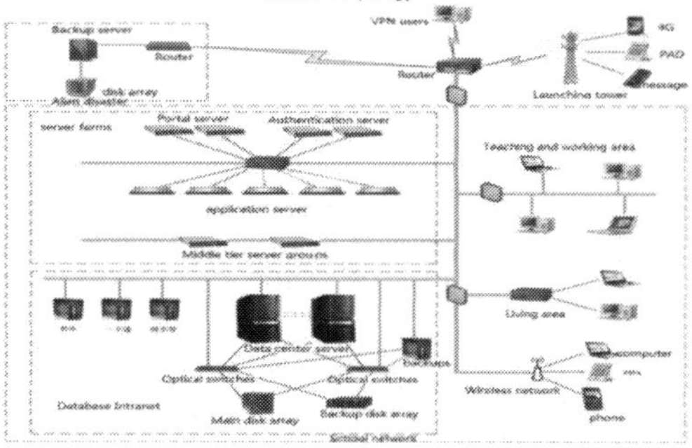

With the construction of the "three links and two platforms" as the core digital campus construction goal, with reference to relevant countries and industry standards, the main construction contents include basic hardware platform construction, application software service platform construction, high-quality education and teaching resource construction, security system construction, the operation and maintenance system construction, information-based team construction, the system security construction and the basic hardware platform construction.

3.1 Construction of basic hardware platform

Database storage exchange area: two professional servers are used to cluster and serve as data center servers. The storage methods are FC runtime storage and backup storage of SATA disks. Storage requires FC interface and IPSan interface, that is, storage for data center database through FC connection. If other servers need to connect to the database server of the new system through IPSan and connect to the storage through the FC port, the databases of other existing systems can also be placed in the intranet of the school database. Server cluster services mainly include: portal, identity authentication, data center application server, using two rack servers or blade servers to virtualize servers and make soft clusters through software such as WMWARE;

The middleware server, in order to enhance the security of the application system to access the database, the single-row middleware server layer, using two high-end rack servers or blade servers, virtualizing the server through software such as WMWARE and making a soft cluster so that it can be virtualized into multiple points. Therefore, any application (new or later) that wants to visit the database needs to be accessed through the middleware server. The application server group uses multiple rack servers or blade servers to virtualize servers and soft clusters through software such as WMWARE.

In the area of teaching, working and living, the way of combining wired network with wireless network will reduce erection costs and improve operational effects. Using load balancing switch or other balancing strategies ensures that mobile devices such as notebook computers, iPads and other wireless devices can access campus resources normally.

Off-campus mobile devices are connected to mobile devices such as 4G mobile phones, iPads, and mobile phones (SMS) through mobile platforms (services provided by mobile providers such as China Mobile, China Telecom, and China Unicom). Strategic incremental replication of critical business data over the IP network between the data center and the disaster recovery center enables offsite backup of data and rapid recovery of data in the event of an unexpected disaster.

Suppose that every 2 people simultaneously use the network to enjoy 1 megabyte of bandwidth. We need to expand the export bandwidth to meet the needs of the school's digital campus construction for export bandwidth. Based on the existing Gigabit fiber and network center computer room of the school, the internal network of the teaching place will be integrated and wired, and the supporting teaching equipment will be added to provide a multimedia teaching environment.

On the basis of the existing network equipment, the network core switch, part of servers, network security equipment, and teacher machine, we need to complete the related supporting environment construction so as to meet the needs of the storage of campus resources, the security of the intranet and the high-speed exchange of large amounts of data.

3.2 Construction of application software service platform

3.2.1 Update the school portal website

The unified identity authentication and authorization platform mainly provides centralized identity authentication and authorization services for each application system. The user realizes single sign-on through the unified information portal to improve the security of the application system of the information management system. By specifying the corresponding centralized authentication technical specifications, a unified application system user management interface is provided, and finally centralized management of all new system user authentication is realized.

3.2.2 Construction of informationalized standard system

In accordance with the actual situation of the school, a set of informatization management standard system conforming to the school itself, including information standards, code coding standards, technical standards, management norms, etc., is provided to provide basic conditions for information exchange and resource sharing, and to ensure that information is collected and exchanged. There is a unified, scientific and standardized classification and description in the transmission process to ensure the orderly construction, use, management and maintenance of the information management system.

3.3 The construction of high-quality teaching resources

(1) Establish a school education resource center based on the basis of the development and construction of digital resources, and enrich the digital education and teaching resources of the whole school through various ways. Build a public learning platform to enrich the content of the course and expand the scope of application. Establish a new network learning model to form a learner-centered learning framework. Teachers are encouraged to produce high-quality courses and web-based courses, and build digital libraries, video and audio libraries, courseware libraries, excellent training cases, reform and innovation courses, and provide high-quality learning resources for teachers, students and others in the areas of online learning, mobile learning and online counseling.

(2) Two new teaching skills training rooms are built to be used in the construction of high-quality courses in schools, and the network sharing of high-quality courses resources can be achieved quickly. They are used in Microteaching to correct and train teachers' teaching skills. They are used to record the courses of "famous teachers' network classes" and to carry out long-distance training and excellence by means of live or on-demand broadcasting. The production and production of quality teaching resources.

3.4 Safety system construction

Information security should be considered and designed from hardware system security, software system security, application management security and other aspects.

3.4.1 Network system security

Considering physical layer security technology and network layer security technology, and physical layer security technology is considered from the aspects of campus network environment security, network operation equipment security, physical isolation of top-secret data, etc. Network layer security technology: between database server and application server, application server, WEB server and campus network add necessary firewall for security filtering, and add intrusion detection security technology, installing anti-virus software in server and user terminal, and installing network virus monitoring and cleaning software.

3.4.2 Software system security

Considering the operating system and application software, the operating system is the basis of normal operation of all computer terminals, workstations and servers, and the security of the operating system is very important. The key server should adopt the server version of the operating system. There are many security vulnerabilities in the operating system because of the design and version problems. In order to strengthen the security management of the operating system, it is necessary to strengthen the security from the aspects of physical security, login security, user security, file system and printer security, registry security, RAS security, data security, application system security and so on. Application software system security is designed through the data access strategy, data encryption, user control, system and information backup, system and information recovery, log system and other aspects of information security.

3.4.3 Database security

The access and operation of database are verified and authorized.

3.4.4 Data transmission security

Data transmission can be carried out by means of HTTPS encrypted transmission. The main function of Https protocol can be divided into two kinds: one is to establish an information security channel to ensure the security of data transmission; the other is to confirm the authenticity of the website. In order to ensure the confidentiality and integrity of data transmission, identity authentication can also be used for dial-up user access.

3.4.5 Data storage security

In order to prevent the abnormal damage of storage devices, the disk fault-tolerant array composed of hot-pluggable SCSI hard disks can be used to backup the system in real-time by RAID5.

3.4.6 System log security

The log system has the function of comprehensive data recording and automatic classification and retrieval. In this system, the log will record all the operations performed in the process from the time a user logs in to the time he exits the system, including the operation of the database and the use of system functions. The logs contain IP addresses, operation types, operation objects and operation execution times of the operating host of the user for future audit verification.

3.5 Operation and maintenance system construction

3.5.1 Work system

Improving the reasonable working system is the key to the success of digitalized campus information. In order to complete the construction of digital campus smoothly under the circumstances of heavy tasks and urgent time, it is necessary to establish a complete working system to ensure the healthy and orderly development of information construction. We should continue to strengthen organizational leadership, and establish a reasonable division of labor and clear responsibilities for the promotion of information coordination mechanism, provide funding and site security, and promote the healthy development of information technology.

3.5.2 Management organization

The leading group of digital campus information construction is the leading organization responsible for planning, organizing and coordinating work. As the daily management organization of the project construction, the leading group of digital campus information construction is responsible for the implementation and guidance of the information construction plan, and supervises and urges departments at all levels to actively participate in the information construction work.

3.5.3 Management mechanism

Establish and improve the organization and management system of information work, project management system, operation and management rules and regulations. We should make unified provisions on information work so as to make information construction work more orderly.

3.6 Information team building

(1) Participate in various computer technology training organized by the Ministry of education.

(2) Plus provincial educational technology training

(3) Participate in technical training for industry organizations.

(4) Organize all staff training in the school so that all teachers can skillfully use all the applications provided by information construction.

3.7 Institutional guarantee

We should make plans for the school information construction, and further clarify the functional departments, and carry out the post responsibilities.

Establish and improve the relevant management system. Strengthen process management, implement target management responsibility system, implement regular meetings, periodic inspection, periodic summary system to ensure the orderly progress of information construction, the whole process has rules to follow. Establish a guarantee and incentive mechanism to ensure the long-term development of school education informatization.

4 Expected results of construction

4.1 Build a perfect educational management information platform

To realize the comprehensive integration of application service platforms such as educational management informatization, educational teaching informatization, educational scientific research informatization and student learning informatization, so as to make the level of school educational management informatization reach the leading level in the province.

4.2 Build a perfect public service platform for educational resources

Ensuring that the platform has the function of opening and sharing high-quality educational resources has become an important node of high-quality educational network teaching resources.

4.3 Realizing the goal of "three links" in an all round way

We should resources, classes, and cyberspace. The ability of teachers and students of applying educational information resources has been greatly improved. Digital campus has become an important means of improving the quality of education and teaching. Information construction especially digital campus construction plays a leading and exemplary role in educational institutions.

https://doi.org/10.1051/itmconf/20192501007

Trade Conflicts and China's Macroeconomic Fluctuations --- An Empirical Analysis Based on Vector Autoregression Model

Chenggang Li[1,2], Yong Gan[1,a]

[1]Faculty of Big Data Statistics and Economics, Guizhou University of Finance and Economics, Guiyang 550025, China
[2]New Structural Financial Research Center, Guizhou University of Finance and Economics, Guiyang 550025, China

Abstract. This paper uses the data from November 2016 to June 2018 to construct a VAR model to empirically analyze the impact of trade wars on the Chinese economy since the trade friction between China and the United States. The empirical results show that the trade conflict between China and the United States will have short-term effects on financial institution loans, net export fluctuations, capital markets, short-term international capital flows, and the RMB exchange rate. After the impact of the trade war, the Chinese economy will have a spontaneous adjustment function, which will cause a certain positive and negative change in economic changes. But over time, the impact of Sino-US trade conflicts on financial institution loans, net export volatility, asset prices, short-term international capital flows, and the RMB exchange rate has gradually weakened until the gradual convergence to the zero axis and the effect disappears.

Keywords: Trade conflict; Macroeconomy; Vector autoregression model; Impulse response

1 Introduction

In 2016, China's exports to the United States accounted for 18% of China's total merchandise exports and 4.4% of GDP. In 2017, Sino-US trade total 3.95 trillion yuan, accounting for 14.2% of China's total import and export volume. For a long time, the United States has been China's largest trade exporter and the largest source of trade surplus. If Sino-US trade relations go bad, it will be difficult for China to find an alternative market for the US market in a short period of time. At the same time, with the rise of the Trump administration's national protectionism, Sino-US trade frictions continue. In January 2018, the Trump administration announced a tariff of up to 30% and 50% on imported large washing machines and photovoltaic products. On July 6, 2018, the United States began to impose a 25% import tariff on Chinese goods valued at $34 billion. Facing the US's important trading partner status with China and the escalating trade friction. Studying the impact of trade wars on the Chinese economy and discussing possible viable policies have been important to an imminent level.

Some scholars have studied the causes of trade wars. Gene considered trade agreements to be the equilibrium result of the bargaining game model between the two governments. Langdon and Bown argue that trade friction is not regular, there is trade friction in the existence of international trade, and the greater the trade scale, the greater trade friction. D Xie and G Zhang (2018)[1] Sino-US trade friction is the product of the contradictions between the economic interests of China and the United States, and can only be gradually resolved in the debugging of mutual economic interests. LJ Huang (2018) [2] attributed the cause of the trade war to the rise of American populism and the containment of China's rise.

There are also scholars studying the impact of trade wars. R Wu and HY Liu(2009)[3] used the trade war model to study the balanced import and export policy implemented by the major powers in intra-industry trade under the monopolistic competition. The conclusions show that the enhancement of product competitiveness will unilaterally increase the scale of trade wars. F Yang and W Sun(2018)[4] through the counting model, using the 2000-2014 WIOD and anti-dumping data to empirically test that the United States is credible for strategic considerations to curb the development of China's high-tech industry. In the trade war, the US government will intervene in the normal operation of Chinese companies in the United States in different ways, thus seriously affecting the investment of Chinese companies in the United States (Schmidt, 2004)[5].

The current scholars' research is mainly based on the qualitative study of basic facts and the reasons or influences and development of trade wars. The scholars' research at the economic analysis level is devoted to constructing the dynamic balance of trade volume changes and exchange rate changes on China's macroeconomic impact. Few scholars have focused their attention on the study of dynamic impact processes. The main innovation of this paper is to set trade conflicts into time-series into virtual variables to act on various indicators of China's macro-economy, making abstract

[a] 253378633@qq.com

https://doi.org/10.1051/itmconf/20192501007

trade warfare into measurable and tangible data, and introducing VAR model into trade conflict analysis system.

2 Variable selection and data source

Trade conflict (*CONFI*). On the basis of full consideration of scientific, measurable principles, and reliability principles, dummy variables are selected as proxy variables for measuring trade conflicts. If one or both of the United States or China announces tariffs in the month, the month is set to 1, otherwise 0.

Financial institution loan (*LOAN*). The increase in the growth rate of credit is one of the most important indicators for measuring financial institution loans. Financial institution loans directly affect the size of M2, and M2 is significantly related to GDP and CPI.

Net export fluctuations (*NETEX*). The net export growth rate is the sequential growth rate. One of the most important parts of the trade war is that the United States has substantially increased tariffs on China. If the United States illegally increases tariffs, our economy is the first to bear the trade volume of the United States.

Capital market (*ASSET*). The Shanghai Composite Index has a sequential growth rate. Using the ring growth rate of the Shanghai Composite Index to measure the strong representativeness of China's asset price fluctuations, and its strong liquidity and measurability are not comparable to other indicators.

Short-term international capital (*CAP*). Actually use the foreign direct investment amount to increase the growth rate. We choose the monthly growth rate of the actual use of foreign investment to measure the flow of short-term international capital in our country.

RMB exchange rate (*ERATE*). The growth rate of the US dollar against the RMB exchange rate. The exchange rate and import and export are a pair of related variables. The total foreign exchange accumulated by the trade surplus will put pressure on the RMB to appreciate. Similarly, the depreciation of the RMB can promote exports.

This paper selects the data from May 2017 to August 2018. The data mainly comes from the statistics of the General Administration of Customs, the WIND database, the People's Bank of China, the RESSET database and the National Bureau of Statistics of China.

3 Data inspection and model setting

3.1 Data stationarity test

In this paper, the unit root test is performed on each indicator by using the ADF method. The presence or absence of drift terms and trend terms is determined based on the timing diagrams of the variables, and the lag order is determined based on the AIC and SC information criteria. At a significance level of 0.05, the six sequences were stable over a 95% confidence interval. Therefore, the test results show that the data is stable and in accordance with the conditions for constructing the VAR model.

3.2 Construction of vector autoregression (VAR) model

VAR model general mathematical expression:

$$Y_t=M_1Y_{t-1}+M_2Y_{t-2}+......+M_pY_{t-p}+N_1X_t......+N_{t-r}+\varepsilon_t \quad (1)$$

Y_t is a k-dimensional endogenous variable column vector. X_t is a d-dimensional exogenous variable vector, P is the lag order of endogenous variables. t is the lag order of the exogenous variable. ε_t is a k-dimensional random perturbation column vector.

Gao(20016)[6] pointed out that the traditional VAR theory requires that each variable in the model is stable, and the data in this paper has passed the unit root test, so the VAR model can be directly established. As shown in Table 1, 3 of the 5 indicators determine that the lag phase 2 is the optimal lag period. Therefore, a vector autoregressive model with lag phase 2 VAR(2) model, is established.

Table 1. VAR Lag Order Selection Criteria

Lag	LogL	LR	FPE	AIC	SC	HQ
0.00	68.27	NA	0.00	-5.93	-5.63*	-5.87
1.00	114.97	62.27*	0.00	-6.95	-4.86	-6.50
2.00	175.88	46.41	1.26*	-9.32*	-5.44	-8.47*

Note: * indicates the hysteresis order selected by the standard. LR: sequentially modified LR test statistic (each test is at 5% level). FPE: final prediction error. AIC: Akaike information standard. SC: Schwarz information standard. HQ: Hannan-Quinn information standard.

4 Impulse response analysis

For the established VAR(2) model, the stability of the AR root must be verified to ensure the validity of the impulse response function results. there is no eigenvalue outside the unit circle, and the established VAR model satisfies the stable condition. Subsequent impulse responses will be based on a stable VAR model. The VAR model is a non-theoretical model that uses an impulse response function to analyze the effect of a standard deviation of a random disturbance on the endogenous variable, how the influence of the disturbance term is propagated to each variable. The horizontal axis of the impulse response diagram indicates the number of lag periods of the impact (unit: month). In order to keep consistent with the time interval, the lag interval is set to 23 months, the solid line indicates the impulse response function, and the broken line indicates the positive and negative twice the standard deviation deviation band.

Figure 1 shows the impulse response of *NASSEP* to *CONFI*. It can be seen from figure 2 that after a shock to *CONFI* in this period, the *NASSEP* will have a negative effect in the early stage, but this negative effect will

https://doi.org/10.1051/itmconf/20192501007

continue to weaken over time, and then gradually converge to zero, and finally the effect disappears. When the trade war occurred with the performance of export enterprises greatly damaged, and part of the capital outflow, the initial impact of the trade war will show a negative impact on the Shanghai Composite Index, that is, the negative reaction of asset prices. However, the impact of this shock on the Chinese stock market is definitely not permanent, but will gradually weaken over time to mean that the impact fades to zero.

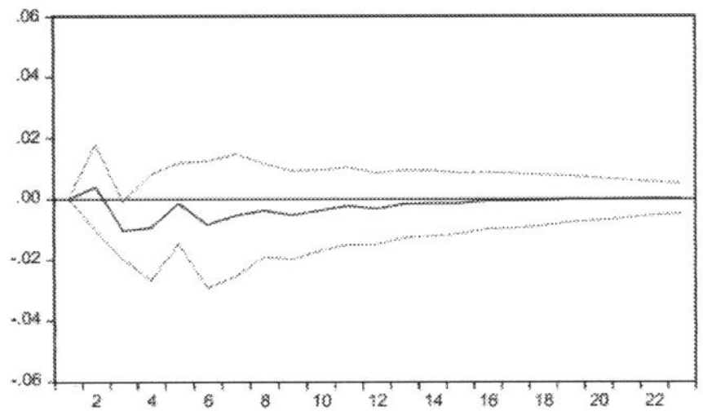

Figure 1. Response of *NASSEP* to *CONFI*

Figure 2 shows the impulse response of *ERATE* to *CONFI*. As can be seen from figure 3, after a shock to *CONFI* in this period, the early stage will have a positive effect on *ERATE*, but this positive effect will continue to weaken over time, then gradually converge to zero, and finally the effect disappears. The exchange rate of this article adopts the direct price method, and the positive reaction represents the rise of the dollar against the Renminbi, that is, the devaluation of the Renminbi. After the trade war, China's exports to the United States fell sharply in the short term, the trade surplus with the United States decreased, and the growth rate of foreign exchange reserves declined, which in turn affected the foreign exchange market, forcing the yuan to depreciate. The devaluation of the Renminbi triggered an automatic adjustment mechanism that played a role in China's exports and entered a new balance.

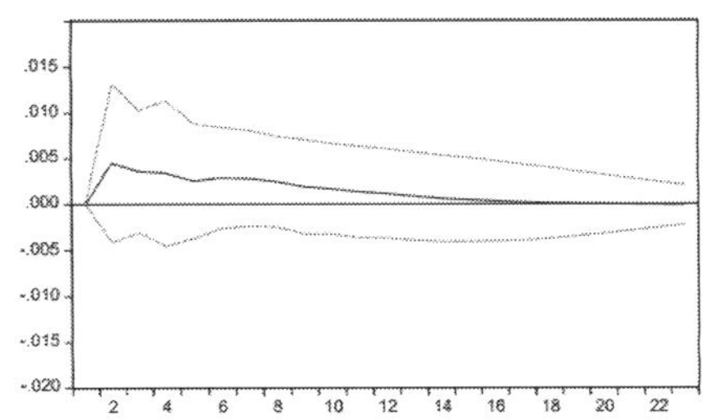

Figure 2. Response of *ERATE* to *CONFI*

Figure 3 shows the impulse response of *NETEX* to *CONFI*. It can be seen from figure 4 that after a shock to *CONFI* in this period, the *NETEX* will have periodic positive and negative alternating effects in the early stage, and the positive and negative effects will gradually weaken with time, and then gradually converge to zero, and the influence disappears. The U.S. government unilaterally took the lead in increasing tariffs on China, which first caused a negative impact on China's exports. The U.S. exports to China increased relatively. With the accumulation of trade surplus, U.S. foreign exchange reserves increased, the Renminbi appreciated against the U.S. dollar, and exports decreased. It is periodically adjusted to form a new balance.

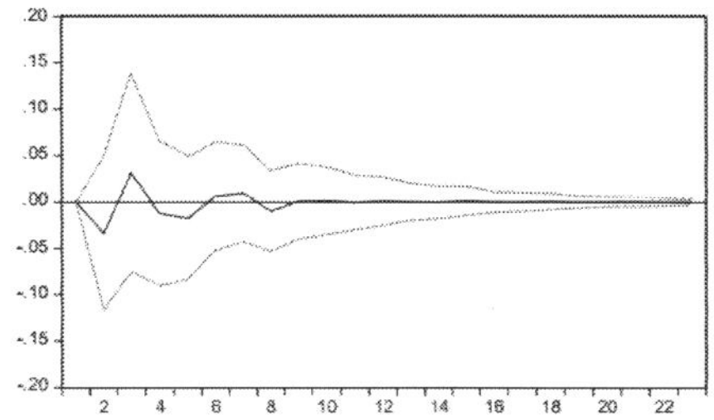

Figure 3. Response of *NETEX* to *CONFI*

Figure 4 shows the impulse response of *LOAN* to *CONFI*. It can be seen from Fig. 5 that after a shock to *CONFI* in this period, the *LOAN* will have a cyclical positive reaction in the early stage, and then reach a peak and then weaken to zero, and then periodically change with the decrease of the amplitude, gradually converge to zero and the effect disappears. After the trade war, the Chinese government adopted an expansionary fiscal policy to stabilize economic growth and a number of RRR cuts to release liquidity. Therefore, the amount of credit will increase in the short term. However, after the increase to the peak, the spontaneous adjustment mechanism came into effect, and the credit growth rate showed a slowing trend. This is then repeated until the effect of the impact is digested, and the corresponding pulse corresponding map converges to the zero axis.

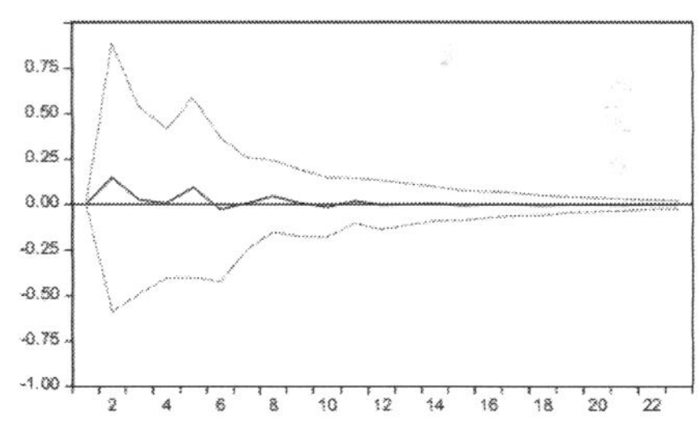

Figure 4. Response of *LOAN* to *CONFI*

Figure 5 shows the impulse response of *CAP* to *CONFI*. It can be seen from figure 5 that after a shock to *CONFI* in this period, the *CAP* will have cyclical positive and negative alternate effects in the early stage, and the growth rate of China's direct use of foreign capital will be negatively affected by the foreign risk aversion. However, when the negative impact of the FDI growth rate peaks, this negative impact gradually weakens until it gradually develops. As the peak decreases, this effect changes periodically, eventually converges to the zero axis and the effect disappears.

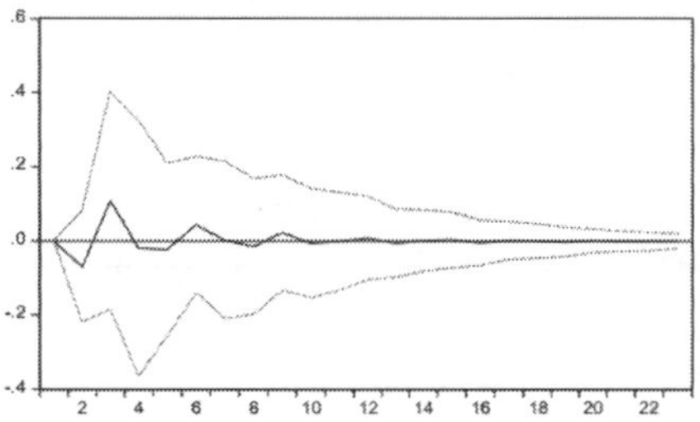

Figure 5. Response of *CAP* to *CONFI*

5 Conclusions

This paper uses the data from October 2016 to August 2018 to construct a VAR model, and analyzes the impact of trade war on financial institution loans, net export fluctuations, asset prices, short-term international capital flows, and RMB exchange rate through an impulse response function. The research results show that: (1) Sino-US trade conflict will have an impact on China's red macro economy in the short term. (2) After the impact of the trade war, the Chinese economy will have a spontaneous adjustment function, which will cause a certain positive and negative change in economic changes. (3) In the long run, the impact of trade wars on various aspects of China's economy will gradually weaken over time and finally enter a new equilibrium.

Acknowledgement

This paper is supported by the General Projects of the National Social Science Fund (17BJY021) of National Planning Office for Philosophy and Social Sciences: Research on the structural reform path of supply-side of the tea industry in China under the background of "One belt and One road".

References

1. D. Xie, F Zhang. The Political Economic Analysis of Trade Frictions between China and the United States. J. China Review of Political Economy, 9(2018): 121-143.
2. L.J. Huang. The Cause, Influence and Trend Analysis of the Upgrading of Sino-US Trade War. J. New Finance, 9(2018): 20-24.
3. R.Q. Wu, H.Y. Liu. Monopolistic Competition, Interest Groups and Trade Wars. J. China Economic Quarterly, 8(2009):829-848.
4. F. Yang, W.Y. Sun, Y. Cheng. Does Technology Catching-Up Inspire Sino-U.S. Trade Friction. J. China Industrial Economics, 10(2018): 99-117.
F. Yang, W.Y. Sun, Y. Cheng. Does Technology Catching-Up Inspire Sino-U.S. Trade Friction. J. China Industrial Economics, 10(2018): 99-117.
5. D. P. Schmidt, Intellectual Property Battles in a Technological Global Economy. J. War Analysis Business Ethics Quarterly, 14(2004): 679-693.
6. T.M. Gao. Econometric methods and modeling. M. Beijing: Tsinghua University Press, (2016): 329-385.

https://doi.org/10.1051/itmconf/20192501008

HTML5 Based Ajax and SSE Technology with Server Intelligent Instant Messaging to Meet the Needs of Transactional Websites

Shuangyuan Li

Jilin Institute of Chemical Technology, 45 Chengde Street, Longtan District, Jilin City, Jilin Province, China

Abstract. With the continuous development of science and technology, Internet technology has been quietly affect the mode of transmission, traditional web site information data only through the web page to load when it is open, need to update the web page information can only be accomplished by way of a page refresh. In today's efficient informatization environment, has highlighted its problems, restricted information updated timely. In this paper, the new Internet programming language of HTML5 is combined with Ajax and SSE technology to study intelligent instant messaging and realize the new application mode.

Keywords: html5; Ajax.; SSE.

Nowadays, the Internet technology covers a wide range of applications, and the advantage of Html5 technology is used to create new application models and bring better experience to users, which is the focus of current research. As a designer, we should consider from the perspective of user demand, pay attention to user experience and meet personalized needs. For example, the stock information website, visitors can get the latest stock market information by refreshing the page, and cannot update the data timely and efficiently. For example, all kinds of e-commerce promotional activities, because the page reload time after the missed a transaction. This waste of time and server resources cannot be ignored, so the immediacy of web page data transmission is becoming increasingly important.

HTML5 is a set of technologies including HTML, CSS and JavaScript that enhance the performance of Web pages and add the functions of Web applications such as local databases. Ajax is called "Asynchronous Javascript And XML" (Asynchronous Javascript And XML). It refers to a web development technology that creates interactive web applications. By exchanging small amounts of data with the server in the background, Ajax can make web pages achieve Asynchronous update. Server-sent Event, or SSE for short, is a component of the HTML 5 specification that can be used to push data from the Server to the browser in real time. By combining the above technologies, intelligent instant messaging can be realized to meet users' demand of real-time information acquisition.

1 Interactive page design

First, design a simple page for interactive demonstration.

```
<form action="http://127.0.0.1/test.php?action=ajax"
method="post" id="action">
<span>username</span><input type="text"
name="usr_id" value="" id="txt1">
<span>password</span><input type="text"
name="usr_psw" value="" id="txt2">
<input type="submit" name="usr_btn"
value="submit" id="sub1">
<pre id="pre_sse"></pre>
    <pre id="pre_ajax"></pre>
    </form>
```

Given the space limitations, the basic tags of the web page are omitted and only the tags set for the implementation function are retained. The <form> tag is used to realize the manual interaction between the web page and the server, and two <pre> tags are reserved to display the data obtained through ajax and SSE. Here, the action address of the <form> tag fills in the server program that is ready to handle the ajax information.

2 Design of data transmission module

Write test.php on the server side to handle ajax transfer data and SSE.

```
<php?
    switch ($_GET['action']) {
    case 'ajax':
    echo 'ajax return to success';
    break;
case 'sse':
    header('Content-Type: text/event-stream');
        header('Cache-Control: no-cache');
```

Shuangyuan Li: lsy@jlict.edu.cn

 https://doi.org/10.1051/itmconf/20192501008

```
        $time = date('Y-m-d H:i:s');
        echo 'retry: 1000'.PHP_EOL;
        echo        'data:        now        is:
'.$time.PHP_EOL.PHP_EOL;
            break;}
?>
```

The code above implements the classification of ajax and sse requests through action values of get. The "ajax request" data is returned when the ajax request is obtained from the web page, and a "data:now is server current time" data is returned every 1000ms when the sse request is obtained.

3 Design of data transmission and processing module

In order to realize the sending and processing of ajax and sse data, a test.js was written to be introduced into the web page. Meanwhile, jquery library was introduced into the web page.

```
$(document).ready(function() {
vares=new
EventSource("http://127.0.0.1/test.php?action=sse");
es.addEventListener("message",function(e){
                //e.data
                $("#pre_sse").html(e.data);
        },false);
        $('#action').submit(function(a) {
                $url1=$("#action").attr("action");
a.preventDefault();
$.post($url1,{usr_id:$('#txt1').val(),usr_psw:$('#txt2').val
(),usr_btn:$('#sub1').val()},function(data,status){
if(status=='success')        {$sat='ajax  Successful  data
exchange';}else{$sat='ajax Data exchange failed';}
$("#pre_ajax").html($("#pre_ajax").html()+"</br>"+$sa
t);  }); }); });
```

Then the basic module of the required function is completed. When you open the prepared web page with the browser, you can see the login interface as shown in Figure 1:

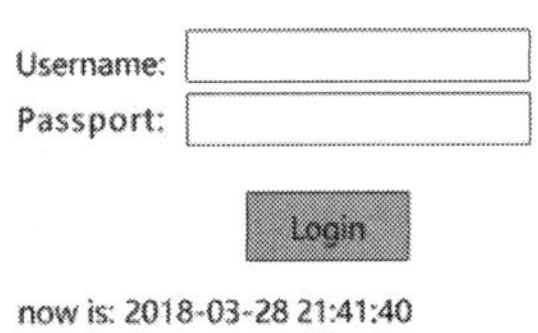

Figure 1. Login interface

And now is: the later time is always changing with the change of time in the server environment. Enter any user name or password box, click login, and there will be an additional line under the time:

Ajax successful data exchange
Ajax successful data exchange
Ajax successful data exchange
Ajax successful data exchange
Ajax successful data exchange

This enables real-time interaction with the server through Ajax and SSE as well as manual interaction with the data.At this point, visitors can update the required information in real time without refreshing the page.

4 Optimal Design

If complete above operation only, its intelligence is reduced greatly. The Php file can be modified as follows for special cases where the data required by the user does not change and there is no need to re-send the useless data to replace the original data.

```
<?php
session_start();
if (isset($_SESSION['value'])){
        $first=false;
}       else{
        $first=true;}
        switch ($_GET['action']) {
                case 'ajax':
                        echo 'ajax return to success';
                        break;
                case 'sse':
                        header('Content-Type: text/event-stream');
                        header('Cache-Control: no-cache');
                        $time = date('Y-m-d H:i:s');
                        echo 'retry: 1000'.PHP_EOL;
                        if ($first) {
                                $_SESSION["value"]=$time;
                                echo        'data:        now        is:
'.$_SESSION["value"].PHP_EOL.PHP_EOL;
                        }       else{
                                if ($_SESSION['value']==$time) {break;}
        else{$_SESSION['value']=$time;
                                echo        'data:        now        is:
'.$_SESSION["value"].PHP_EOL.PHP_EOL;}}
                                break;}
?>
```

Through the above code is managed to user data needed for temporary storage by the session on the server, every time when the trigger SSE request, the server will authenticate users need $time data is the data with the last changed, when there is no change, then you won't send change data to the client to repeat, to avoid the client due to rewrite data additional CPU and memory usage, and both the optimization of resource usage is especially important in mobile terminal. Since the $time data set is generated by the current time, this determines that it is always updated per second, so this feature is not represented. In practice, it can be replaced by other required data.

Users continues to increase, although is enabled on the server session variable, but still can cause the server memory footprint is cumulative, and the default session variables automatically destroyed time for 24 min, in the case of 1 s a SSE request frequency, obviously too long, so want to rewrite the survival time of the session variable, and the memory used by the session released when.

The specific modified code is as follows:

```
<?php
session_start();
if (isset($_SESSION['value'])){
    $first=false;
}   else{
    $first=true;}
    switch ($_GET['action']) {
        case 'ajax':
            echo 'ajax return to success';
            break;
        case 'sse':
        $later=1000;// Every 1000 is 1s, in ms
        header('Content-Type: text/event-stream');
        header('Cache-Control: no-cache');
        setcookie(session_name(), session_id(), time()
+ $later/1000*60, "/");
        $time = date('Y-m-d H:i:s');
        echo 'retry: '.$later.PHP_EOL;
        if ($first) {
            $_SESSION["value"]=$time;
            echo 'data: now is:
'.$_SESSION["value"].PHP_EOL.PHP_EOL;
        }   else{
            if ($_SESSION['value']==$time) {break;}
    else{
            $_SESSION['value']=$time;
                echo 'data: now is:
'.$_SESSION["value"].PHP_EOL.PHP_EOL;}}
            break;}?>
```

With the above code Settings, the session storage time is changed to 60 times the SSE refresh cycle, which in the example is 60s(60000ms). In the actual application, users may need to temporarily suspend and continue to monitor the changes in the data during use. Therefore, HTML, js and PHP files need to be modified. The specific implementation method is as follows:

Html

```
<form action="http://127.0.0.1/test.php?action=ajax"
method="post" id="action">
        <span>username</span><input type="text"
name="usr_id" value="" id="txt1">
        <span>passport </span><input type="text"
name="usr_psw" value="" id="txt2">
        <input type="submit" name="usr_btn"
value="submit" id="sub1">
        <a id="pause" href=""> Suspension of
communication </a>
        <pre id="pre_sse"></pre>
        <pre id="pre_ajax"></pre>
    </form>
```

Js:

```
$(document).ready(function() {
tmp=true;
functionSsestart(){
vares = new
EventSource("http://127.0.0.1/test.php?action=sse");
es.addEventListener("message",function(e){
        //e.data
    $("#pre_sse").html(e.data); },false);   };
Ssestart();
        $('#action').submit(function(a) {
            $url1=$("#action").attr("action");
a.preventDefault();
$.post($url1,{usr_id:$('#txt1').val(),usr_psw:$('#txt2').val
(),usr_btn:$('#sub1').val()},function(data,status){
if(status=='success')
                {$sat='ajax Successful data
exchange';}else{$sat='ajax Data exchange failed';}
$("#pre_ajax").html($("#pre_ajax").html()+"</br>"+$sa
t);}); });
        $('#pause').click(function(a) {
a.preventDefault();
if (tmp) {
$.post('http://127.0.0.1/test.php?action=pause',{action:'p
ause'},function(data,status){
if(status=='success'){
alert(data);   }});
tmp=false;
  $('#pause').html(' Get communication ');
}else   {
$.post('http://127.0.0.1//test.php?action=continue',{actio
n:'pause'},function(data,status){
if(status=='success'){
alert(data);   }});
tmp=true;
            $('#pause').html(' Suspension of
communication ');
Ssestart();}});});
```

Php:

```
<?php
session_start();
if (isset($_SESSION['value'])){
    $first=false;}  else{
    $first=true;
    $_SESSION['sse_pause']=false;}
    switch ($_GET['action']) {
        case 'ajax':
            echo 'ajax Return to success';
            break;
        case 'sse':
        if(!$_SESSION['sse_pause']){
            $later=1000;// Every 1000 is 1s, in ms
header('Content-Type: text/event-stream');
        header('Cache-Control: no-cache');
        setcookie(session_name(), session_id(), time()
+ $later/1000*60, "/");
        $time = date('Y-m-d H:i:s');
        echo 'retry: '.$later.PHP_EOL;
    if ($first) {
            $_SESSION["value"]=$time;
            echo 'data: now is:
'.$_SESSION["value"].PHP_EOL.PHP_EOL;
        }   else{
            if ($_SESSION['value']==$time) {break;}
    else{$_SESSION['value']=$time;
                echo 'data: now is:
'.$_SESSION["value"].PHP_EOL.PHP_EOL;}}
        }else{
$_SESSION['sse_pause']=false;}
            break;
            case 'pause':
    $_SESSION['sse_pause']=true;
            echo ' Successfully suspended ';
```

```
            break;
            case 'continue':
            $_SESSION['sse_pause']=false;
                  echo ' Successfully continued ';
        break;}
 ?>
```

Then, we can switch the pause and continue state of SSE through the hyperlink click event, so as to further define the user's needs. Then, we can make the hyperlink look like a button with CSS. The final page is shown in figure 2:

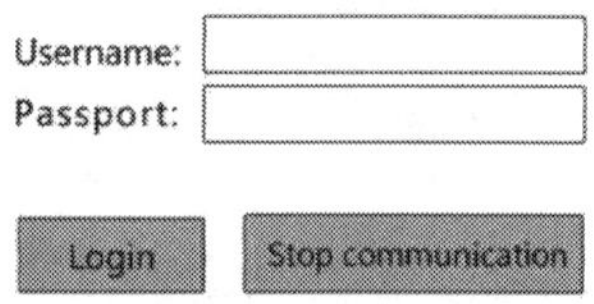

Figure 2. The login screen after compilation

5 Concludes

Through Ajax technology and SSE, instant messaging of the server is realized, which reduces the burden of the server. SEE can be used to push data from the server side to the browser side in real time, which is easier to operate and has less server side changes. Ajax can shift the work of the previous server burden to the client, use the idle capacity of the client to process, reduce the burden of the server and bandwidth, and minimize the burden of redundant requests and responses on the server, thus realizing the new application mode of intelligent instant messaging.

References

1. J.C. Xu, D.Y. Kong, Y.Y. Luo, Learning Support Technology of Mobile Online Education Platform Based on HTML5, College of Computer &Information Engineering, Henan Normal University Journal Natural Science Edition, **03**, 143-147 (2015).
2. R.Y. Rui, D.M. Zhang, The Research and Design of the Information System Based on Ajax and MVC Pattern, College of Electronic information, Electronic Technology Application Journal,**02**, 128-131 (2014).
3. S.J. Ren, X. Zhou, Y.M. Ren, L.L. Li, Multi-Thread Downloading Technology Based on HTML5, Journal of Computer System Application, **26(11)**, 11-18 (2017).
4. L. Yang, Research on Algorithm of Crawling Ajax Dynamic Web Pages Based on User Interface State Changes, Beijing Jiaotong University (2016).

Comparative Analysis of Infrastructure and Ad-Hoc Wireless Networks

Shanna Li[1,a]

[1]Information Technology Center, Beijing Jiaotong University,100044 Beijing, China

Abstract. The paper introduces the difference between infrastructure and ad hoc mode in the 802.11 Wi-Fi framework. We evaluate and compare the performance of ad hoc versus infrastructure through a series of experiments. We evaluate the performance depending of the mobility of the nodes and range of the area covered by the nodes.

1 Introduction

The IEEE 802.11 has two basic modes of operation: ad hoc mode and infrastructure mode (STA-AP). In ad hoc mode, each node transmits data directly to other nodes without access point. In infrastructure mode, all communication needs to go through the access point (AP) which connects wireless devices (Stations) to wired network. Under different scenarios , which is better, ad hoc mode or STA-AP mode ? In this case, 'better' means that more packets server node received in the same period of time when the same application was installed on the client node. In this paper, we can draw conclusions from a series of experiments using NS-3 simulator. We'll compare infrastructure and ad hoc networks to see which network can work best. The main method is comparing the number of the received packets through FlowMonitor using FlowMonitorHelper.

2 Ad hoc and Infrastructure Wireless Networks

2.1 Ad hoc Wireless Networks

There is no access point in ad hoc network. Nodes are within range of each other they can communicate directly with no access point. [1] Moreover, Nodes organize themselves into a network and route among themselves. Each node participates in routing by forwarding data for other nodes.[2]

In the Windows operating system, ad-hoc is a communication mode (setting) that allows computers to directly communicate with each other without a router. [3]

2.2 Infrastructure Wireless Networks

In infrastructure mode (STA-AP), all communication needs to go through the access point (AP), and access point plays key role in connecting wireless devices (Stations) to wired network.

Let's take two laptops positioned next to each other as an example. They can be connected to the same wireless network, but they are not directly communicating with each other. What happens is, one device sends packets to the access point and the packets are sent to the other laptop. To connect all the devices, you'd need an infrastructure mode network with a central access point. [4]

3 NS-3 Introduction

3.1 NS-3

Network Simulator 3(NS-3) is free software, licensed under the GNU GPLv2 license, and is publicly available for research, development, and use.[5]NS-3 is modular design network simulator can be connected to a real network. It has logging facility for debugging and tracing for getting output. Most of the users focus on wireless simulation includes models for Wi-Fi and routing protocols such as AODV and OLSR. NS-3 is split over number of modules having one or more models for real network device and protocols.[6]

The first is to download and build an official release from the main web site. After we finished downloading and building ns-3, we wrote some scripts that will create a WiFi link between the nodes and generate traffic between the nodes.

3.2 FlowMonitor

FlowMonitor is a network monitoring framework for the NS-3 which can be easily used to collect and store network performance data from a NS-3 simulation instead of WireShark. FlowMonitor can automatically detect all flows passing through network. NS-3 provides

[a] Corresponding author: lsn@bjtu.edu.cn

FlowMonitorHelper class to create FlowMonitor easily. The helper will take care of about everything.

4 Simulation experiments

4.1 Experimental purpose

A series of experiments have been done using NS-3 under different scenarios. Meanwhile, we made comparative analysis between ad hoc mode and infrastructure mode.

We mainly focused on the packets server node received in the same period of time when the same application was installed on the client node.

4.2 3 nodes topology

There are 3 nodes topology which is equilateral triangle.

Each node will be installed ad hoc mode and infrastructure mode. Application is OnOff using OnOffHelper. Generate traffic from n0 to n2, as follows.

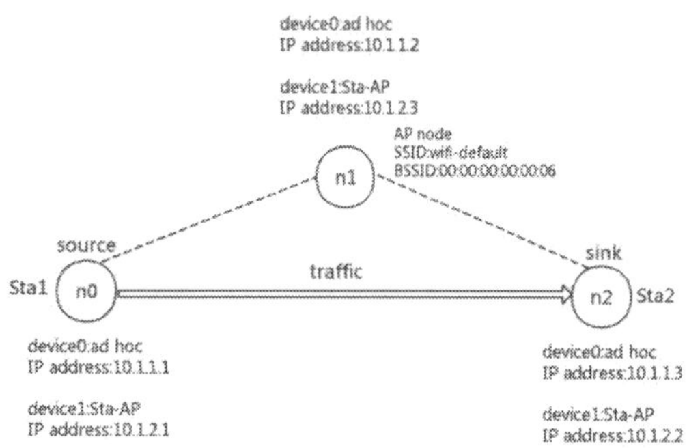

Figure 1. 3 nodes topology.

We can see from the figure 2 that ad hoc mode is better within a certain distance. STA-AP mode is better beyond a certain distance.

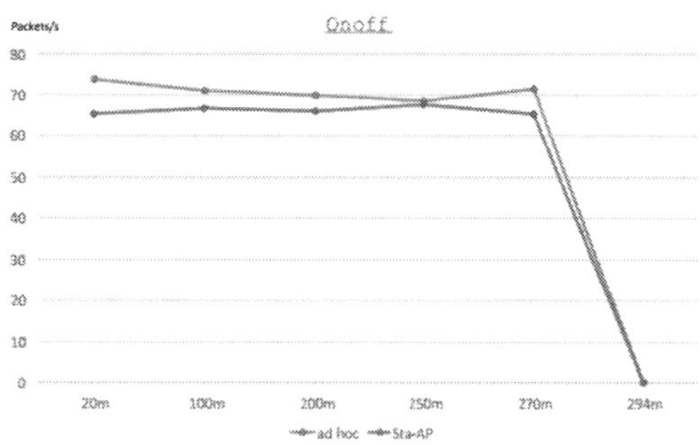

Figure 2. packets/s with different distance.

Since STA-AP mode is better beyond a certain distance , if we try to add routing on the nodes in ad hoc mode , we can find ad hoc mode is better than STA-AP mode after adding AODV routing protocol.STA-AP mode is better than ad hoc mode after adding OLSR routing protocol.

4.3 5 nodes topology

We will simulate topology like figure3 in different simulator.Each node will be installed ad hoc protocol or STA-AP Protocol.The nodes will be installed routing protocol when they are in ad hoc mode.Generate traffic flow1 from n0 to n2.Generate traffic flow2 from n3 to n4

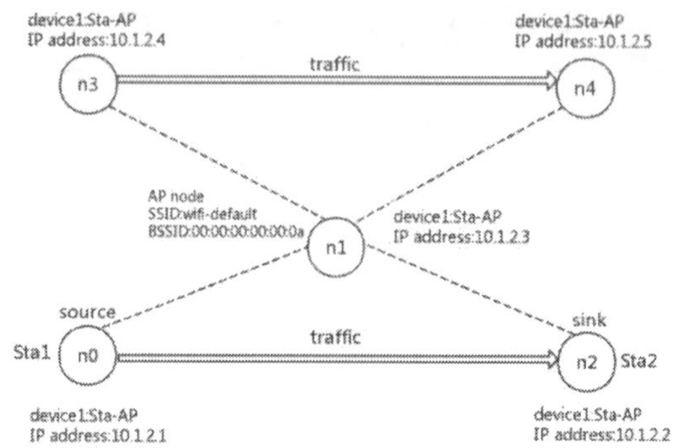

Figure 3. 5 nodes topology.

We can draw conclusions from experiment that no matter AP node is static or moving, the number of packets received in ad hoc mode is always two times that of STA-AP mode.

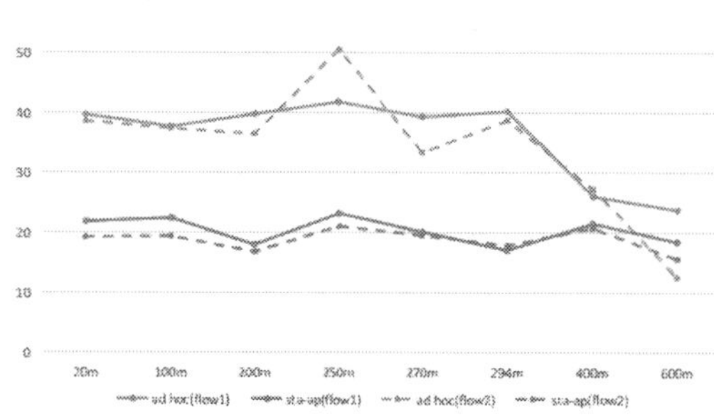

Figure 4. packets/s with different distance.

Ad hoc mode is better than STA-AP mode because STA-AP mode transfers a packet two times as long as ad hoc mode.

5 Conclusion

Ad hoc mode is better within a certain distance. STA-AP mode is better beyond a certain distance. After adding routing in ad hoc mode, which is better depends on routing protocol. Ad hoc mode is better than STA-AP mode because STA-AP mode transfers a packet two times as long as ad hoc mode.

In addition, ad hoc networks are very fast. Throughput rate is twice as fast as STA-AP networks. But limited wireless transmission range is the fact. By comparison, infrastructure networks can connect to a wired network and extend your wireless network's range. In the future, we will explore more complicated scenarios to get better comparison between ad hoc mode and infrastructure mode.

References

1. Morteza M. Zanjireh; Hadi Larijani (May 2015). A Survey on Centralised and Distributed Clustering Routing Algorithms for WSNs (PDF). IEEE 81st Vehicular Technology Conference. Glasgow, Scotland. doi:10.1109/VTCSpring.2015.7145650.
2. Morteza M. Zanjireh; Ali Shahrabi; Hadi Larijani (2013). ANCH: A New Clustering Algorithm for Wireless Sensor Networks (PDF). 27th International Conference on Advanced Information Networking and Applications Workshops. WAINA 2013. doi:10.1109/WAINA.2013.242.
3. Chai Keong Toh, Ad Hoc Mobile Wireless Networks. United States: Prentice Hall Publishers (2002).
4. Chris Hoffman, What's the Difference Between Ad-Hoc and Infrastructure Mode Wi-Fi? https://www.howtogeek.com/180649/htg-explains-whats-the-difference-between-ad-hoc-and-infrastructure-mode/ (2016)
5. https://www.nsnam.org/docs/release/3.29/tutorial/html/introduction.html#about-ns3
6. Rakesh Kumar Jha, Pooja Kharga; Advanced Open Source Simulator: NS-3, International Journal of Computer Sciences and Engineering **3**,67 (2015).

https://doi.org/10.1051/itmconf/20192501010

Research on Trajectory Planning of Six Degrees of Freedom Robot

Hao Zhou

Wuhan Business University, Wuhan 430056 China

Abstract. With the continuous development of industrial automation, the demand for industrial robots in the manufacturing field is gradually increasing. In order to meet the needs of different occasions and functions, the planning of the trajectory of the robot becomes the research direction of the six-degree-of-freedom robot. The research object of this paper is a six-degree-of-freedom industrial robot. According to engineering needs, a structure of a handling robot is designed. The kinematics of the robot and its trajectory planning are studied, and the simulation analysis is made.

1 The introduction

Industrial robot [1] is an electromechanical integration device in the industrial field, mainly a humanoid robot with multiple degrees of freedom. Such robots tend to be autonomous and can be programmed repeatedly. Since the first industrial robot appeared in the United States, more and more attention has been paid to industrial robots by scholars.

Compared with foreign countries, although China is the world's largest market, in the high-end field, the robot market has been basically monopolized by foreign countries. According to the latest data, the top-selling model in the Chinese market is multi-joint robot, among which there are more six-axis robots. However, many products in China are basically dependent on imports. The competitiveness of domestic industrial robots is very poor, and the research foundation is very weak.

The system of the six-degree of robot [4] requires strong coupling, strong non-linearity, and uncertainty in some aspects, such as parameters and interference of the external environment. This brings about certain difficulties in control. With the rapid development of modern industry, people have strict requirements on quality, especially in laser cutting, welding and other occasions more stringent. This puts forward higher requirements for robot tracking accuracy [5]. How to make the manipulator [6] stable, accurate and control its speed has become the top priority. These are things that need to be explored. How to realize the high-precision movement of robot has become a key factor restricting the level of robot in our country and even enhancing the competitiveness.

2 Dynamic analysis

Industrial robots are usually multi-rigid-body coupling, multi-dimensional and high-precision motion devices [7]. In addition to the general equipment design requirements, it also needs to have flexibility and accuracy. Robot mechanical structure design often needs to consider the linkage and motion. The robot design first analyzes and draws lessons from the existing robot. After major innovations and even improvements, we can realize the maximum value of this robot. This requires repeated tests on the model [8]. In the analysis of the robot, it is necessary to carry out dynamic analysis and verify the robot separately. Figure 1 is a schematic of the robot.

This robot needs to achieve θ_1 specific action according to the difference of six angles. For example, when A is used, waist rotation can be achieved. However, its range of action and speed are also required. The maximum is 160°/*s*; At θ_2, the pitch of the big arm can be achieved. Its Angle range is -145 to 90, and its maximum speed is the same as that at θ_1; At θ_3, the pitch of the forearm can be achieved. Its Angle ranges from -125 to +128, and its maximum speed is 220°/*s*. At θ_4, you can rotate the wrist, and its Angle range is, the maximum speed is 500°/*s*; At θ_5, you can flip the wrist, which has the same Angle range and maximum speed as at θ_4; At θ_6, you can achieve wrist deflection, and it's Angle range is, the maximum speed is 330°/*s*. As can be seen from the figure, wrist movement is mainly controlled by l4-l6. When the robot moves, there are six degrees of freedom in total. At this time, the structure improves the flexibility of the robot [9].

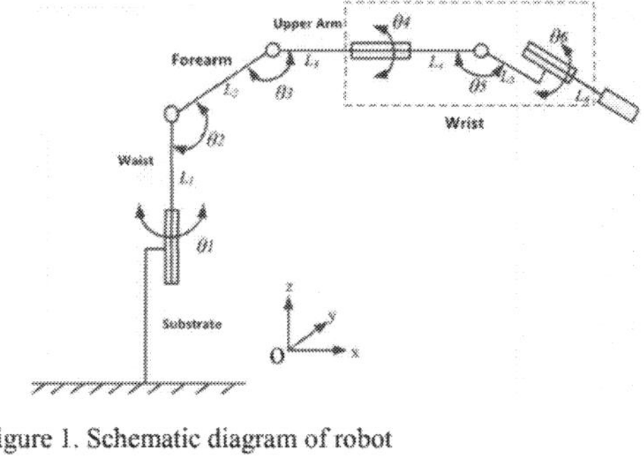

Figure 1. Schematic diagram of robot

https://doi.org/10.1051/itmconf/20192501010

3 Trajectory planning

Before tracking tasks, mechanical arms [10] usually need to understand tracking targets and assign tasks to different joints. Generally, the operation of the robot is curvilinear motion. At this time, displacement and velocity need to be determined to achieve the desired trajectory planning. Trajectory planning is the basis of tracking tasks, usually joint space or cartesian coordinate space. Trajectory planning is the main content of motion planning. Trajectory planning [11] mainly considers inserting an intermediate point between the start and the end to make its path correspond to the corresponding time, so as to realize the movement of the robot along the trajectory. Generally, manual input path and constraint conditions are used to determine the target position, time, speed and other parameters, and finally trajectory is generated based on calculation [12]. Trajectory planning often requires its function to be continuous and smooth, and even needs to consider the obstacles encountered in the middle. Its planning flow chart is shown in figure 2.

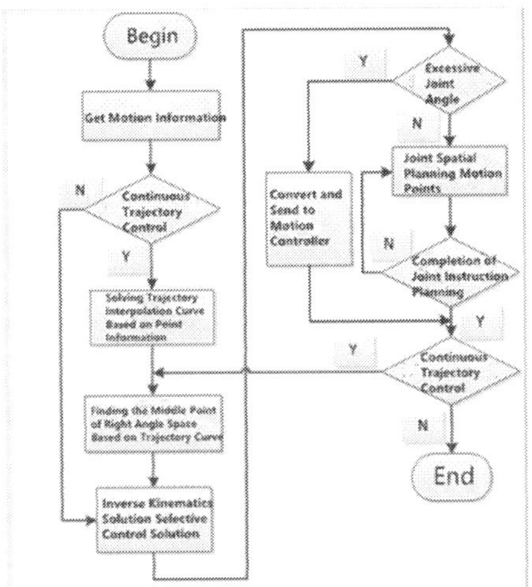

Figure 2. Trajectory planning process

When the robot moves to the target point, the planner usually puts forward some requirements to the user, and usually provides some explicit constraints, such as smoothness or continuity. At this time, the planner uses some functions to operate on the corresponding nodes according to the requirements, so as to formulate different path segments, and then drives the manipulator to reach the specified path point according to the controller, and then reaches the target position.

4 Simulation analysis

In general, the transformation of each joint required by the planning of spatial trajectory can be basically regarded as a function of time, that is, all joints pass through a certain point at the same time, so the planning of trajectory needs to have a strong real-time performance. The setting and planning of constraint conditions are usually carried out in space, without considering obstacles, and generally applicable to point-to-point.

The way to select the joint quantity to show the robot's motion is to describe the joint space. However, joint space planning is roughly divided into two steps: on the one hand, the assumed path point coordinates are calculated by inverse kinematics solution to calculate the vector values of their key nodes, and then the vector values of each joint are integrated into a smooth order, and finally it is made into a function of the path points. This trajectory planning can not only ensure the continuity of joints, but also demonstrate its real-time performance. Its disadvantage is that it is difficult to determine the trajectory of the end, which is only suitable for point-to-point. In addition, the smoothness of its velocity should even be considered. Sometimes the overshoot of speed causes the motor to oscillate, and then affects its response time. If the acceleration is large, it will directly affect the torque of the motor, at the same time, it will accelerate the loss of machinery and bring unnecessary trouble to the system.

For cartesian space, its trajectory planning is developed by changing the posture of the end-effector in space, mainly considering its transformation sequence. Because the requirements of tasks are different, the paths used by users in the task space are also different, such as arc, line and spline curve, etc., so according to the different path trajectories, this kind of planning can be summarized as arc trajectory planning and linear function interpolation. This kind of space description method is more intuitive, and the trajectory of its end is very clear, which is a kind of suitable trajectory planning for continuous path. The path points of this method may be difficult to become joint space problems. Sometimes, the inverse solution of kinematics needs to be solved many times in each interpolation cycle, and even the problem of joint Angle needs to be considered. In addition, the control of joint movement needs to be considered, resulting in a huge amount of calculation.

If the end of the manipulator wants to perform pose operation, it is necessary to control the action of these operations as a function of time, such as speed, etc. Then, the principle of inverse kinematics is adopted to solve joint variables, and its motion trajectory can be clearly displayed. If the pose cannot be directly measured, it usually relies on joint space to find the inverse solution, so joint space coordinates or cartesian space coordinates are used to switch, resulting in a large amount of computation. FIG. 3 shows simulation with joint space model on the left and cartesian space model on the right.

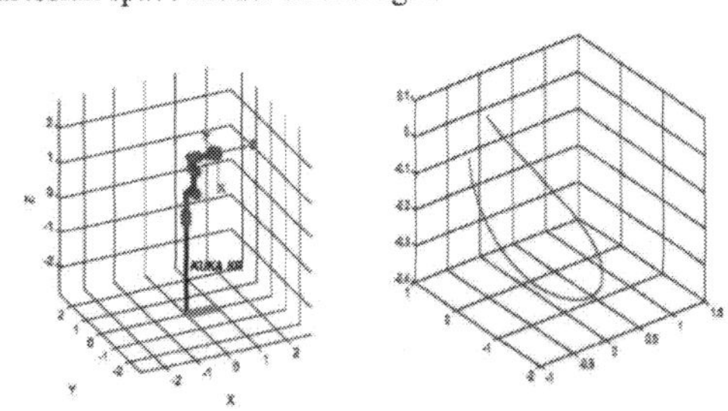

Figure 3. Simulation of two methods

For robots, there must be two problems with planning: first, the constraints of the basis, which can be listed as speed and displacement of each joint. On the other hand, we need to consider the outside world to determine whether obstacles affect the movement of robots.

5 Conclusion

This paper mainly makes a simple introduction to the six-degree of robot, designs the trajectory planning process, emphatically explores the planning process of joint space and cartesian space, and simulates its trajectory planning with MATLAB software, hoping to provide theoretical basis for the further realization of the follow-up trajectory tracking research.

6 Acknowledgement

This paper is supported by University-level scientific research project of Wuhan Business University: "Algorithm and Realization of optimal trajectory for industrial robot (Number: 2017KY008)".

References

1. Le Ying, Ku Wei, Lu Yi, Zhang Haiwei, Zhao Donglei. Trajectory planning of NURBS based on optimization of six-degree of industrial robot [J]. Modular machine tool and automation processing technology, 2017 (11): 41-43+47.
2. Ma Dani, li Chuanjiang, Zhang Ziqiang. Trajectory planning of 7-degree of robot based on genetic algorithm [J]. Laboratory research and exploration, 2016, 35 (09): 33-37.
3. Topaz Kushiro. Trajectory planning simulation of tensor product surface of six-degree of polishing robot [J]. Computer simulation, 2015, 32 (07): 348-351+377.
4. Gong Chikun, Yu Guoying, Xiong Jiguang, Huang Chenglin. Design, analysis and implementation of six-degree of robot [J]. Modern manufacturing engineering, 2014 (11): 60-63.
5. Chen Weihua, Zhao Zian, Wu Shaobin. Research on arc trajectory planning algorithm of six-degree of robot [J]. Manufacturing automation, 2013, 35 (22): 5-6+14.
6. Qiu Ningjia, Sui Zhen, Li Mingzhe, Zheng Chengxiang. Trajectory planning algorithm for six degrees of freedom robot space marking [J]. Journal of Jilin university (engineering), 2013, 43 (05): 1307-1313.
7. Gao Guoqin, Hu Hongyu, Hu Zhi. Trajectory planning of parallel robot in six-degree of surface machining [J]. Machinery design and manufacturing, 2010 (05): 167-168. (in Chinese)
8. Zhao Jianbo, Gao Feng, Yue Yi. Trajectory planning of 6-ppps orthogonal 6-degree of parallel robot [J]. Mechanical design and research, 2007 (03): 62-65.
9. Ma Guoqing, Liu li, Yu Zhenglin, Cao Guohua. Trajectory generation and experimental research of six-degree of parallel robot [J]. Journal of Changchun university of science and technology (natural science edition), 2015, 38 (05): 53-57+63.
10. Qu Linjin, Wang Xingju, Liu Wei. Motion simulation of six-degree of arc welding tandem robot based on virtual prototype [J]. Welding machine, 2014, 44 (09): 60-63+105.
11. Li yuan, Wu Jianxin, Guo Yuhong, Li Bowei. Development and application of six-degree of manipulator based on Galil controller [J]. Mechanical engineering and automation, 2015 (05): 169-171.
12. Wang Guoming. Motion analysis and control of six-degree of series robot based on MATLAB / SimMechanics module [J]. Journal of Binzhou university, 2014, 30 (03): 89-93.

Research on LEACH-Based Wireless Sensor Network Routing

Junke Lv [1,a]

[1]*Xingzhi College, Zhejiang Normal University, Jinhua, Zhejiang, China*

Abstract. Routing technology is one of the main supporting technologies of wireless sensor networks. Only by using routing algorithm reasonably or finding better routing optimization algorithm, can the function of wireless sensor networks be maximized. Therefore, the research of routing technology for wireless sensor networks has important theoretical and practical significance. Based on the analysis of existing routing protocols in wireless sensor networks, this paper focuses on LEACH protocol.

1 Introduction

Wireless Sensor Networks (WSNs) have been widely applied to battlefield investigation, rehabilitation therapy and field environment monitoring [1]. Numerous sensing nodes are deployed in the above-mentioned application environment. Sensing nodes can sense the environment data in real time and then transmit the data to the data management center so as to realize environment monitoring. However, due to limited energy supplied by sensing nodes, the energy consumption of these nodes is the key factor affecting the data collection efficiency of WSNs and shortening the network lifework. Once the nodes run out of energy, they cannot sense the environment data, which forms loopholes in WSNs coverage and shortens its lifetime[2-4].

Consequently, it's the research focus to enhance the energy utilization of WSNs. Currently, the inter-cluster

2 Problem description

The Low Energy Adaptive Clustering Hierarchy (LEACH) protocol generates cluster heads at random and takes into account the residual energy of node. Specifically, a node (supposed as node i) generates randomly a uster head in this round if $\gamma > \lambda(i)$. The threshold of node i, namely $\lambda(i)$, is defined as shown in Equation (1):

$$\lambda(i)=\begin{cases}\dfrac{p}{1-p\times\left(r \bmod \dfrac{1}{p}\right)}, & i\in G\\ 0, & i\notin G\end{cases} \tag{1}$$

Where: p represents cluster head proportion, namely the larger the number of cluster heads in networks, the greater the possibility that the node becomes a cluster head. r represents the number of current round while G indicates the set of nodes failing to become cluster heads in the previous round (r -1). According to Equation (1), the nodes that have become cluster heads in the previous round are not considered as candidates for cluster heads in this round, aiming to balance node energy.

Notwithstanding the LEACH protocol takes into account energy balancing, there are still some shortcomings as follows:

(1) The threshold doesn't consider the residual energy of node. If a node with a little residual energy is chosen as the cluster head, its energy will be used up quickly, which makes direct impact on network lifetime;

(2) Under the LEACH protocol, the proportion of cluster heads p is fixed, which doesn't consider network energy distribution information;

(3) The spacing between nodes is not considered when setting the threshold. If the spacing is too large, the number of hops for data transmission will be increased and thus the energy consumption will be increased.

Thus, based on the LEACH protocol, the paper revises its threshold and meanwhile considers the heterogeneous sensor networks, namely there is a difference in the initial energy of node.

3 Network model

The network model[8-9] shown in the Figure 2 can be considered, namely the source node forwards the data packet to the destination node (sink) through the relay nodes. The relay nodes between the source node and the sink nodes are also called forwarding nodes.

In addition, since the paper considers heterogeneous networks with three-level energy, namely node energy is divided into three levels and node energy varies from level to level, these nodes of various energy levels are respectively called advanced nodes, intermediate nodes and normal nodes. Advanced nodes contain highest

[a] Corresponding author: ljk@zjnu.cn

energy while normal nodes have lowest energy. These nodes of various levels have different proportion. It's supposed that the proportion of advanced nodes and intermediate nodes in network nodes are m and m_0 respectively. It's supposed that the energy of normal nodes is E_0 and that of advanced nodes and intermediate nodes are represented by $E_0(1+\alpha)$, $E_0(1+\beta)$ respectively, where α and β are coefficients.

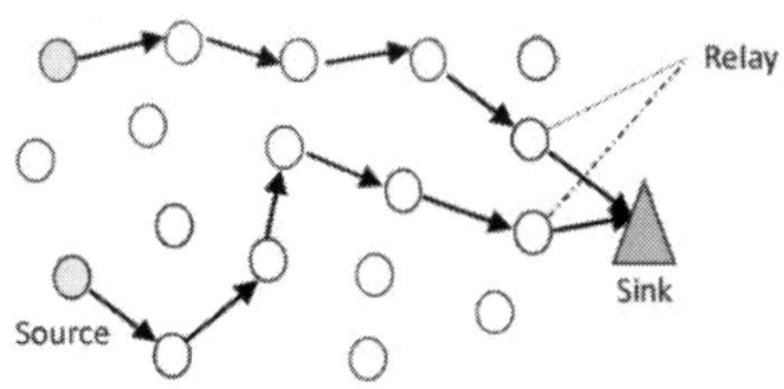

Figure 1. Network Model

4 Performance simulation

4.1 Simulation parameters and performance indicator

In order to better analyze the performance of the CTICR protocol, a simulation platform is established with the assistance of MATLAB and the LEACH and LEACH-D protocols are adopted as reference to compare their performance. It's supposed that 100 nodes are randomly distributed within $100m\times100m$ network area. Specific simulation parameters are shown in Table 1. Each experiment is carried out independently for repeatedly 100 times and the average value is taken as the final experimental data.

Table 1. Simulation Parameter

Parameter	Value
Simulation area	$100m\times100m$
Number of nodes	80
Node distribution	Random distribution
E_0	$0.5J$
E_{elec}	50nJ/bit
E_{frris}	10nJ/(bit*m^2)
E_{tworay}	0.0013pJ/bit/m^4
E_{DA}	5nJ/bit/signal

In addition, three indicators including network lifetime, stability duration and the number of data packet successfully received by the Base Station shall be adopted to assess the protocol. Network lifetime refers to the number of rounds when the last failure node occurs in the network; the stability duration refers to the number of rounds when the first failure node occurs in the network.

4.2 Data analysis

The CTICR protocol considers the heterogeneous networks with three-level energy. Thus, during the experiment simulation, $m=0.4$, $m_0=0.4$ while $\alpha=2$, $\beta=3.5$.

(1) Stability duration and network lifetime

The stability duration and network lifetime of the LEACH, DDEE and CTICR protocols are shown in Table 2. Data of 10 experiments are listed in Table 2.

Table 2. List of stability duration and network lifetime

Experiment	Stability duration (rounds)			Network lifetime (rounds)		
	LEACH	DDEEC	CTTCR	LEACH	DDEEC	CTTCR
1	969	1355	1717	5536	5673	8638
2	926	1355	1716	5553	5670	8637
3	970	1342	1718	5537	5673	8636
4	967	1357	1716	5532	5674	8643
5	972	1365	1714	5538	5676	8640
6	945	1358	1720	5539	5675	8640
7	936	1350	1718	5530	5668	8638
8	978	1355	1719	5534	5670	8640
9	976	1359	1716	5538	5673	8641
10	969	1355	1716	5530	5675	8641

According to Table 2, the proposed CTICR protocol has the longest stability duration reaching 1,717 rounds while that of the LEACH and DDEEC protocols are 969 rounds and 1,355 rounds respectively. The cause is that the CTICR protocol reduces the energy consumption and balances network energy consumption through revising the threshold so as to prolong the stability duration. In addition, according to Table 2, the CTICR protocol has the longest network lifetime, far higher than that of the LEACH protocol.

It's not hard to figure out that the CTICR protocol can effectively improve network utilization rate, balance energy consumption and prolong network lifetime according to the experimental data. The mainly cause is that the CTICR protocol always attempts to choose the optimal node as the cluster head in each round so as to balance the energy consumption.

5 Conclusion

Data-centric wireless sensor networks have limited computing power, limited storage capacity, limited wireless communication capacity and limited power supply capacity. How to obtain as much and effective feature information as possible and transmit it to user nodes for processing in such a limited resource environment is the focus of current research. Therefore, designing energy-efficient routing strategies to prolong the lifetime of wireless sensor networks has become a key issue. Based on the analysis of existing routing protocols in wireless sensor networks, this paper focuses on LEACH protocol.

References

1. X.L. Xue. Research on Multi-hop Non-uniform Clustering Routing Algorithms for WSN Based on LEACH Protocol [D]. School of Information, East China University of Technology, (2010).
2. L.M. Sun, C. Ye, Y. Liao. Routing Mechanism for Sensor Networks [J]. *Computer Science*, 31(1) 54-57, (2004).

https://doi.org/10.1051/itmconf/20192501011

3. X.Y. Mo. Wireless Sensors Research and Design of Network Clustering Routing Protocols [D]. School of Information, Zhejiang University, (2006).
4. X. Zheng, Research and Optimization of Energy Consumption Performance of LEACH-based Wireless Sensor Networks Routing Protocols [D]. Shanghai: Department of Computer Science and Engineering, Shanghai Jiaotong University.

Feedback Numbers of Goldberg Snark, Twisted Goldberg Snarks and Related Graphs

Xinyue Zhang[1], Yijin Wang[1] and Sijia Zhang[1,a]

[1]*School of Information Engineering, Dalian Ocean University, Dalian, 116023, China*

Abstract. A subset of vertices of a graph G is called a feedback vertex set of G if its removal results in an acyclic subgraph. The minimum cardinality of a feedback vertex set is called the feedback number. In this paper, we determine the exact values of the feedback numbers of the Goldberg snarks G_n and its related graphs G_n^*, Twisted Goldberg Snarks TG_n and its related graphs TG_n^*. Let $f(n)$ denote the feedback numbers of these graphs, we prove that $f(n)=2n+1$, for $n\geq 3$.

1 Introduction

Let $G = (V, E)$ be a graph or digraph without multiple edges, with vertex set $V(G)$ and edge set $E(G)$. A subset $F\subset V(G)$ is called a feedback vertex set if the subgraph $G-F$ is acyclic, that is, if $G-F$ is a forest. The minimum cardinality of a feedback vertex set is called the feedback number (or decycling number proposed first by Beineke and Vandell [1]) of G. A feedback vertex set of this cardinality is called a minimum feedback vertex set.

Apart from its graph-theoretical interest, the minimum feedback vertex set problem has important application to several fields. For example, the problems are in operating systems to resource allocation mechanisms that prevent deadlocks [2], in artificial intelligence to the constraint satisfaction problem and Bayesian inference, in synchronous distributed systems to the study of monopolies and in optical networks to converters placement problem (see [3, 4]).

Determining the feedback number is quite difficult even for some elementary graphs. However, the problem has been studied for some special graphs and digraphs, such as hypercubes, meshes, toroids, butterflies, cube-connected cycles, directed split-stars (see [3, 4, 5, 6, 7, 8, 9, 10, 11, 12, 13]). In fact, the minimum feedback set problem is known to be NP-hard for general graphs [14] and the best known approximation algorithm is one with an approximation ratio two [5].

Snarks are simple nontrivial connectes cubic graphs of chromatic index four [16]. The importance of the snar-ks does not only depend on the four colour theorem. Indeed, there are several important open problems such as the classical cycle double cover conjecture [18]. The smallest snark is the Petersen graph and it was the first discovered. In [17], it gave a survey of some results on some well known families of snarks, e.g. Flower snarks, Loupekine snarks and Goldberg snarks.

Goldberg Snarks is referred to Loupekine by Goldberg himself. In fact, Goldberg Snarks are cartwheel snarks [19]. Both Goldberg Snarks and twisted Goldberg Snarks are graphs on $8n$ vertices with

$$V(G_n)=\{v_j^i \mid 0\leq i\leq n-1, 1\leq j\leq 8\}$$

• For every odd $n\geq 3$, G_n is called the ***Goldberg Snark graph*** and adjacencies are defined as shown in Fig.1, where the vertex labels i are read modulo n.

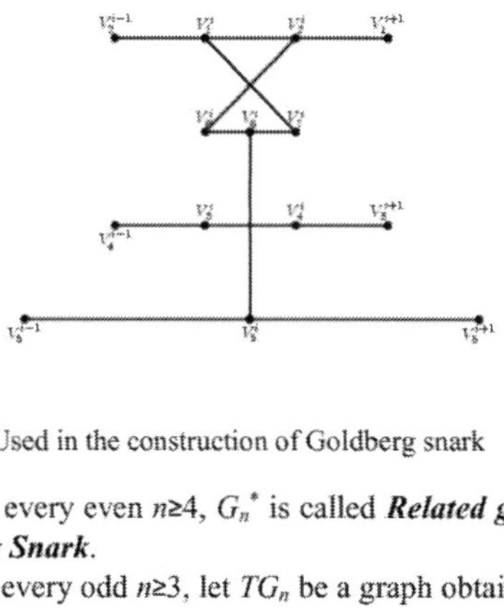

Figure 1. Used in the construction of Goldberg snark

• For every even $n\geq 4$, G_n^* is called ***Related graphs of Goldberg Snark***.

• For every odd $n\geq 3$, let TG_n be a graph obtained from G_n by replacing the edges $v_2^{n-1}v_1^0$ and $v_4^{n-1}v_3^0$ with $v_2^{n-1}v_3^0$ and $v_4^{n-1}v_1^0$, respectively. We denote TG_n as ***Twisted Goldberg Snark***.

• For every even $n\geq 4$, TG_n^* is called ***Related graphs of Twisted Goldberg Snark***.

[a] Corresponding author: zhangsijia@dlou.edu.cn

The example of G_3, G_4^*, TG_3 and TG_4^* are shown in Fig.2.

However, both Goldberg Snarks and twisted Goldberg Snarks can be obtained via the Loupekine construction from the Petersen graph [15].

In this paper, we determine the exact values of the feedback number of the Goldberg snarks G_n and its related graphs G_n^*, the twisted Goldberg snarks TG_n and its related graphs TG_n^*. Let $f(n)$ denote the feedback number of these graphs, we prove that $f(n)=2n+1$, for $n \geq 3$.

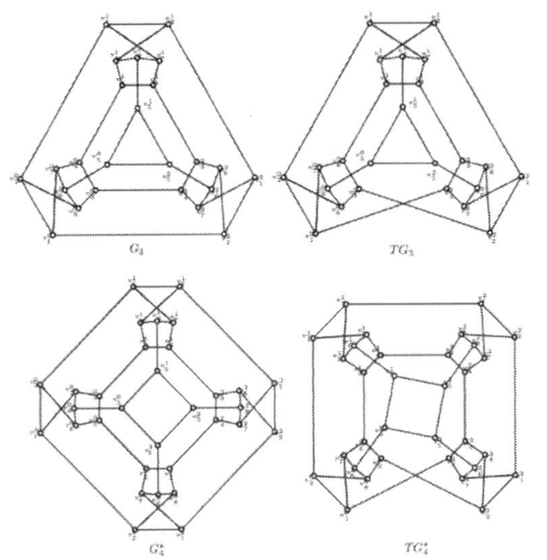

Figure 2. Graph G_3, G_4^*, TG_3 and TG_4^*

2 Acyclic Vertex Set of G_n and G_n^*

Let $n \bmod 2 = k$, then $n = 2m + k$, $m \geq 1$ *and* $0 \leq i \leq k$. Thus $k=0$ and $k=1$. Then, we discuss 2 cases as follows.

Case 1. If $n \bmod 2 = 1$ and $n \geq 3$

Let $V_a(G_n) = F_1^n \cup F_2^n$, where

$$F_1^n = \{v_2^0, v_3^0, v_8^0, v_6^0, v_7^0\}$$

$$F_2^n = \bigcup_{i=1}^{n-1} \{v_2^i, v_3^i, v_8^i, v_6^i, v_7^i, v_5^i\}$$

Case 2. If $n \bmod 2 = 0$ and $n \geq 4$.

Let $V_a(G_n^*) = F_1^n \cup F_2^n \cup F_3^n$,where

$$F_1^n = \{v_2^0, v_3^0, v_8^0, v_6^0, v_7^0\}$$

$$F_2^n = \{v_2^1, v_3^1, v_8^1, v_6^1, v_7^1, v_5^1\}$$

$$F_3^n = \bigcup_{i=2}^{n-1} \{v_2^i, v_3^i, v_8^i, v_6^i, v_7^i, v_5^i\}$$

Lemma 2.1. $G[V_a(G_n)]$ is acyclic for n mod 2=1 and $n \geq 3$.

Proof: Since $V_a(G_n) = F_1^n \cup F_2^n$, Then if we want to prove $G[V_a(G_n)]$ is acyclic, which is equivalent to verify that $G[F_1^n \cup F_1^n]$ is acyclic.

Firstly, we prove the $G[F_1^n \cup F_1^n]$ is a forest by induction on n.

We first prove the basic step for n=3.

Combining case 1 and the definition of G_n, we have

$$F_1^3 = \{v_2^0, v_3^0, v_8^0, v_6^0, v_7^0\}$$

$$F_2^3 = \{v_2^1, v_3^1, v_8^1, v_6^1, v_7^1, v_5^1, v_2^2, v_3^2, v_8^2, v_6^2, v_7^2, v_5^2\}$$

Obviously, the induced subgraph of vertex set F_1^3 and the induced subgraph of vertex set F_2^3 are acyclic graphs(see Fig.3 and Fig.4) and each graph of $G[F_1^3]$ and $G[F_2^3]$ is a tree.

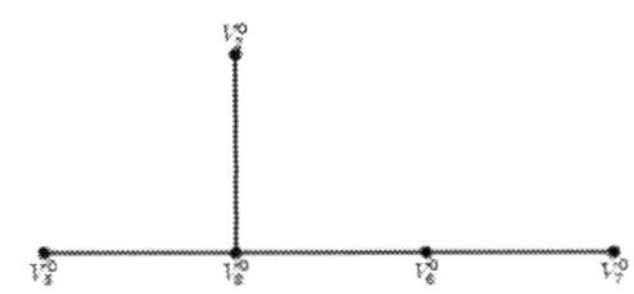

Figure 3. Subgraph of $G[F_1^3]$

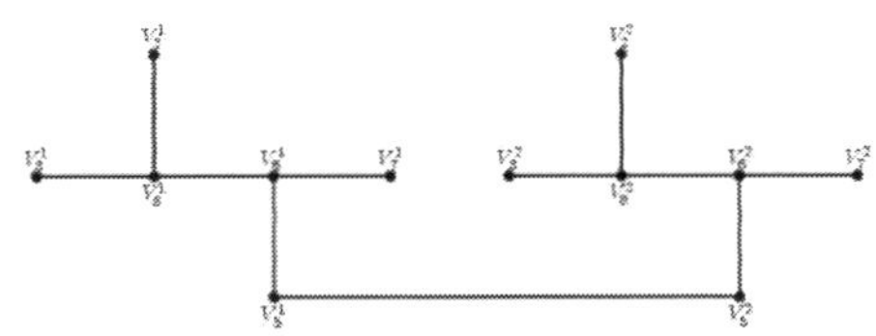

Figure 4. Subgraph of $G[F_2^3]$

Since $F_1^3 \cap F_2^3 = \emptyset$, then the induced subgraph of vertex set $F_1^3 \cup F_2^3$ is acyclic. That is, $G[F_1^3 \cup F_2^3]$ is a forest.

Suppose $G[F_1^n \cup F_2^n]$ is acyclic, we now prove that $G[F_1^{n+2} \cup F_2^{n+2}]$ is acyclic.

Since

$$F_1^{n+2} = \{v_2^0, v_3^0, v_8^0, v_6^0, v_7^0\}$$

$$F_2^{n+2} = \bigcup_{i=1}^{n+2-1} \{v_2^i, v_3^i, v_8^i, v_6^i, v_7^i, v_5^i\}$$

Then we have

$$F_1^{n+2} = F_1^n$$

$$F_2^{n+2} = \bigcup_{i=1}^{n-1} \{v_2^i, v_3^i, v_8^i, v_6^i, v_7^i, v_5^i\} \cup \bigcup_{i=n}^{n+1} \{v_2^i, v_3^i, v_8^i, v_6^i, v_7^i, v_5^i\}$$

$$= F_2^n \cup \bigcup_{i=n}^{n+1} \{v_2^i, v_3^i, v_8^i, v_6^i, v_7^i, v_5^i\}$$

For convenience, we denote T as vertex set $\bigcup_{i=n}^{n+1} \{v_2^i, v_3^i, v_8^i, v_6^i, v_7^i, v_5^i\}$, then we denote the induced subgraph of vertex set $\bigcup_{i=n}^{n+1} \{v_2^i, v_3^i, v_8^i, v_6^i, v_7^i, v_5^i\}$ as $G[T]$.

Obviously, $G[T] \cong G[F_2^3]$ (see Fig. 5), then $G[T]$ is a tree.

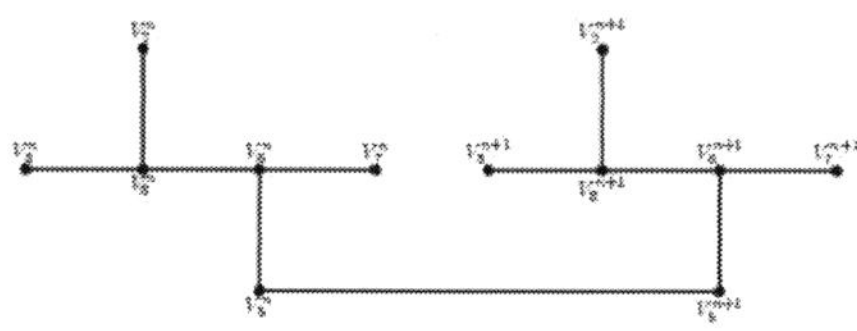

Figure 5. Subgraph of $G[T]$

Since $T \cap F_2^n = \emptyset$, then $G[T \cup F_2^n]$ is a forest.

Since $T \cap F_1^n = \emptyset$, then $G[T \cup F_1^n \cup F_2^n]$ is a forest. That is, $G[F_1^{n+2} \cup F_2^{n+2}]$ is acyclic.

Combining induction step with basic step, the $G[F_1^n \cup F_2^n]$ is a forest. Thus, $G[V_a(G_n)]$ is acyclic.

The lemma holds.

Lemma 2.2. $G[V_a(G_n^*)]$ is acyclic for $n \bmod 2 = 0$ and $n \geq 4$.

Proof: Since $V_a(G_n^*) = F_1^n \cup F_2^n \cup F_3^n$, Then if we want to prove $G[V_a(G_n^*)]$ is acyclic, which is equivalent to verify that $G[F_1^n \cup F_2^n \cup F_3^n]$ is acyclic.

Firstly, we prove the $G[F_1^n \cup F_2^n \cup F_3^n]$ is a forest by induction on n.

We first prove the basic step for n=4.

Combining case 2 and the definition of G_n^*, we have

$$F_1^4 = \{v_2^0, v_3^0, v_8^0, v_6^0, v_7^0\}$$

$$F_2^4 = \{v_2^1, v_3^1, v_8^1, v_6^1, v_7^1, v_5^1\}$$

$$F_3^4 = \{v_2^2, v_3^2, v_8^2, v_6^2, v_7^2, v_5^2, v_2^3, v_3^3, v_8^3, v_6^3, v_7^3, v_5^3\}$$

Obviously, $G[F_1^4]$, $G[F_2^4]$ and $G[F_3^4]$ are acyclic graphs, and each graph of $G[F_1^4], G[F_2^4]$ and $G[F_3^4]$ is a tree.

Since $F_1^4 \cap F_2^4 = \emptyset$, then the induced subgraph of vertex set $F_1^4 \cup F_2^4$ is acyclic.

Since $F_1^4 \cap F_3^4 = \emptyset$, then the induced subgraph of vertex set $F_1^4 \cup F_3^4$ is acyclic.

Since $F_2^4 \cap F_3^4 = \emptyset$, then the induced subgraph of vertex set $F_2^4 \cup F_3^4$ is acyclic.

Thus ,we have $F_1^4 \cap F_2^4 \cap F_3^4 = \emptyset$, then the induced subgraph of vertex set $F_1^4 \cup F_2^4 \cup F_3^4$ is acyclic.

That is, $G[F_1^4 \cup F_2^4 \cup F_3^4]$ is a forest. The vertices set is shown as Fig 6.

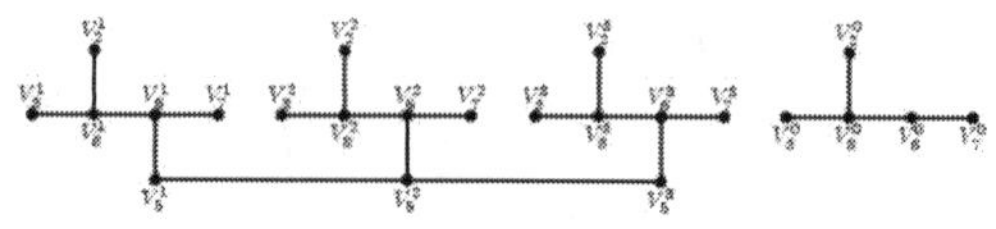

Figure 6. Subgraph of $G[F_1^4 \cup F_2^4 \cup F_3^4]$

Suppose $G[F_1^n \cup F_2^n \cup F_3^n]$ is a forest, we now prove that $G[F_1^{n+2} \cup F_2^{n+2} \cup F_3^{n+2}]$ is a forest.

Since

$$F_1^{n+2} = \{v_2^0, v_3^0, v_8^0, v_6^0, v_7^0\}$$

$$F_2^{n+2} = \{v_2^1, v_3^1, v_8^1, v_6^1, v_7^1, v_5^1\}$$

$$F_3^{n+2} = \bigcup_{i=1}^{n+2-1} \{v_2^i, v_3^i, v_8^i, v_6^i, v_7^i, v_5^i\}$$

Then, we have

$$F_1^{n+2} = F_1^n$$

$$F_2^{n+2} = F_2^n$$

$$F_3^{n+2} = \bigcup_{i=2}^{n-1} \{v_2^i, v_3^i, v_8^i, v_6^i, v_7^i, v_5^i\} \cup \bigcup_{i=n}^{n+1} \{v_2^i, v_3^i, v_8^i, v_6^i, v_7^i, v_5^i\}$$

$$= F_3^n \cup \bigcup_{i=n}^{n+1} \{v_2^i, v_3^i, v_8^i, v_6^i, v_7^i, v_5^i\}$$

For convenience, we also denote T as vertex set $\bigcup_{i=n}^{n+1} \{v_2^i, v_3^i, v_8^i, v_6^i, v_7^i, v_5^i\}$, then we denote the induced subgraph of vertex set $\bigcup_{i=n}^{n+1} \{v_2^i, v_3^i, v_8^i, v_6^i, v_7^i, v_5^i\}$ as $G[T]$.

Obviously, $G[T] \cong G[F_3^4]$, then $G[T]$ is a tree.

Since $T \cap F_3^n = \emptyset$,then $G[T \cup F_3^n]$ is a forest.

Since $T \cap F_1^n = \emptyset$,then $G[T \cup F_1^n \cup F_2^n]$ is a forest.

Since $T \cap F_2^n = \emptyset$,then $G[T \cup F_1^n \cup F_2^n \cup F_3^n]$ is a forest. That is, $G[F_1^{n+2} \cup F_2^{n+2} \cup F_3^{n+2}]$ is acyclic.

Combining induction step with basic step, the $G[F_1^n \cup F_2^n \cup F_3^n]$ is a forest. Thus, $G[V_a(G_n^*)]$ is acyclic.

The lemma holds.

3 Acyclic Vertex Set of TG_n and TG_n^*

Let $n \bmod 2 = k$, then $n = 2m+k$, $m \geq 1$ *and* $0 \leq i \leq k$. Thus $k=0$ and $k=1$. Then, we discuss 2 cases as follows.

Case 1. If $n \bmod 2 = 1$ and $n \geq 3$

Let $V_a(TG_n) = F_1^n \cup F_2^n$, where

$$F_1^n = \{v_2^0, v_3^0, v_8^0, v_6^0, v_7^0, v_2^{n-1}, v_3^{n-1}, v_8^{n-1}, v_6^{n-1}, v_7^{n-1}, v_5^{n-1}\}$$

$$F_2^n = \bigcup_{i=1}^{n-2} \{v_2^i, v_3^i, v_8^i, v_6^i, v_7^i, v_5^i\}$$

Case 2. If $n \bmod 2 = 0$, and $n \geq 4$

Let $V_a(TG_n^*) = F_1^n \cup F_2^n$, where

$$F_1^n = \{v_2^0, v_3^0, v_8^0, v_6^0, v_7^0, v_2^{n-1}, v_3^{n-1}, v_8^{n-1}, v_6^{n-1}, v_7^{n-1}, v_5^{n-1}\}$$

$$F_2^n = \bigcup_{i=1}^{n-2} \{v_2^i, v_3^i, v_8^i, v_6^i, v_7^i, v_5^i\}$$

Lemma 3.1. $G[V_a(TG_n)]$ is acyclic for $n \bmod 2 = 1$ and $n \geq 3$.

Proof: Since $V_a(TG_n) = F_1^n \cup F_2^n$, Then if we want to prove $G[V_a(TG_n)]$ is acyclic, which is equivalent to verify that $G[F_1^n \cup F_2^n]$ is acyclic.

Firstly, we prove the $G[F_1^n \cup F_2^n]$ is a tree by induction on *n*.

We first prove the basic step for *n*=3.

Combining case 1 and the definition of TG_n, we have

$$F_1^3 = \{v_2^0, v_3^0, v_8^0, v_6^0, v_7^0, v_2^2, v_3^2, v_8^2, v_6^2, v_7^2, v_5^2\}$$

$$F_2^3 = \{v_2^1, v_3^1, v_8^1, v_6^1, v_7^1, v_5^1\}$$

Obviously, by the definition of TG_n, we have that $G[F_1^3]$ and $G[F_2^3]$ are acyclic graphs, and each graph of $G[F_1^3]$ and $G[F_2^3]$ is a tree.

Since $F_1^3 \cap F_2^3 = \emptyset$, then the induced subgraph of vertex set $F_1^3 \cup F_2^3$ is acyclic. That is, $G[F_1^3 \cup F_2^3]$ is a tree. The vertices set is shown as Fig 7.

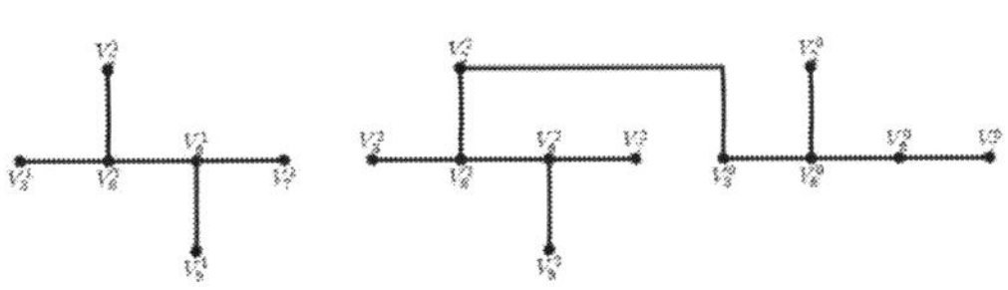

Figure 7. Subgraph of $G[F_1^3 \cup F_2^3]$

Suppose $G[F_1^n \cup F_2^n]$ is a tree, we now prove that $G[F_1^{n+2} \cup F_2^{n+2}]$ is a tree.

Since

$$F_1^{n+2} = \{v_2^0, v_3^0, v_8^0, v_6^0, v_7^0, v_2^{n+1}, v_3^{n+1}, v_8^{n+1}, v_6^{n+1}, v_7^{n+1}, v_5^{n+1}\}$$

$$F_2^{n+2} = \bigcup_{i=1}^{n+2-2} \{v_2^i, v_3^i, v_8^i, v_6^i, v_7^i, v_5^i\}$$

$$= \bigcup_{i=1}^{n-2} \{v_2^i, v_3^i, v_8^i, v_6^i, v_7^i, v_5^i\} \cup \bigcup_{i=n-1}^{n} \{v_2^i, v_3^i, v_8^i, v_6^i, v_7^i, v_5^i\}$$

$$= F_2^n \cup \bigcup_{i=n-1}^{n} \{v_2^i, v_3^i, v_8^i, v_6^i, v_7^i, v_5^i\}$$

Then we have

$$F_1^{n+2} \cong F_1^n$$

$$F_2^{n+2} = F_2^n \cup \bigcup_{i=n-1}^{n} \{v_2^i, v_3^i, v_8^i, v_6^i, v_7^i, v_5^i\}$$

For convenience, we denote T as vertex set $\bigcup_{i=n-1}^{n} \{v_2^i, v_3^i, v_8^i, v_6^i, v_7^i, v_5^i\}$, then we denote the induced subgraph of vertex set $\bigcup_{i=n-1}^{n} \{v_2^i, v_3^i, v_8^i, v_6^i, v_7^i, v_5^i\}$ as $G[T]$.

Obviously, $G[T] \cong G[F_2^3]$, then $G[T]$ is a tree.

Since $T \cap F_2^n = \emptyset$, then $G[T \cup F_2^n]$ is a tree.

Since $T \cap F_1^n = \emptyset$, then $G[T \cup F_1^n \cup F_2^n]$ is a tree. That is, $G[F_1^{n+2} \cup F_2^{n+2}]$ is acyclic.

Combining induction step with basic step, the $G[F_1^n \cup F_2^n]$ is a tree. Thus, $G[V_a(TG_n)]$ is acyclic.

The lemma holds.

Lemma 3.2. $G[V_a(TG_n^*)]$ is acyclic for $n \bmod 2 = 0$ and $n \geq 4$.

Proof: Since $V_a(TG_n^*) = F_1^n \cup F_2^n$, Then if we want to prove $G[V_a(TG_n^*)]$ is acyclic, which is equivalent to verify that $G[F_1^n \cup F_2^n]$ is acyclic.

Firstly, we prove the $G[F_1^n \cup F_2^n]$ is a tree by induction on *n*.

We first prove the basic step for *n*=4.

Combining case 2 and the definition of TG_n^*, we have

$$F_1^4 = \{v_2^0, v_3^0, v_8^0, v_6^0, v_7^0, v_2^3, v_3^3, v_8^3, v_6^3, v_7^3, v_5^3\}$$

$$F_2^4 = \{v_2^1, v_3^1, v_8^1, v_6^1, v_7^1, v_5^1, v_2^2, v_3^2, v_8^2, v_6^2, v_7^2, v_5^2\}$$

Obviously, $G[F_1^4]$ and $G[F_2^4]$ are acyclic graph, and each graph of $G[F_1^4]$ and $G[F_2^4]$ is a tree. Since $F_1^4 \cap F_2^4 = \emptyset$, then the induced subgraph of vertex set $F_1^4 \cup F_2^4$ is acyclic. That is, $G[F_1^4 \cup F_2^4]$ is a tree. The vertices set is shown as Fig 8.

 https://doi.org/10.1051/itmconf/20192501012

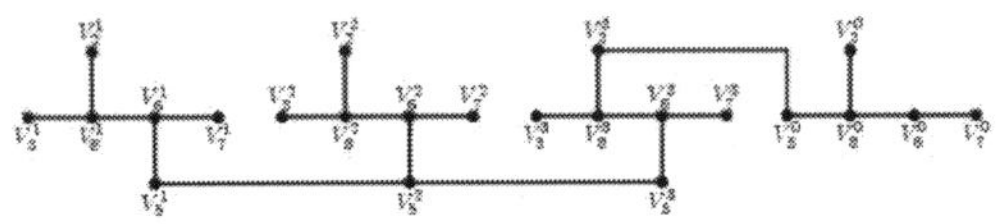

Figure 8. Subgraph of $G[F_1^4 \cup F_2^4]$

Suppose $G[F_1^n \cup F_2^n]$ is a tree, we now prove that $G[F_1^{n+2} \cup F_2^{n+2}]$ is a tree.

Since

$$F_1^{n+2} = \{v_2^0, v_3^0, v_8^0, v_6^0, v_7^0, v_2^{n-1}\} \cup \{v_3^{n+1}, v_8^{n+1}, v_6^{n+1}, v_7^{n+1}, v_5^{n+1}\}$$

$$F_2^{n+2} = \bigcup_{i=1}^{n+2-2} \{v_2^i, v_3^i, v_8^i, v_6^i, v_7^i, v_5^i\}$$

Then we have

$$F_1^{n+2} \cong F_1^n$$

$$F_2^{n+2} = F_2^n \cup \bigcup_{i=n-1}^{n} \{v_2^i, v_3^i, v_8^i, v_6^i, v_7^i, v_5^i\}$$

For convenience, we also denote T as vertex set $\bigcup_{i=n-1}^{n} \{v_2^i, v_3^i, v_8^i, v_6^i, v_7^i, v_5^i\}$, then we denote the induced subgraph of vertex set $\bigcup_{i=n-1}^{n} \{v_2^i, v_3^i, v_8^i, v_6^i, v_7^i, v_5^i\}$ as $G[T]$.

Obviously, $G[T] \cong G[F_2^4]$, then $G[T]$ is a tree.

Since $T \cap F_2^n = \emptyset$, then $G[T \cup F_2^n]$ is a tree.

Since $T \cap F_1^n = \emptyset$, then $G[T \cup F_1^n \cup F_2^n]$ is a tree. That is, $G[F_1^{n+2} \cup F_2^{n+2}]$ is acyclic.

Combining induction step with basic step, the $G[F_1^n \cup F_2^n]$ is a tree. Thus, $G[V_a(TG_n^*)]$ is acyclic.

The lemma holds.

4 Feedback Number of graphs

By the Lemma 2.1 and Lemma 2.2, we obtain

Lemma 4.1. $V(G_n) \setminus V_a(G_n)$ is feedback vertex set of G_n .

Lemma 4.2. $V(G_n^*) \setminus V_a(G_n^*)$ is feedback vertex set of G_n^* .

By the Lemma 3.1 and Lemma 3.2, we obtain

Lemma 4.3. $V(TG_n) \setminus V_a(TG_n)$ is feedback vertex set of TG_n .

Lemma 4.4. $V(TG_n^*) \setminus V_a(TG_n^*)$ is feedback vertex set of TG_n^* .

For convenience, we denote $f(n)$ as the feedback numbers of Goldberg Snark, Twist Goldberg Snark and their related graphs.

Lemma 4.5. For $n \geq 3$, the upper bound of feedback number is

$$f(n) \leq 2n+1$$

Proof: By Lemma 4.1, we have the feedback number of $V(G_n)$ as follows.

$$\begin{aligned}
&|V(G_n) \setminus V_a(G_n)| \\
&\leq |V(G_n) \setminus (F_1^n \cup F_2^n)| \\
&= |V(G_n)| - |(F_1^n \cup F_2^n)| \\
&= 8n - [5 + 6(n-1)] \\
&= 2n+1
\end{aligned}$$

By Lemma 4.2, we have the feedback number of $V(G_n^*)$ as follows.

$$\begin{aligned}
&|V(G_n^*) \setminus V_a(G_n^*)| \\
&\leq |V(G_n^*) \setminus (F_1^n \cup F_2^n \cup F_3^n)| \\
&= |V(G_n^*)| - |(F_1^n \cup F_2^n \cup F_3^n)| \\
&= 8n - [5 + 6 + 6(n-2)] \\
&= 2n+1
\end{aligned}$$

By Lemma 4.3, we have the feedback number of $V(TG_n)$ as follows.

$$\begin{aligned}
&|V(TG_n) \setminus V_a(TG_n)| \\
&\leq |V(TG_n) \setminus (F_1^n \cup F_2^n)| \\
&= |V(TG_n)| - |(F_1^n \cup F_2^n)| \\
&= 8n - [11 + 6(n-2)] \\
&= 2n+1
\end{aligned}$$

By Lemma 4.4, we have the feedback number of $V(TG_n)$ as follows.

$$\begin{aligned}
&|V(TG_n^*) \setminus V_a(TG_n^*)| \\
&\leq |V(TG_n^*) \setminus (F_1^n \cup F_2^n)| \\
&= |V(TG_n^*)| - |(F_1^n \cup F_2^n)| \\
&= 8n - [11 + 6(n-2)] \\
&= 2n+1
\end{aligned}$$

Then, we have the upper bound of feedback number of is $f(n) \leq 2n+1$

Lemma 4.6. For $n \geq 3$, the lower bound of feedback number is

$$f(n) \geq 2n+1$$

Proof: By reference [20], Beineke and Vandell prove a lower bound of general graphs $G(V, E)$:

$$f(G) \geq \left\lceil \frac{|E|-|V|+1}{\Delta-1} \right\rceil$$

Since $|V| = 8n$, $|E| = 12n$ and $\Delta = 3$. Thus, we obtain a lower bound of these graphs as follows:

$$f(n) \geq \left\lceil \frac{|E|-|V|+1}{\Delta-1} \right\rceil = \left\lceil \frac{12n-8n+1}{3-1} \right\rceil$$
$$= \left\lceil \frac{4n+1}{2} \right\rceil = \lceil 2n+1 \rceil$$

By the Lemma 4.5 and Lemma 4.6, we obtain the feedback number of these graphs as follows.

Theorem1. For $n \geq 3$, the feedback number of these graphs is $f(n) = 2n+1$.

Acknowledgment

The work was supported by NNSF of China (No.61802046) and Key Research Items in Natural Science Foundation of Liaoning (No.20170520327) and Doctoral Start up Fund of Dalian Ocean University (No.HDYJ201818).

References

1. L. W. Beineke, R. C. Vandell, Decycling graphs, J. Graph Theory, **25**, 59-77, (1997).
2. I. Niven, H. S. Zuckerman, An Introduction to the Theory of Numbers (5th ed.).John Wiley and Sons, New York, (1991).
3. I. Caragiannis, C. Kaklamanis, P. Kanellopoulos, New bounds on the size of the minimum feedback vertex set in meshes and butterflies. Information Processing Letters, **83**, 75-80, (2002).
4. P. Festa, P. M. Pardalos, M. G. C. Resende, Feedback set problems. Handbook of Combinatorial Optimization (D.-Z. Du, P.M. Pardalos eds.), Vol. A, Kluwer, Dordrecht, pp. 209, (1999).
5. V. Bafna, P. Berman, T. Fujito, A 2-approximation algorithm for the undirected feedback vertex set problem. SIAM J. Discrete Mathematics, **12**, 289-297, (1999).
6. S. Bau, L. W. Beineke, Z. Liu, G. Du, R. C. Vandell, Decycling cubes and grids. Utilitas Math., **59**, 129-137, (2001).
7. R. Bar-Yehuda, D. Geiger, J. S. Naor, R. M. Roth, Approximation algorithms for the feedback vertex set problem with applications to constraint satisfaction and Bayesian inference. SIAM J. Comput., **27**, 942-959, (1998).
8. R. Focardi, F. L. Luccio, D. Peleg, Feedback vertex set in hypercubes. Information Processing Letters, **76**, 1-5, (2000).
9. Y. D. Liang, On the feedback vertex set in permutation graphs. Information Pro cessing Letters, **52**, 123-129, (1994).
10. F. L. Luccio, Almost exact minimum feedback vertex set in meshes and butterflies. Information Processing Letters, **66**, 59-64, (1998).
11. G. W. Smith, Jr. and R. B. Walford, The identification of a minimal feedback vertex set of a directed graph. IEEE Trans. Circuits and Systems, **22**, 9-15, (1975).
12. C.-C. Wang, E. L. Lloyd, M. L. Soffa, Feedback vertex sets and cyclically reducible graphs. J. Assoc. Comput. Mach., **32**, 296-313, (1985).
13. F.-H. Wang, C.-J. Hsu, J.-C. Tsai, Minimal feedback vertex sets in directed split stars. Networks, **45**, 218-223, (2005).
14. M.R. Garey, D.S. Johnson, Computers and Intractability, Freeman, San Francisco, CA, (1979).
15. Mohammad Ghebleh, The circular chromatic index of Goldberg snarks. Discrete Mathematics, **307**, 3220-3225, (2007).
16. A.Cavicchioli, T.E. Murgolo, B. Ruini and F. Spaggiari. Special Classes of Snarks. Acta Applicandae Mathematicae, **76**, 57-88, (2003).
17. A. Cavicchioli, M. Meschiari, B. Ruini, and F. Spaggiari. A Survey on Snarks and New Results: Products, Reducibility and a Computer Search. Journal of Graph Theory, **28(2)**, 57-86, (1998).
18. M. Abreu, D. Labbate, R. Rizzi, J. Sheehan, Odd 2-factored snarks. European Journal of Combinatorics, **36**, 460-472, (2014).
19. John J. Watrins, Snarks. Annals New York Academy of Sciences, **576**, 606-622, (2006).
20. L. W. Beineke, R. C. Vandell, Decycling graphs, J. Graph Theory, **25**, 59-77, (1997).
21. S.J. Zhang, X.R. Xu, C. Yin, N.Cao, Y.S. Yang, Feedback Numbers of Augmented Cubes AQn, Utilitas Mathematica, **97**, 183-192, (2015)
22. S.J. Zhang, X.R. Xu, C. Yin, et al. The feedback number of Knödel graph W3, n, ARS Combinatoria, **140**, 397-409, (2018).
23. X.R.Xu,C.Yin,S.J.Zhang, et al.Improved Feedback Vertex sets in Kautz Digraph Kautz Digraph K(d, n),CIS 2014, **161-165**, (2014).
24. X.R. Xu, S.P. Dino, H.F. Zhang, et al.D ecycling number of crossed cubes CQn, CIS 2017, 145-150, (2017)
25. Forbes A.D.. Snark Design. Utilitas Mathematica, **107**,167-192, (2018).

 https://doi.org/10.1051/itmconf/20192501013

Feedback Numbers of Möbius Ladders

Yijin Wang[1], Xinyue Zhang[1] and Sijia Zhang[1,a]

[1]*School of Information Engineering, Dalian Ocean University, Dalian, 116023, China*

Abstract. A subset $F \subset V(G)$ is called a feedback vertex set if the subgraph $G-F$ is acyclic. The minimum cardinality of a feedback vertex set is called the feedback number of G, which is proposed by Beineke and Vandell [1]. In this paper, we consider a particular topology graph called Möbius ladders M_{2n}. We use $f(M_{2n})$ to denote the feedback number of M_{2n}. This paper proves that $f(M_{2n}) = \left\lceil \frac{n+1}{2} \right\rceil, n \geq 3$.

1 Introduction

It is well-known that the underlying topology of an interconnection network can be represented by a connected graph $G=(V,E)$, where V is the set of processors and E is the set of communication links in the network. In this paper, we use graphs and interconnection networks interchangeably.

Let G=(V, E) be a graph or digraph without multiple edges, with vertex set V(G) and edge set E(G). A subset $F \subset V(G)$ is called a feedback vertex set if the subgraph G-F is acyclic, that is, if G-F is a forest. The minimum cardinality of a feedback vertex set is called the feedback number (or decycling number proposed first by Beineke and Vandell [1]) of *G*. A feedback vertex set of this cardinality is called a minimum feedback vertex set.

Apart from its graph-theoretical interest, the minimum feedback vertex set problem has important application to several fields. For example, the problems are in operating systems to resource allocation mechanisms that prevent deadlocks [2], in artificial intelligence to the constraint satisfaction problem and Bayesian inference, in synchronous distributed systems to the study of monopolies and in optical networks to converters placement problem (see [3, 4]).

Determining the feedback number is quite difficult even for some elementary graphs. However, the problem has been studied for some special graphs and digraphs, such as hypercubes, meshes, to roids, butterflies, cube-connected cycles, directed split-stars (see [3, 4, 5, 6, 7, 8, 9, 10, 11, 12, 13]). In fact, the minimum feedback set problem is known to be NP-hard for general graphs [14] and the best known approximation algorithm is one with an approximation ratio two [5].

In this paper, we consider the feedback number of Möbius Ladders M_{2n}. Let $f(M_{2n})$ denote the feedback number of Möbius ladders. By using an approach to construct an acyclic subgraph of M_{2n}, we proves that:

$$f(M_{2n}) = \left\lceil \frac{n+1}{2} \right\rceil, n \geq 3.$$

2 Preliminary

R. L.Guy and F. Harary consider the graph M_L (also called the Möbius ladder) in1966, which we picture as a ladder with the ends joined after a twist, so that the graph is naturally embedded in a Möbius band [16].

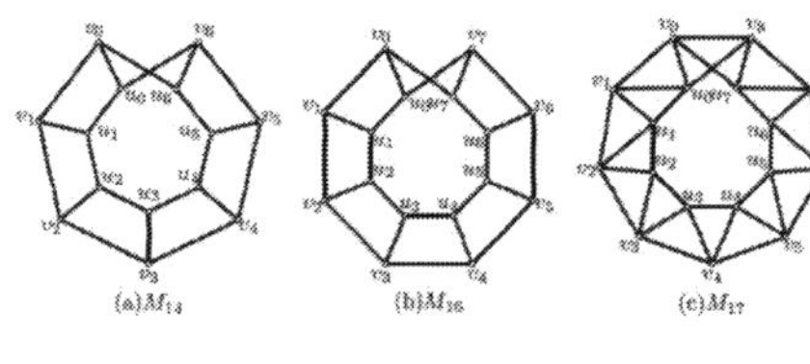

Figure 1. Examples of Möbius ladders

One particular molecular graph which is of interest is the molecular Möbius ladder, which was first synthesized by Walba et al. It was a significant achievement in chemistry because of its topologically interesting molecular structure. Simon proved that its associated embedded molecular graph was topologically chiral [17].

Although many authors only consider even L, but there exists odd L which be mentioned in ref. [18]. And as evidenced by the number of publications, there are many more established results for even L Möbius ladders than for odd. Obviously, the two cases (L even or odd) change the structure of these graphs quite radically:

Case1. When L is even, M_L is three-regular and Hamiltonian (See Fig.1(a)-(b)).

Case2. When L is odd, M_L is four-regular and therefore two-factorable (See Fig.1(c)).

[a] Corresponding author: zhangsijia@dlou.edu.cn

https://doi.org/10.1051/itmconf/20192501013

In this paper, we study only Case 1, and only even $L \geq 6$. Unless otherwise stated, assume that M_L means an even Möbius Ladder.

Definition 2.1. A Möbius Ladder is defined to be a graph on $2n(n \geq 3)$ vertices with

$$V(M_{2n}) = \{v_i, u_i : 0 \leq i \leq n-1\}$$

and

$$E(M_{2n}) = \{v_i u_i : 0 \leq i \leq n-1\} \cup \{v_i v_{i+1}, u_i u_{i+1} : 0 \leq n-1\} \cup \{u_{n-1} v_0, v_{n-1} u_0\}$$

Obviously, M_{2n} is three-regular and Hamiltonian.

3 Feedback vertex set of M2*n*

Since $N = 2n$, let $n \bmod 2 = k$, then $n = 2m + k$, $m \geq 1$ and $k \in [0,1]$.

Let $V_a^1(M_{2n}) = F_1^n \cup F_2^n \subset V(M_{2n})$, then we discuss two cases as follows.

Case 1. If $n \bmod 2 = 1$ and *odd* $n \geq 3$, let

$$F_{1,1}^n = \bigcup_{\substack{i=0,\\ i \bmod 2=0}}^{n-1} \{v_i\} \cup \bigcup_{\substack{i=0,\\ i \bmod 2=1}}^{n-2} \{u_i\}$$

$$F_{1,2}^n = \bigcup_{\substack{i=0,\\ i \bmod 2=1}}^{n-2} \{v_i\}$$

Case 2. If $n \bmod 2 = 0$ and *even* $n \geq 4$, let

$$F_{2,1}^n = \bigcup_{\substack{i=0,\\ i \bmod 2=0}}^{n-1} \{v_i\} \cup \bigcup_{\substack{i=0,\\ i \bmod 2=1}}^{n-2} \{u_i\}$$

$$F_{2,2}^n = \bigcup_{\substack{i=0,\\ i \bmod 2=1}}^{n-2} \{v_i\}$$

$$F_{2,3}^n = \{u_{n-1}\}$$

Definition 3.1. The open neighborhood and the closed neighborhood of a vertex $v \in V(M_{2n})$ are denoted by $N(v) = \{u \in V(M_{2n}) : vu \in E(M_{2n})\}$ and $N[v] = N(v) \cup \{v\}$, respectively. For a vertex set $S \subseteq V(M_{2n})$, $N(S) = \bigcup_{v \in S} N(v)$ and $N[S] = \bigcup_{v \in S} N[v]$.

Definition 3.2. For any vertex $u_j \in F_{i,2}^2$, $i \in [1,2]$ and $j \in [0, n-1]$, denote $T_{1,j} = N[u_j]$, where $N[u_j]$ is the closed neighborhood of a vertex u_j and the induced subgraph of $T_{1,j}$ as $G[T_{1,j}]$.

In fact, for any j, $G[T_{1,j}]$ is isomorphic to $K_{1,3}$. That is, for any j, $G[T_{1,j}]$ is a tree, where vertex v_j is a root vertex of tree $G[T_{1,j}]$ and vertex set $N(v_j)$ are leaf vertices of tree $G[T_{1,j}]$.

By the Definition 2.1, all the vertices in $F_{i,1}^n$ and $F_{i,2}^n$ are isolated vertex set for $i \in [1,2]$, respectively. Then the induced subgraph of $F_{i,1}^n$ is acyclic and the induced sub-graph of $F_{i,2}^n$ is acyclic. By the Definition 3.2, we obtain $N(F_{i,2}^n) = F_{i,1}^n$.

Lemma 3.1. $G[V_a^1(M_{2n})]$ is acyclic for $n \bmod 2 = 1$ and *odd* $n \geq 3$.

Proof.

Since

$$V_a^1(M_{2n}) = F_{1,1}^n \cup F_{1,2}^n = N(F_{1,2}^n) \cup F_{1,2}^n = N[F_{1,2}^n]$$

Then if we want to prove $G[V_a^1(M_{2n})]$ is acyclic, which is equivalent to verity that $G[N[F_{1,2}^n]]$ is acyclic.

Firstly, we prove that $G[N[F_{1,2}^n]]$ is a tree by induction on *n*.

We first prove the basic step for $n = 3$.

Since

$$F_{1,1}^3 = \{v_0, v_2\} \cup \{u_1\},\ F_{1,2}^3 = \{v_1\}$$

And

$$T_{1,1}^3 = N[v_1] = N\{v_1\} \cup \{v_1\} = \{v_0, v_2\} \cup \{v_1\} = F_{1,1}^3 \cup F_{1,2}^3 = N[F_{1,2}^3]$$

$$G[T_{1,1}^3] \cong K_{1,3}$$

Then $G[T_{1,1}^3]$ is a tree. That is, $G[F_{1,1}^3 \cup F_{1,2}^3]$ is a tree.

Suppose $G[F_{1,1}^n \cup F_{1,2}^n]$ is a tree, we now prove that $G[F_{1,2}^{n+2} \cup F_{1,2}^{n+2}]$ is a tree.

Since

$$F_{1,1}^{n+2} = \bigcup_{\substack{i=0,\\ i \bmod 2=0}}^{n+2-1} \{v_i\} \cup \bigcup_{\substack{i=0,\\ i \bmod 2=1}}^{n+2-2} \{u_i\}$$

$$= \bigcup_{\substack{i=0,\\ i \bmod 2=0}}^{n-1} \{v_i\} \cup \bigcup_{\substack{i=n,\\ i \bmod 2=0}}^{n+1} \{v_i\} \cup \bigcup_{\substack{i=0,\\ i \bmod 2=1}}^{n-2} \{u_i\} \cup \bigcup_{\substack{i=n-1,\\ i \bmod 2=1}}^{n} \{u_i\}$$

$$= F_{1,1}^n \cup \bigcup_{\substack{i=n,\\ i \bmod 2=0}}^{n+1} \{v_i\} \cup \bigcup_{\substack{i=n-1,\\ i \bmod 2=1}}^{n} \{u_i\}$$

$$= F_{1,1}^n \cup \{v_{n+1}\} \cup \{u_n\}$$

and

$$F_{1,2}^{n+1} = \bigcup_{\substack{i=0,\\ i \bmod 2=1}}^{n+2-2}\{v_i\} = \bigcup_{\substack{i=0,\\ i \bmod 2=1}}^{n-2}\{v_i\} \cup \bigcup_{\substack{i=n-1,\\ i \bmod 2=1}}^{n}\{v_i\}$$

$$= F_{1,2}^{n} \cup \{v_n\}$$

Then

$$F_{1,1}^{n+2} \cup F_{1,2}^{n+2} = F_{1,1}^{n} \cup F_{1,2}^{n} \cup \{v_{n+1}, u_n, v_n\}$$

$$= F_{1,1}^{n} \cup F_{1,2}^{n} \cup T_{1,n}^{n+2}$$

Since $G[T_{1,n}^{n+2}] \cong K_{1,3}$,then $G[T_{1,n}^{n+2}]$ is a tree.

By the induction hypothesis, $G[F_{1,1}^{n} \cup F_{1,2}^{n}]$ is a tree.

Tree $G[T_{1,n}^{n+2}]$ and tree $G[F_{1,1}^{n} \cup F_{1,2}^{n}]$ just have one common leaf vertex v_{n-1}, then $G[F_{1,1}^{n} \cup F_{1,2}^{n} \cup T_{1,n}^{n+2}]$ is a tree.

Combining induction step with basic step, $G[F_{1,2}^{n} \cup F_{1,2}^{n}]$ is a tree.

Thus, $G[V_a^1(M_{2n})] = G[F_{1,1}^{n} \cup F_{1,2}^{n}]$ is acyclic.

The lemma holds.

Lemma 3.2. $G[V_a^2(M_{2n})]$ is acyclic for $n \bmod 2 = 0$ and even $n \geq 4$.

Proof.

Since

$$V_a^2(M_{2n}) = F_{2,1}^{n} \cup F_{2,2}^{n} \cup F_{2,3}^{n}$$

$$= N(F_{2,2}^{n}) \cup F_{2,2}^{n} \cup \{u_{n-1}\}$$

$$= N[F_{2,2}^{n}] \cup \{u_{n-1}\}$$

Then if we want to prove $G[V_a^2(M_{2n})]$ is acyclic, which is equivalent to verity that $G[N[F_{2,2}^{n}] \cup \{u_{n-1}\}]$ is acyclic.

Firstly, we prove that $G[N[F_{2,2}^{n}] \cup \{u_{n-1}\}]$ is a tree by in-duction on n.

We first prove the basic step for $n = 4$.

Since

$$F_{2,1}^{4} = \{v_0, v_2\} \cup \{u_1\},\ F_{2,2}^{4} = \{v_1\},\ F_{2,3}^{4} = \{u_3\}$$

And

$$T_{2,1}^{4} = N[v_1] = N(v_1) \cup \{v_1\} = \{v_0, v_2, u_1\} \cup \{v_1\}$$

$$= F_{2,1}^{4} \cup F_{2,2}^{4} = N[F_{2,2}^{2}]$$

Since $G[T_{2,1}^{4}] \cong K_{1,3}$, then $G[T_{2,1}^{4}]$ is a tree. That is, $G[F_{2,1}^{4} \cup F_{2,2}^{4}]$ is a tree.

Suppose $G[F_{1,2}^{n} \cup F_{1,2}^{n}]$ is a tree, we now prove that $G[F_{1,2}^{n+2} \cup F_{1,2}^{n+2}]$ is a tree.

Since

$$F_{1,1}^{n+2} = \bigcup_{\substack{i=0,\\ i \bmod 2=0}}^{n+2-1}\{v_i\} \cup \bigcup_{\substack{i=0,\\ i \bmod 2=1}}^{n+2-2}\{u_i\}$$

$$= \bigcup_{\substack{i=0,\\ i \bmod 2=0}}^{n-1}\{v_i\} \cup \bigcup_{\substack{i=n,\\ i \bmod 2=0}}^{n+1}\{v_i\} \cup \bigcup_{\substack{i=0,\\ i \bmod 2=1}}^{n-2}\{u_i\} \cup \bigcup_{\substack{i=n-1,\\ i \bmod 2=1}}^{n}\{u_i\}$$

$$= F_{1,1}^{n} \cup \bigcup_{\substack{i=n,\\ i \bmod 2=0}}^{n+1}\{v_i\} \cup \bigcup_{\substack{i=n-1,\\ i \bmod 2=1}}^{n}\{u_i\}$$

$$= F_{1,1}^{n} \cup \{v_{n+1}\} \cup \{u_n\}$$

and

$$F_{1,2}^{n+1} = \bigcup_{\substack{i=0,\\ i \bmod 2=1}}^{n+2-2}\{v_i\}$$

$$= \bigcup_{\substack{i=0,\\ i \bmod 2=1}}^{n-2}\{v_i\} \cup \bigcup_{\substack{i=n-1,\\ i \bmod 2=1}}^{n}\{v_i\}$$

$$= F_{1,2}^{n} \cup \{v_n\}$$

Then

$$F_{1,1}^{n+2} \cup F_{1,2}^{n+2}$$

$$= F_{1,1}^{n} \cup F_{1,2}^{n} \cup \{v_{n+1}, u_n, v_n\}$$

$$= F_{1,1}^{n} \cup F_{1,2}^{n} \cup T_{1,n}^{n+2}$$

Since $G[T_{1,n}^{n+2}] \cong K_{1,3}$,then $G[T_{1,n}^{n+2}]$ is a tree.

By the induction hypothesis, $G[F_{1,1}^{n} \cup F_{1,2}^{n}]$ is a tree.

Tree $G[T_{1,n}^{n+2}]$ and tree $G[F_{1,1}^{n} \cup F_{1,2}^{n}]$ just have one common leaf vertex v_{n-1}, then $G[F_{1,1}^{n} \cup F_{1,2}^{n} \cup T_{1,n}^{n+2}]$ is a tree.

Combining induction step with basic step, $G[F_{1,2}^{n} \cup F_{1,2}^{n}]$ is a tree.

Thus, $G[V_a^1(M_{2n})] = G[F_{1,1}^{n} \cup F_{1,2}^{n}]$ is acyclic.

The lemma holds.

By Lemma 3.1 and Lemma 3.2, we obtain the Lemma 3.3 as follows.

Lemma 3.3. $V(M_{2n}) \setminus V_a^i(M_{2n})$ **is** The feedback vertex set of M2n for $i \in [1,2]$.

4 Feedback Number of M2n

By reference [1], Beineke and Vandell prove a lower bound of general graphs $G(V, E)$:

$$f(G) \geq \left\lceil \frac{|E| - |V| + 1}{\Delta - 1} \right\rceil$$

Lemma 4.1. Denote $f(M_{2n})$ as the feedback number of M_{2n}, the lower bound of the feedback number is

$$f(M_{2n}) \ge \left\lceil \frac{n+1}{2} \right\rceil$$

Proof.

Since $|V(M_{2n})| = 2n$, $|E(M_{2n})| = 3n$ and M_{2n} is 3-regular graph. Then, we obtain a lower bound as follows:

$$f(M_{2n}) \ge \left\lceil \frac{|E|-|V|+1}{\Delta - 1} \right\rceil = \left\lceil \frac{3n-2n+1}{2} \right\rceil = \left\lceil \frac{n+1}{2} \right\rceil$$

Lemma 4.2. Denote $f(M_{2n})$ as the feedback number of M_{2n}, the upper bound of the feedback number is

$$f(M_{2n}) \le \left\lceil \frac{n+1}{2} \right\rceil$$

Proof. By Lemma 3.3, we have

$$f(M_{2n}) \le V(M_{2n}) \setminus V_a^i(M_{2n})$$

Then

$$f(M_{2n}) \le \begin{cases} 2n - (n + \frac{n-1}{2}) & \text{for odd } n \\ 2n - [(n-1) + (\frac{n}{2} - 1) + 1] & \text{for even } n \end{cases}$$

$$= \left\lceil \frac{n+1}{2} \right\rceil$$

By the Lemma 4.1 and Lemma 4.2, we obtain the feedback number of M_{2n} as follows.

Theorem1. For $n \ge 3$, the feedback number of M_{2n} is $f(M_{2n}) = \left\lceil \frac{n+1}{2} \right\rceil$

Acknowledgment

The work was supported by NNSF of China (No.61802046) and Key Research Items in Natural Science Foundation of Liaoning (No.20170520327) and Doctoral Start up Fund of Dalian Ocean University (No.HDYJ201818).

References

1. L. W. Beineke, R. C. Vandell, Decycling graphs, J. Graph Theory, **25**, 59-77, (1997).
2. I. Niven, H. S. Zuckerman, An Introduction to the Theory of Numbers (5th ed.). John Wiley and Sons, New York, (1991).
3. I.Caragiannis, C. Kaklamanis, P. Kanellopoulos, New bounds on the size of the minimum feedback vertex set in meshes and butterflies. Information Processing Letters, **83**, 75-80, (2002).
4. P. Festa, P. M. Pardalos, M. G. C. Resende, Feedback set problems. Handbook of Combinatorial Optimization (D.-Z. Du, P.M. Pardalos eds.), Vol. A, Kluwer, Dordrecht, pp. 209, (1999).
5. V. Bafna, P. Berman, T. Fujito, A 2-approximation algorithm for the undirected feedback vertex set problem. SIAM J. Discrete Mathematics, **12**, 289-297, (1999).
6. S. Bau, L. W. Beineke, Z. Liu, G. Du, R. C. Vandell, Decycling cubes and grids. Utilitas Math., **59**, 129-137, (2001).
7. R. Bar-Yehuda, D. Geiger, J. S. Naor, R. M. Roth, Approximation algorithms for the feedback vertex set problem with applications to constraint satisfaction and Bayesian inference. SIAM J. Comput., **27**, 942-959, (1998).
8. R. Focardi, F. L. Luccio, D. Peleg, Feedback vertex set in hypercubes. Information Processing Letters, **76**, 1-5, (2000).
9. Y. D. Liang, On the feedback vertex set in permutation graphs. Information Processing Letters, **52**, 123-129, (1994).
10. F. L. Luccio, Almost exact minimum feedback vertex set in meshes and butterflies. Information Processing Letters, **66**, 59-64, (1998).
11. G. W. Smith, Jr. and R. B. Walford, The identification of a minimal feedback vertex set of a directed graph. IEEE Trans. Circuits and Systems, **22**, 9-15, (1975).
12. C.-C.Wang, E. L. Lloyd, M. L. Soffa, Feedback vertex sets and cyclically reducible graphs. J. Assoc. Comput. Mach., **32**, 296-313, (1985).
13. F.-H. Wang, C.-J. Hsu, J.-C. Tsai. Minimal feedback vertex sets in directed splitstars. Networks, **45**, 218-223, (2005).
14. M. R. Garey, D. S. Johnson, Computers and Intractability, Freeman, San Francisco, CA, (1979).
15. R. Kralovic and P. Ruzicka, Minimum feedback vertex sets in shuffle-based interconnection networks. Information Processing Letters, 86 (4) (2003), 191-196.
16. J. C. Bermond and C. Peyrat, De Bruijn and Kautz networks: a competitor for the hypercube? In Hypercube and Distributed Computers (F. Andre and J. P. Verjus eds.). North-Holland: Elsevier Science Publishers, 1989, 278-293.
17. J.-M. Xu, Y.-Z. Wu, J. Huang, C.Yang, Feedback numbers of Kautz digraphs. Discrete Math., 307(13)(2007), 1589-1599.
18. J.-M. Xu, Topological Structure and Analysis of Interconnection Networks. Kluwer Academic Publishers, Dordrecht/Boston/London, 2001.
19. S.J.Zhang, X.R.Xu, C.Yin, N.Cao, Y.S.Yang, Feedback Numbers of Augmented Cubes AQn, Utilitas Mathematica, 97,183-192, (2015)
20. S.J.Zhang, X.R.Xu,C.Yin,et al. The feedback number of Knödel graph W3, n, ARS Combinatoria, 140, 397-409, (2018).

A Seismic Signal Denoising Method Based on Wavelet Comprehensive Threshold

Jingsong Yang, Jie Li[a], Han Wang

Institute of Disaster Prevention, Vibration Key Laboratory of Precision Measurement Technology and Instrument065201, China

Abstract. The wavelet comprehensive threshold is used to inherit and develop the advantages of hard threshold and soft threshold denoised method. Based on the small wavelet coefficients of the noise signal and the large wavelet coefficients of the seismic signal, the simulation experiment of the Ricker signal and the noise reduction experiment is carried out. The simulation results show that the MSE of the wavelet comprehensive threshold is the closest to the original signal waveform after noise reduction, and the energy of the high frequency part of the waveform is reduced and the low frequency part is suppressed. Finally, the actual seismic waveform, for example, the noise reduction of the actual waveform can be the first time of the waveform, and the waveform of the effective signal energy, noise signal energy is suppressed.

1 Introduction

In the process of seismic signal acquisition, it is affected by external environment and the uncertainty of the sensor itself. The signal is mixed with secondary noise, environmental noise and instrument noise, which leads to the occurrence of earthquake misjudgment and missed judgment (Zheng Zuoya et al., 2007; Fan Tao, 2014). Among the three types of noise, instrument noise has a weak influence on seismic signals, so it mainly reduces the misjudgment and missed judgment by eliminating the interference caused by secondary noise and environmental noise (Li Ying et al., 2006).

For the problem that wavelet threshold denoising has soft and hard threshold function which can not effectively eliminate the influence of noise signal on seismic signal, the wavelet integrated threshold method is proposed to improve the threshold function. After the improvement, the wavelet coefficients of the wavelet integrated threshold function are infinitely close to the wavelet coefficients of the real function, which not only maintains the continuity of the signal but also preserves the high frequency signal to achieve noise reduction.

2 Wavelet integrated threshold denoising method

2.1 Wavelet integrated threshold denoising method principle

Threshold function method is also called wavelet threshold denoising method. Donoho et al. have demonstrated that wavelet threshold denoising methods are superior to other classical noise reduction methods (Bruni et al., 2006). Currently, commonly used threshold noise reduction methods include soft and hard threshold denoising methods. The hard threshold method compares the absolute value of the signal wavelet coefficient with the threshold of the wavelet coefficient to achieve the preservation of the wavelet coefficients in the high-frequency part of the signal, but the discontinuity is likely to occur at the threshold zero, resulting in the absence of effective signals (Chong et al, 2015; Mousavi et al.2016), the hard threshold function is shown in formula (1); the soft threshold method improves the signal missing phenomenon in the hard threshold method, but loses the high-frequency signal energy, and the soft threshold function is as shown in formula (2).

$$hard(\omega,\lambda)=\begin{cases}\omega(|\omega|\geq\lambda)\\0(|\omega|<\lambda)\end{cases}\tag{1}$$

$$soft(\omega,\lambda)=\begin{cases}\mathrm{sgn}(\omega)(|\omega|-\lambda)(|\omega|\geq\lambda)\\0(|\omega|<\lambda)\end{cases}\tag{2}$$

In the formula w is the signal wavelet coefficient; λ is the threshold value (non-negative value); sgn is the symbol function, when the noisy signal is greater than 0, sgn=1; when the noisy signal is less than 0, sgn=-1. Aiming at the insufficiency of high-frequency signal energy loss in the process of noise reduction by soft threshold method, wavelet comprehensive threshold method combined with hard threshold method to improve the high-frequency part of the signal and use the soft threshold method to maintain signal continuity in the low-frequency part of the signal, propose wavelet The integrated threshold function is shown in equation (3).

[a] Corresponding author: 1009278271@qq.com

$$new(\omega,\lambda)=\begin{cases}\omega(|\omega|\geq\lambda)\\ sng(\omega)(|\omega-\lambda|)(\omega\leq\lambda)\end{cases} \quad (3)$$

where $\omega_{j,k}$ is the true wavelet coefficient, $\hat{w}_{j,k}$ is the improved wavelet coefficient, To improve the wavelet coefficient, $b=\frac{|w_{j,k}|-\lambda}{|w_{j,k}|}$ when $|w_{j,k}|=\lambda$, b=0, $\hat{w}_{j,k}$ =0, solve the hard threshold method in the threshold zeroing part of the discontinuity phenomenon. With the increase of $|w_{j,k}|$, b=1 and $\hat{w}_{j,k}\approx w_{j,k}$. Solve the problem of high-speed signal energy loss in the soft threshold method. Wavelet integrated threshold denoising preserves the high frequency signal while changing the threshold function while maintaining signal continuity. Experimental results show that the improved threshold function has a good effect on seismic signal noise reduction.

SNR (Signal to Noise Ratio) and MSE (Average Variance) are a way to evaluate the merits of the noise reduction method. Assuming the seismic signal vector is $a=[a_0, a_1, a_2, ...a_{N-1}]^T$, there is a formula (4):

$$a_i=f_i+n_i \quad i=0,1,2,...N-1 \quad (4)$$

where f_i is the function f Sampling, n_i is a Gaussian white noise distributed $N(0,\sigma)$. The goal of noise reduction is that the mean variance MSE of the fitted value $\hat{f}$ is the smallest, and the expression of MSE is as shown in formula (5)

$$R(\hat{f},f)=\frac{1}{N}\left\|\hat{f}-f\right\|^2=\frac{1}{N}\sum_{i=0}^{N-1}(\hat{f}_i-f_i)^2 \quad (5)$$

From equation (5), the smaller the $\hat{f}_i-f_i$ is, the smaller the MSE value is, after noise reduction. The closer the waveform is to the original signal waveform.

2.2 Wavelet characteristic energy spectrum coefficient

Wavelet characteristic energy spectrum coefficient is a representation of the noise reduction method. It can visually observe the energy distribution of the signal in the low frequency and high frequency parts, and it is convenient to observe the noise reduction result and draw conclusions quickly. The wavelet characteristic energy spectrum coefficients are decomposed by i scales and the total energy is unchanged, as in formula (6), where f(n) is the discrete sampling sequence of the seismic signal, A is the low frequency part of the signal, and D is the high frequency part of the signal, $A_i f(n), D_i f(n)$, is the component of each frequency after the scale transformation, $E_i^A f(n), E_i^D f(n)$ is the low-frequency signal component energy and the high-frequency signal component energy at the decomposition scale i, respectively.

$$f(n)=A_i f(n)+D_i f(n)+...+D_i f(n) \quad (6)$$

$$E_i^A f(n)=\sum_{i=1}^{N}(A_i f(i))^2 \quad (7)$$

$$E_i^D f(n)=\sum_{i=1}^{N}(D_i f(n))^2, i=1,2,...,N \quad (8)$$

Define the ratio between the energy of each component in the wavelet decomposition and the total energy, that is, the wavelet characteristic energy spectrum coefficient, expressed by the parameters hE_i^A and hE_i^D, respectively:

$$hE_i^A=\frac{E_i^A f(n)}{Ef(n)}, hE_i^D=\frac{E_i^D f(n)}{Ef(n)} \quad j=1,2,...,N \quad (9)$$

3 Wavelet integrated threshold noise reduction experiment

3.1 Simulated seismicsignal denoising experiment

The experimental research processed signal is for the down hole near-seismic signal frequency band. Then ear-shock signal is coif wavelet as the wavelet basis function, and the wavelet characteristic energy spectrum coefficient of the signal after 6 decompositions is calculated. Observed near the characteristic energy spectrum coefficient at the third decomposition scale the seismic signal energy is strong, so the wavelet characteristic energy spectrum coefficient on the third decomposition is selected. The down-seismic near-seismic signal acquisition process includes near-seismic signals and noise signals. The frequency of the peak energy of the near-seismic signals is mainly concentrated at 3-6 Hz. According to the random noise source and the performance law of the noise itself, the noise is divided into three categories (Table 1):

Table 1 Noise classification

Noise type	Frequency range (Hz)	Noise reduction difficulty
Environmental noise	3-20	Difficult
Secondary noise	5-30	Difficult
Instrument noise	1-2	Easy

In order to compare the noise reduction ability of the wavelet integrated threshold method and the soft threshold method for secondary noise and environmental noise, select the near-shock signal. The Rake wavelet signal with similar wavelet coefficient characteristics was simulated. The Rake wavelet signal adds a noise frequency range of 3-30 Hz, including ambient noise and secondary noise. Fig.1(a) shows the waveform of the Rake wavelet and the waveform of the noise-reconciled wavelet. The soft threshold and wavelet integrated threshold denoising experiment of the noisy rake wavelet

[a] Corresponding author: 1009278271@qq.com

https://doi.org/10.1051/itmconf/20192501014

waveform are shown in Fig. 1(b).

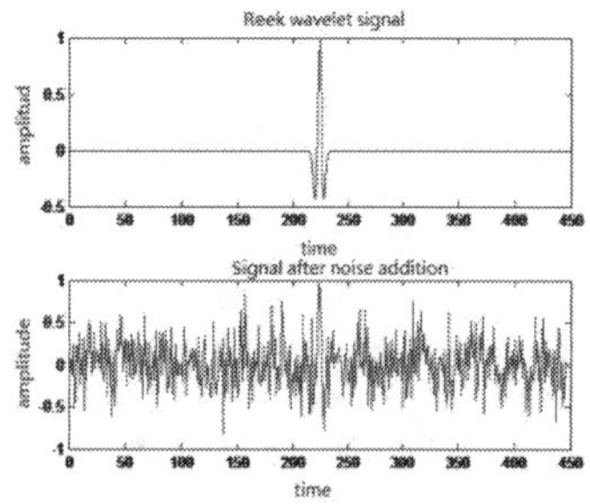

(a) The rexson waveform and the noised waveform

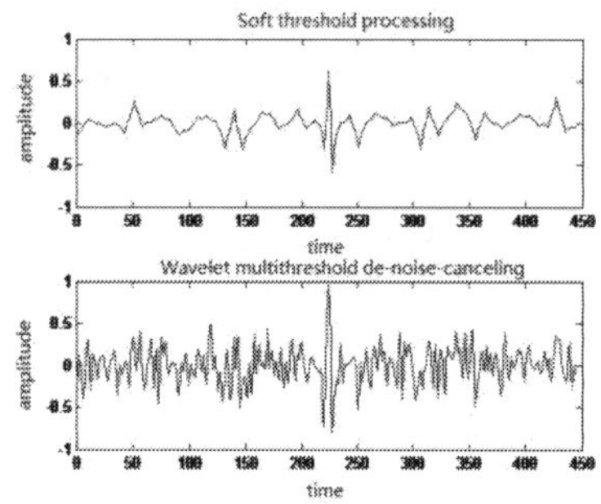

(b) Wave form comparison of the results of the two threshold noise reduction methods

Figure 1. Rexson waveform and noise reduction waveform

In Figure 1(a), the signal of the Rake wavelet after the noise is 210s at the first arrival. After the noise is added, the high-frequency signal of the waveform is suppressed, and the seismic signal and the noise signal cannot be distinguished. Comparing the waveforms of the two methods of noise reduction in Figure 1(b), the soft threshold method suppresses the amplitude of the high-frequency signal. The noise near the zero-frequency is similar to the waveform after the noise-added, and the noise reduction effect is not obvious. The wavelet comprehensive threshold method improves the high-frequency signal. Amplitude reduces the amplitude of noise at zero frequency. By calculating the SNR and MSE (Table 2), the wavelet integrated threshold method is improved on two indicators. The wavelet integrated threshold method has the smallest MSE value after noise reduction, and the signal after noise reduction is more similar to the original signal.

Table 2 SNR and MSE from the de-noised signal in simulation

The noise reduction method	SNR	MSE
Hard threshold	18.5736	0.2907
Soft threshold	19.3285	0.2897
Wavelet synthesis threshold	19.4136	0.2784

4 Results and discussion

The wavelet integrated threshold denoising method uses the hard threshold method to improve the high-frequency signal energy, and uses the soft threshold method to preserve the signal smoothness of the low-frequency part of the signal, and improves the signal de-noising ability while ensuring signal continuity. The soft threshold, the wavelet integrated threshold method and the soft threshold method based on S transform are used to denoise the signal to observe the noise reduction. Experiments show that the wavelet high-frequency signal is recovered and the noise energy spectrum coefficient is suppressed by the wavelet integrated threshold method. The waveform MSE value is the smallest after the wavelet comprehensive threshold denoising, and the waveform after noise reduction is the closest to the original signal waveform. The noise reduction effect is as obvious as the soft threshold denoising method based on S transform. However, the wavelet comprehensive threshold method has a lot of problems of slow data processing, and the redundancy problem existing in the algorithm should be improved or the improvement of the threshold function should be further proposed. The improved wavelet integrated threshold method should be able to adapt to signals with similar characteristics to the near-seismic signals, increasing the breadth and universality of the application.

Acknowledgments

This work was funded by the department of Science and technology of Hebei province (Grant No. 16275417); China Scholarship Council.

References

1. Wei Xueqiang, Yuan Hongke, Qin Jingjing, Zuo Ying. Time-frequency analysis of generalized s-transform seismic signals [J]. Earthquake disaster prevention technology, 11 (2017): 808-813.
2. Geng Guanshi, Yu Yanxiang. Empirical relationship between source rupture scale and magnitude in western China [J]. Earthquake disaster prevention technology, 10 (2015): 68-76.
3. Zheng Zuoya, Lu Xiushan, Li Kexing. Construction of a class of wavelet basis functions and its application in measurement data processing [J]. Surveying and mapping science, (2007):9-11.
4. Tang Shoufeng, Tong Minming, Pan Yuxiang, He Xinmin, Lai Xiaosong. Analysis of microseismic signal of coal and rock fracture by wavelet signature spectroscopy [J]. Acta instrumentation sinica, (2011): 1521-1527.
5. Li Ying, Zhang Shuzhen, Xu Kangsheng. Application of wavelet noise reduction method in seismic signal processing [J]. Journal of northwest seismology, (2006): 159-162.
6. S. Mostafa Mousavi, Charles A. Langston. Hybrid Seismic Denoising Using Higher-Order Statistics and Improved Wavelet Block Thresholding [J]. Bulletin of the Seismological Society of America, (2016):1380-1393.
7. Vittoria Bruni, Domenico Vitulano. Wavelet-based signal de-noising via simple singularities approximation. [J]. Signal Processing, 2006. 86(4): 859-876.

[a] Corresponding author: 1009278271@qq.com

A Brief Review on Safety Strategies of Physical Human-robot Interaction

Nana Wang[1,a], Yi Zeng[1], Jie Geng[2]

[1]*China National Institute of Standardization, 100191 Beijing, China*
[2]*College of Quality and Safety Engineering, China Jiliang University, 310018 Hangzhou, China*

Abstract. Nowadays, intelligent robotics are found in many places and always seem to be growing in complexity. The need to consider the human-robot interaction was further motivated by a growing number of collisions occurred among humans and robotics. The potential accidents need to be concerned and addressed urgently. This paper briefly reviewed some relevant researches on physical Human-robot Interactions, especially for the safety strategy issues. The suggestion to solve the physical Human-robot Interaction safety issues has been also proposed given to the review works.

1 Introduction

Nowadays, intelligent robotics are growing in complexity. Its application field has been extended from traditional industrial fields to medical treatment, logistics, housekeeping and other service fields. The need to consider the human-robot interaction was further motivated by a growing number of collisions occurred among humans and robotics. The potential accidents need to be concerned and addressed urgently.

It is understandable there has to have requirements and enhanced skills for humans and a demand of evolved robots in some more human-friendly machines. For a safe pHRI, safety is the basic requirement of a robot when working with humans. Human safety is generally guaranteed through slowing down or stopping motion when robot is approaching to human. Further, coexistence allows robotics sharing the workspace with humans. Collaboration is a special coexistence scenario that robotics interact with human directly. Safe collaboration has to be consistently guaranteed in a pHRI scenario [1].

The safety issue is always the first and core consideration should be guaranteed during the robot design phase. Safety strategies should be implemented. Current pHRI safety strategies cover pre-collision safety strategy and post-collision safety strategy [1]; or passive safety strategy and active safety strategy. Preventing pHRI collision is commonly used for active safety strategy; while reducing the collision forces during the special emergency scenario is a usual way for passive safety strategies in the robot design phase. Since there are various safety strategies for dealing with pHRI, some pHRI safety strategies are reviewed in the paper.

2 Active (pre-collision) pHRI safety strategies

2.1 Safety strategy for pedestrian behavior prediction

A probabilistic model was developed in [2] that can predict the behaviour of a pedestrian for mobile robots in the office and shopping mall HRI environment. The proposed safety strategy is for protecting mobile robots; however, it can be learned also for protecting human safety issue. This safety strategy was divided into two scenarios:

1) *efficient mode* can accurately predict the pedestrian behaviours; a probability of collision for human and robot can be estimated.

2) *safety mode* cannot support the prediction of the pedestrian behaviours, and the robot must do actions with a certain level of the safety emphasis.

In detailed modelling, the parameters refer to a set of behaviour patterns q, positions s, output directions o, position output distributions aq(S), and direction output distributions bq(s,o). Then, the robot will learn these model parameters through collecting behaviour data, classifying the data; and determining the output distributions of positions and directions. In the end, the trajectory will be generated to support making decision of different modes. For each mode, the different ranges of warning areas are also introduced to predict the collision risk, and the velocity control has been used to achieve these two safety strategies.

2.2 Pre-collision HRI safety strategy

Pre-collision safety strategies are generally dealing with safety at different time horizons. They have three

[a] Corresponding author: wangnn@cnis.gov.cn

components [3]:

-Safe Planning (long-term safety) is a pathway planning with safety criteria. The method aims to place the robot in a better position when human is approaching to avoid unanticipated safety events. The planning module uses search strategies, like the best-first planning approach, or randomized planning. The method planned the safest path by searching contiguous regions without obstacles. It also leads to the goal and minimize a measure of danger criterion.

-Trajectory Scaling (medium term safety) is the path planning method that generates the velocity and acceleration profile to be followed along the path under the pHRI context. With an estimation of the danger from dynamic factors, it provides a relative safety path planning result.

-Reactive Control (short-term safety) is the key element of the safety module that estimates the danger level with danger index. With the calculated danger index, the virtual force to push the robot away from the human is generated.

Meanwhile, user monitoring technology is an alternative method sensing users' position and reactions. The information is used as inputs to the various safety modules.

2.3 Learning-based safety strategy

Learning-based safety strategy is initially designed for a robotic manipulator operating in an unstructured pHRI environment [4]. During reproduction,

- Kinematic Redundancy of the robot regulates the dynamic movement when the robot generates an infinite number of inverse control strategies.
- Task Redundancy regulates the stiffness of the robot when the task can be achieved through an infinite number of solutions.

After having several observations of a similar task, the robot creates a skill simulation model. The model considered the variations and correlations observed along the movement. If a part of a movement was consistent observed in different trials, the part should probably be reproduced in this specific manner.

2.4 Withdrawal strategy for human safety

Withdrawal strategy for human safety can be used when human and robot are approaching to each other in a very close range. The strategy aims to enlarge the distance from the robot to the human. Virtual force model regulates the end-effector velocity so that the robot can move away from human and meanwhile go to a nearest parking position [5].

2.5 Constraint-based safety strategy

Designing task-consistent collision avoidance strategies [6] productively combined task execution and safety actions in the HRI environment. Constraints affecting the task are concerned in the HRI safety strategy. Here, tasks' constraints are consistent and there is not necessary to have prioritization. Three task-oriented classifications (hard constraints, skill constraints, and soft constraints) support the exploitation of possible constraints redundancy while preserving the final task execution and completion. Moreover, unconstrained velocities can be exploited to perform evasive motions. Evasive motions aim to minimize the level of danger in HRI. For this, the danger field is introduced for assessing danger in HRI. Such measure concerns robotics as danger sources in its pHRI workspace. Both the distance and velocity between the human and robotics have to be predicted. The value of danger filed is computed and a state machine template to manage velocity constraints then will be proposed.

An integrated framework for social mapping [7] allowed robots to navigate in a pHRI environment. It demonstrates socially behaviour at the acceptable level. particularly one of "comfort, naturalness, sociability" responds the performed action by detecting the social map.

3 Passive (post-collision) pHRI safety strategies

Past research works also investigated the impacts of robotics from perspectives of realistic threats to human jobs, resources and safety, identity threats to human identity and distinctiveness, attitude toward robots, and support for robotics [8]. Participants were asked to watch videos of supposedly robotics and perceived that robots in general will be a significant threatening source to humans in future.

A new approach of human robot interaction (Human Hybrid Robot – HHR) [9] combined human and technical elements to supporting manual assembly tasks by taking advantages of individual abilities and technical benefits.

Assembly stations where human-robot collaborative tasks are carried out was designed [10]. Both passive and active pHRI safety strategies were combined to apply to guarantee the human safety and the overall system's productivity. A lot of clearance for robots has been required for fenceless separation monitoring. However, requirements for close cooperation of human and robotics are reduced in the collaborative and cooperative context. Here, the human is not constrained. The cooperation requires far more sensing technics for collision detection and collision avoidance. Regarding user's acceptance, operators feel more comfortable when they are aware of the underlying safety functionalities.

The requirements where humans and robots collaborate in an assembly process were studied in [11]. The robots assist working people in the assembly process. The requirements in terms of different aged operators in an ergonomic workplace are identified in line. The study also indicated that although "the corresponding technologies are already available, appropriate safety standards to ensure occupational safety are missing". The missing safety standards to response pHRI context especially focusing on the collaborative scenario is a main barrier to direct introduce robots into the pHRI working context.

A method for improving human performance has been

introduced in [12]. The overall challenges are positively influenced by the method. The results lead to an enhanced pHRI experience.

A method presented by [13] is a systematic approach successfully in research projects. The method adapted a hazard identification technique, HAZOP (Hazard Operability), coupled with UML (Unified Modeling Language).

In the early design phase of a robot, planning for safety to identify the potential HRI hazards received less attention than techniques. Planning for safety is an important way to reduce potential hazards under the HRI context. Safety criteria need to identify in the planning phase [3]. With the safe planning and designing, the robot will improve the performance as well [14]. Some robotic standards included the commonly used industrial risk assessment methods to guarantee the pHRI safety. However, these standards [15-16] rarely meet the requirements for dealing with close pHRI scenarios. Appropriate policies for controlling the relevant risks and associated control strategies need to be examined [17-18].

4 Conclusion

Safety is the most essential requirement of human-robot interaction. In addition to taking hardware and software measures to ensure the objective attributes of robot safety. It is also necessary to further study the subjective attributes of human feelings and psychology in the process of human-robot interaction, so as to evaluate the safety problems more objectively and accurately.

References

1. Heinzmann, J., & Zelinsky, A. (2003). Quantitative safety guarantees for physical human-robot interaction. *The International Journal of Robotics Research, 22*(7-8), 479-504.
2. Tamura, Y., Le, P. D., Hitomi, K., & Chandrasiri, N. P. (2012). Development of pedestrian behavior model taking account of intention. *IEEE/RSJ International Conference on Intelligent Robots & Systems.*
3. Kulić, D., & Croft, E. (2007). Pre-collision safety strategies for human-robot interaction. *Autonomous Robots, 22*(2), 149-164.
4. Calinon, S., D'halluin, F., Sauser, E. L., Caldwell, D. G., & Billard, A. G. (2010). Learning and reproduction of gestures by imitation. *IEEE Robotics & Automation Magazine, 17*(2), 44-54.
5. Ricardez, G. A. G., Yamaguchi, A., Takamatsu, J., & Ogasawara, T. (2013, November). Withdrawal strategy for human safety based on a virtual force model. *In Intelligent Robots and Systems (IROS), 2013 IEEE/RSJ International Conference* on (pp. 1119-1124). IEEE.
6. Ceriani, N. M., Zanchettin, A. M., Rocco, P., Stolt, A., & Robertsson, A. (2013, November). A constraint-based strategy for task-consistent safe human-robot interaction. In Intelligent Robots and Systems (IROS), *2013 IEEE/RSJ International Conference* on (pp. 4630-4635). IEEE.
7. Charalampous, K., Kostavelis, I., & Gasteratos, A. (2016). Robot navigation in large-scale social maps: An action recognition approach. *Expert Systems with Applications, 66*, 261-273.
8. Złotowski, J., Yogeeswaran, K., & Bartneck, C. (2017). Can we control it? Autonomous robots threaten human identity, uniqueness, safety, and resources. *International Journal of Human-Computer Studies, 100*, 48-54.
9. Weidner, R., Kong, N., & Wulfsberg, J. P. (2013). Human Hybrid Robot: a new concept for supporting manual assembly tasks. *Production Engineering, 7*(6), 675-684.
10. Michalos, G., Makris, S., Tsarouchi, P., Guasch, T., Kontovrakis, D., & Chryssolouris, G. (2015). Design considerations for safe human-robot collaborative workplaces. *Procedia CIrP, 37*, 248-253.
11. Faber, M., Bützler, J., & Schlick, C. M. (2015). Human-robot cooperation in future production systems: analysis of requirements for designing an ergonomic work system. *Procedia Manufacturing, 3*, 510-517.
12. Guerrero, C. R., Marinero, J. C. F., Turiel, J. P., & Muñoz, V. (2013). Using "human state aware" robots to enhance physical human–robot interaction in a cooperative scenario. *Computer methods and programs in biomedicine, 112*(2), 250-259.
13. Guiochet, J. (2016). Hazard analysis of human–robot interactions with HAZOP–UML. *Safety science, 84*, 225-237.
14. Macfarlane, S., & Croft, E. A. (2003). Jerk-bounded manipulator trajectory planning: design for real-time applications. *IEEE Transactions on Robotics and Automation, 19*(1), 42-52.
15. ISO 10218:1992. Manipulating industrial robots - Safety manual.
16. Gaskill, S. P., & Went, S. R. G. (1996). Safety issues in modern applications of robots. *Reliability Engineering & System Safety, 53*(3), 301-307.
17. Calinon, S., D'halluin, F., Sauser, E. L., Caldwell, D. G., & Billard, A. G. (2010). Learning and reproduction of gestures by imitation. *IEEE Robotics & Automation Magazine, 17*(2), 44-54.
18. Gaskill, S. P., & Went, S. R. G. (1996). Safety issues in modern applications of robots. *Reliability Engineering & System Safety, 53*(3), 301-307.

Comparative Analysis of Transmission and Switching Technologies

Yanhong Chen[1,a], Xiaoxia Wang[1] and Qinghua Wu[1]

[1]*High-tech Research Institute, No.12 Fangongting South Street, Qingzhou City, Shandong Province, China*

Abstract. This paper compares the advantages and disadvantages of OTN, SDH, WDM, ASON and other transmission and switching technologies, as well as the carrying schemes, and focuses on the analysis of the advantages of OTN-based ASON network in networking, capacity expansion, protection and other aspects.

In the era of uwb metropolitan area network, optical network is evolving from SDH to OTN in order to meet the requirements of large broadband, IP, high reliability and other ip-centric services.

1 OTN, SDH AND WDM

SDH focuses on the electrical layer processing of business, has flexible scheduling, management and protection capabilities, and has perfect OAM functions. However, SDH is unable to meet the needs of rapid business growth because it takes vc-4 as the basic cross-scheduling particle and adopts single-channel line, and capacity growth and scheduling particle are limited. WDM focuses on the optical layer processing of services, and the transmission characteristics of multi-wavelength channels make it have the advantage of large-capacity transmission, but it is still inferior to SDH in scheduling, protection, management and other aspects.

The line characteristic of OTN is that the transmission setting of any digital customer signal is independent of the customer specific characteristics (that is, customer independence). SDH/MSTP has a variety of service transmission functions, rich management and protection functions. WDM improves bandwidth utilization and implements transparent service transmission. OTN inherits the advantages of WDM network capacity and SDH network flexibility and perfectly meets the current business requirements. OTN not only applies SDH's operability and manageability to WDM, but also has the advantages of SDH's flexibility and reliability and WDM's large capacity. Pairs of these techniques are shown in table 1.

OTN effectively inherits the advantages of SDH and WDM, perfectly supports the current business requirements, and gradually realizes the goal of "one network, multiple business hosting". OTN has created a new situation that optical layer is independent of electrical layer. It can complete the functions of signal transmission, multiplexing, routing, switching, monitoring and other functions on optical layer, and guarantee its performance index and survivability. OTN supports various upper layer technologies and is an ideal base transport network to adapt to the evolution of various communication networks.

Table 1. Comparison of OTN, SDH and WDM Carrying schemes

OTN compared with SDH		OTN compared with traditional WDM	
OTN	**SDH**	**OTN**	**WDM**
Broad bandwidth, convenient capacity expansion	Narrow bandwidth	Multiple networking capabilities	Poor networking skills
Large particle scheduling	Pellet scheduling	Strong and flexible scheduling ability	Business scheduling is inflexible
High efficiency of business encapsulation and transparent business transmission	low business packaging efficiency	A variety of sound protection mechanisms	The protection mechanism is imperfect
Multistage series monitoring	Single stage monitoring	Rich overhead management	Simple OSC, unable to accurately manage channels
Out-of-band FEC	No FEC or in-band FEC		

2 OTN, SDH and ASON

Both SDH and OTN are typical transmission network

[a] Corresponding author: 395179801@qq.com

technology systems. And ASON is has nothing to do with the specific transmission technology of network architecture, its greatest progress is in the original system of transmission network technology increases the control plane, and transferring the ownership of the original management plane function in the control plane, adopts the distributed control mechanism to replace the past a single centralized management mode, introduced the concept of dynamic exchange, thus will exchange, transmission, data real together, the relationship between the three is shown in figure 1.

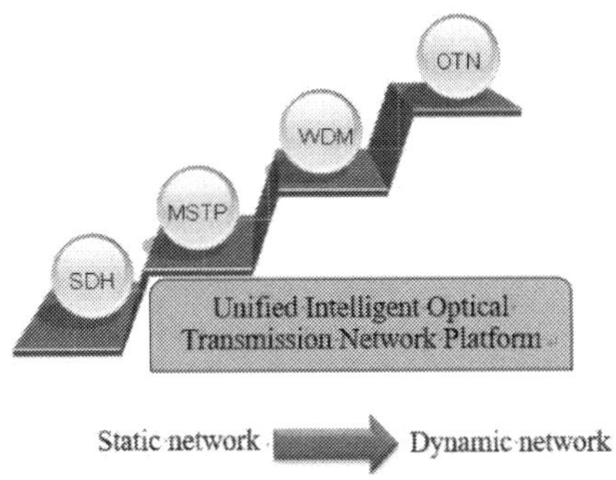

Figure 1. Relationship between SDH, OTN and ASON

After the traditional optical transmission network USES the ASON technology, makes the traditional concept of multi-layer network structure becomes simple and flat, optical network layer to carry business directly, avoiding the traditional Internet business to upgrade when received multiple restrictions, can satisfy the user dynamic allocation of resources, effective protection of resilience and wavelength requirements for the application of new business and so on. The concept and idea of ASON can be extended to different transmission network technologies and has universal adaptability. Therefore, it can be said that the concept of ASON is not only a historical breakthrough in the concept of traditional.

3 ASON network based on OTN

With the development of the network, for the large-grain broadband service, the pure information transmission capacity has been unable to measure the efficiency of the transmission network, and the network and service survivability are more dependent on the framework of flexible transmission network to guarantee. Therefore, the concept of network readiness was proposed. That is:
Network readiness = information transmission capability + business control capability + network operation capability

Therefore, the transmission capacity relying on OTN alone cannot meet the requirements of the grid, and an otn-based ASON network is needed, as shown in figure 2. In general, the advantages of otn-based ASON network are reflected in the following six aspects.

3.1 Networking

First, it can realize flexible and efficient scheduling and networking of large granule services. Based on ODUk's high-capacity electrical cross matrix, multiple optical line directions are supported to ensure flexible scheduling of large-particle services in the electrical layer. The basic particles of dispatching business are GE and 2.5g POS, which can improve the efficiency. Combined with wavelength - based scheduling, efficiency and flexibility can be improved. Second, network survivability has been greatly improved. Traditional WDM has limited protection methods because of its single alarm detection means, no switching protocol is defined and no powerful cross-scheduling module. OTN supports electric cross matrix, can provide special automatic protection switching overhead, support comprehensive alarm detection, with a good foundation to provide a variety of protection methods.

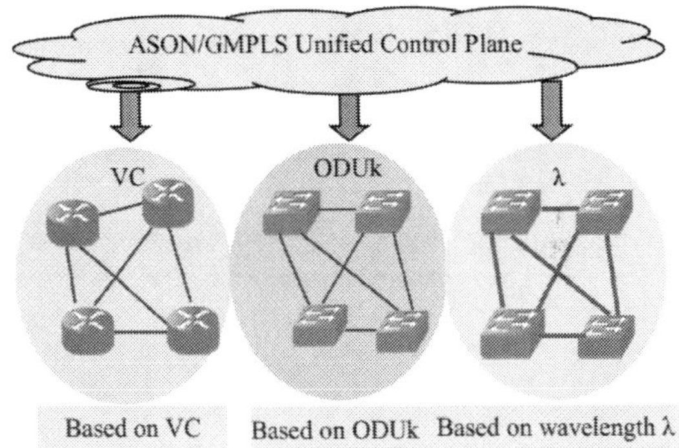

Figure 2. Multi-layer ASON Network Based on OTN

3.2 Capacity expansion

Automatic resource discovery for network expansion. The network has capacity expansion needs. When nodes need to be added, the nodes on both sides of the newly added nodes can automatically find new nodes, update the database, and automatically display the new topology on the network management. When the business is damaged, the business automatically finds out that the new route through the new node can realize the non-damage recovery of the business.

3.3 Clock

Clock information transparent transmission, can provide multiple SDH subnet mixed transmission. G. 709 provides an asynchronous mapping mode from stm-n to OPUk, in which OPUk signal is generated by the clock of OTN device itself and is independent of stm-n signal, and a positive/negative/zero adjustment mechanism is used to tolerate a certain frequency deviation. In this way, multi-subnet mixed transmission can be realized. OTN technology can better adapt to the construction requirements of trunk network at all levels.

3.4 Protection

One is to provide wavelength level optical channel

protection, photonic network connection protection. These protection methods have been widely used in traditional WDM systems. The other is to provide protection of subnet connection based on ODUk. This is a relatively mature protection method of OTN at present, which has little relation with network topology. It provides protection by using the double-generation selective receiving function of electrical layer intersection, which can be applied to ring, chain and Mesh. Third, provide ring network protection based on ODUk. OTN can support the ring network protection of SDH MSP ring, for example, because the electrical crossover ability brings great flexibility, the electric layer alarm carried by OTUk frame is the trigger condition of ring network inversion; Fourth, MESH protection based on ODUk and wavelength. This protection method has the characteristics of ASON. Combined with ROADM's OTN/ASON equipment, it can provide multiple path recovery in both ODUk and wavelength layers, greatly improving the network survivability.

3.5 Business

One is the multilayer ASON network, with more transmission options. Otn-based ASON supports ODUk ASON, which enriches the ASON network layer and enables more modes of delivery for demanding customer businesses. For small granular businesses with remote scheduling, end-to-end ASON scheduling and management can be supported by means of SDH network and OTN network docking. The second is to provide various business Level agreements (slas) Level of business. Otn-based ASON provides SLA business of ODUk; ROADM provides wavelength SLA business. Third, to provide full service access to adapt to future network development. OTN defines a variety of mapping methods, so that different types of client side signals have a suitable path to adapt to the OTN network; OTN defines virtual cascaded frames that are used to deliver large granular services over ODUk; G.709 provides encapsulation of package-based user data, that is, Ethernet frames are encapsulated directly through the GFP (Generic Frame Protocol). GFP encapsulation protocol (g.7041) is a general method to encapsulate arbitrary packet signals into fixed rate signals (such as OPUk), which can guarantee the support of new business in the future.

3.6 Management

Provides end-to-end channel OAM capability. Traditional WDM devices can only monitor a small amount of optical layer information, such as optical power, and cannot realize the monitoring based on business channel. The operation and maintenance management remains unchanged, and they cannot provide the protection based on business channel and other functions. OTN, because it draws on the advantages of SDH, defines perfect and rich monitoring bytes in the frame structure, which can realize monitoring based on business channels. Serial monitoring bytes carry information of source and host nodes, which makes monitoring function more powerful. The improvement of end-to-end channel OAM function enables OTN network to have the operation, maintenance and management functions similar to SDH network, and to provide protection and other functions based on business channels. The embedded network management channel reduces the management cost. Traditional WDM systems cannot provide embedded network management channels, and its management information needs to be realized through external independent optical modules. OTN provides special general communication channels, which can realize embedded network management. The embedded network management channel adopts the electric monitoring mode, which can avoid the waste of resources in the optical monitoring mode. Each line of business can provide a network management channel to achieve redundant backup; The use of embedded network management does not affect the use of non-embedded network management, traditional monitoring methods can still support.

References

1. Zeng Shan, Zhang Haibo, Zhang Liangkai. *Application of otn transmission network technology in power communication system* (Electronic Test, Issue no.12, 2018).
2. Mengqi Chen, *Study on the carrying mode of large particle and large connection based on OTN technology (*Telecom Engineering Technics and Standardization, Issue no.9, 2018).
3. Ming Gao. *Study on ASON programming method based on OTN* (Communications Management and Technology, Issue no.1, 2014).

ITM Web of Conferences **25**, 01017 (2019) https://doi.org/10.1051/itmconf/20192501017
ICICCI 2018

Study on SDN Technology Based on OpenFlow and Its Application Prospect

Yanhong Chen[1,a], Peng Zhang[1], and Shuhua Zhou[1]

[1]*High-tech Research Institute, No.12 Fangongting South Street, Qingzhou City, Shandong Province, China*

Abstract. Openflow-based SDN separates the control plane of the network from the data plane of the switch and router, providing a new idea for the future development of the Internet. This paper starts with the connotation of OpenFlow and SDN, analyzes the key technologies of SDN, and prospects the application prospect of SDN.

Introduction

The traditional Internet has become an indispensable part of people's work, study and life after more than 40 years of development. Compared with its flexible and colorful application layer, its network layer is increasingly rigid and closed. The Internet based on TCP/IP couples control logic and data forwarding tightly with the network devices, in most cases it is necessary to configure the router or switch separately. On the contrary surface, some emerging businesses such as the data center, cloud computing, and some new technologies need to join and update kinds of agreements onto the control plane. On one hand the deployment process is complicated and huge, on the other hand it will take a lot of time and energy. In 2006, Nick McKeown, a professor at Stanford university, was inspired by his research project Ethane and proposed the concept of Open Flow, which was a brand-new network architecture concept with Open and programmable as the core. This concept was further extended to Software Defined Networking in 2009. In 2011, the establishment of the Open Network Foundation became an important milestone in the development of SDN/OpenFlow. In 2012, the positive actions of the industry pushed SDN to a climax. The proposal of SDN architecture provides more possibilities for the design, management and use of network resources, and facilitates the innovation and development of network.

1 Connotation of SDN technology based on OpenFlow

The Ethane project attempted to use a centralized controller to enable network administrators to easily define network-based security control policies and apply these to various network devices, thus realizing the security control of the entire network communication. Therefore, the earliest concept of OpenFlow is to separate the two functional modules of data plane and control plane of traditional network devices and manage and configure various network devices through centralized controller and standardized interface. Based on the programmable characteristics brought by OpenFlow to the network, professor McKeown further proposed the concept of SDN. The core idea of SDN is to separate the control plane of the network from the data forwarding plane and realize programmable control. The tightly coupled traditional network is divided into three layers: application layer, control layer and infrastructure layer. Control functions are transferred to the server, and the upper application is abstracted into multiple logical entities. By decoupling, the control layer and the forwarding layer are separated and opened, so that the third-party value-added applications can control the network business more intelligently, thus realizing the network programming. A SDN is mainly composed of two devices: controller and OpenFlow switch. The controller allocates a forwarding path for each flow in SDN by collecting statistical data of each OpenFlow switch; The OpenFlow switch sends the flow to the corresponding port according to the instructions of the controller, as shown in figure 1.

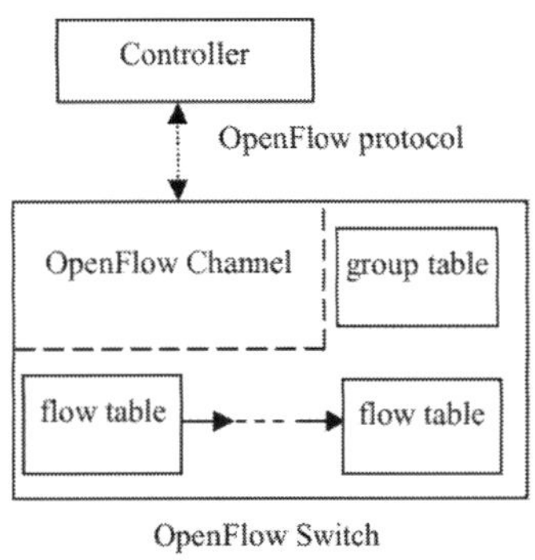

Figure 1. Overall Architecture of OpenFlow

[a] Corresponding author: 395179801@qq.com

Therefore, the generation of SDN is closely related to OpenFlow protocol. Although strictly defined, OpenFlow only refers to one of a variety of communication protocols between SDN control plane and data plane, in fact, OpenFlow has taken its good flexibility and normalization as the de facto standard of SDN communication protocol, which is similar to TCP/IP as the communication standard of the Internet. Therefore, SDN based on OpenFlow protocol is generally regarded as a narrow SDN in the industry, and this concept is also the default concept in the industry.

2 Key technologies of SDN based on OpenFlow

2.1 Network operating system

In the SDN category, the Network operating system (NOS) is also called the Network controller. Currently, the popular NOS include NOX, Beacon, Trema, Maestro and so on. All the intelligent and core functions of the network are reflected in the network controller, which schedules and manages the forwarding strategy of the forwarding surface and supports different businesses running on the network controller through the non-intelligent fast forwarding surface equipment. NOS is like the operating system of OpenFlow network, which manages traffic by operating on the switch. Therefore, the switch also needs to support corresponding management functions.

From the perspective of the whole network, NOS should abstract all kinds of resources in the network and provide an easy-to-use interface for network management. It does not complete the management tasks of the network itself, but realizes specific management tasks through various "applications" running on NOS. Managers and developers can focus on developing these applications without spending time analyzing the underlying details. When traffic passes through the switch, if no corresponding matching table item is found, it is forwarded to the network controller running NOS and a decision mechanism is triggered to determine which application the traffic belongs to. Applications running on NOS use traffic information to build a network view and determine traffic behavior. It is because of NOS that SDN has the ability to establish different logical networks and implement different traffic management strategies for different applications.

2.2 Abstract modeling of forwarding surface

One of the key technologies of SDN is the abstract modeling of the forwarding surface, which is similar to the Virtual File System (VFS) subsystem in the Linux operating System. VFS abstracts a common file system, providing a unified data structure definition and operation method for the upper layer, and ADAPTS different file systems for the lower layer, such as ext2, ext3, NFS and so on. For the abstract model of SDN forwarding surface, the ONF standard organization proposed and standardized the OpenFlow protocol, in which the forwarding surface device is abstracted as a forwarding model driven by multi-level flow table.

2.3 OpenFlow protocol

OpenFlow protocol is the basis for SDN to realize the separation of control and forwarding. In order to promote the development of SDN and unify OpenFlow standard, ONF was established in March 2011. ONF mainly focuses on promoting SDN based on OpenFlow protocol to become a new network standard. Its main research achievements include defining SDN basic architecture, OpenFlow standard and OpenFlow configuration and management protocol. Since the first release of the OpenFlow specification in October 2009, ONF has released 1.1, 1.2, 1.3, and the latest version of OpenFlow 1.4 in October 2013.

The OpenFlow specification is mainly composed of port, flow table, communication channel and data structure, and its data grouping processing principle is as follows. After the SDN switch receives the data packet, it first looks for matching flow entries on the local flow table. Data groups match from the first flow table and may go through multiple flow tables, called pipelining. The flow entry in the flow table contains three parts, matching: matching the existing flow entry according to the input port of data grouping, header field and the information passed by the previous flow table; Count: count the groups that match successfully; Operations: including output grouping to port, encapsulation to controller, discarding, and so on. If a data group successfully matches a flow entry in the flow table, the count of the flow entry is updated and the operation in the flow entry is performed. If not, the first message or message digest of the data stream is forwarded to the controller, which decides the forwarding port.

2.4 Network virtualization

Network virtualization enables the creation of logically independent networks on the same Shared physical network resources to meet the application trends of multi-tenancy, traffic isolation and logical network freedom control. FlowVisor is a network virtualization platform based on OpenFlow controller. By adding virtual abstraction layer to the controller, SDN application layer can only see the local part of the whole network view diagram, provide more abstract network resource description, and realize more flexible programming. From the point of the current research progress, people have used SDN network virtualization advantage in solving cloud computing/data center network overlap, cross subnet IP address of the virtual machine migration, migration across the data center business difficulties, STP/MSTP slow convergence speed, loop link resources waste, unable to multiple tenants provide cross section such as bandwidth issues such as the extensive research and practice.

FlowVisor generates independent network sharding by splitting the flow table space. Network sharding is an element of FlowVisor's management function. It is defined by a set of text configuration files. A text configuration file contains rules that control various network activities, ranging from the source IP address of traffic to port number or data packet header information. Through network sharding, FlowVisor divides the physical network into multiple logical networks, allowing multiple controllers to control an OpenFlow switch at the same time, but each controller can control only one virtual network that passes through the OpenFlow switch. Therefore, the test platform established by FlowVisor can allow multiple network tests to be performed simultaneously in different virtual networks without affecting the forwarding speed of the flow. FlowVisor has been widely applied to the experimental platform of multiple research institutions. At the global open network summit, it provides a demonstration environment for various SDN innovative applications to share the same set of physical network resources.

3 Application prospect of SDN based on OpenFlow

3.1 Application of SDN in data center network

Cloud computing data center is one of the fields with the fastest development of network standards and the most advanced technology types. Especially in the public service cloud, the hosting network which provides users with data isolation by VLAN mode can no longer meet the needs of continuous updating. On the one hand, the number of vlans is limited; On the other hand, users hope to apply for virtual network resources flexibly, including IP address resources, bandwidth resources, firewall, load balancer and other network value-added services resources, just like leasing virtual machines, storage and other resources. Therefore, the new cloud computing data center network should have four capabilities: it can provide a number of scalable isolation networks, and it can provide reusable IP address resources for different tenants; A virtual network with guaranteed bandwidth for different tenants; Provides flexible firewall and load balancing modules for different tenants. SDN architecture can better achieve the above capabilities, data center is undoubtedly the first stage of SDN commercial focus.

3.2 Application of SDN in optical transmission network

The most prominent advantage of introducing SDN into optical transmission network is that the SDN controller has a global view of the whole network, can grasp the topology and network state and other information of the whole network, improve the convergence speed and network performance such as delay, and ensure the predictability of system routing and performance. At present, the OpenFlow protocol has been extended to the field of transmission network, adding granular support for time slot, port, label, wavelength and so on. Power, attenuation, nonlinear cost, dispersion cost, and other additional costs related to network physical layer parameters can be abstracted as digital model input SDN controller, which realizes the management and control of network parameters. SDN controllers that master the parameters of the physical layer of the whole network can also select appropriate modulation formats and spectral resources according to the length of optical transmission channel and the number of cross-sections. In addition, there are various types of optical network equipment veneer. If programmable software under SDN architecture and customized speed/code type optical modules are adopted, normalization of veneer hardware can be realized, the number of spare parts can be reduced, and rapid opening and deployment of various types of businesses can be realized.

3.3 Application of SDN in government and enterprise networks

Government and enterprise networks have many types of business, complex network equipment functions and many types, which require high security of the network, centralized management and control, high flexibility of the network, and the ability to meet the requirements of customization. The architecture of SDN forwarding and control separation can make network equipment universal and simple. SDN separates the complex business functions and is implemented by the upper application server, which can not only reduce the cost of equipment hardware, but also simplify the enterprise network and make the hierarchy clearer. At the same time, the logic centralization of SDN control can realize the centralized management and control of enterprise network, centralized deployment and management of enterprise security policies, and more flexible customized network functions can be applied in the controller or upper layer to better meet the needs of enterprise network. As the enterprise network is generally constructed, managed and maintained by the enterprise's own information department, which is closed and can be uniformly planned, deployed and upgraded, SDN deployment is highly feasible.

3.4 Application of SDN in Solid-shift Fusion

Under the background of full-service operation, the current communication operators have two networks, namely fixed network and mobile network, and the edge gateway of these two networks is assumed by different devices. If SDN technology is applied, the control plane of gateway device can be extracted and uniformly deployed to NOS of cloud data center that also adopts SDN technology. Since the control plane can be programmed by script and the operator can develop it to meet the functional requirements of customers, most of the business can be completed in the control plane. At the same time, the gateway device becomes the forwarding surface device and can act as xGW/xGXN/BRAS simultaneously. Based on the above operations, the data forwarding surface of fixed network and mobile device can be unified, so as to achieve the integration of fixed network and mobile network.

4 Conclusion

At present, SDN related technologies are not mature enough and the degree of standardization is not high enough. SDN still has a long way to go and network reform must go through a long process. And because the whole industry is facing reshuffle, it is difficult to judge whether each manufacturer can support open standards, and the development of system technology is uncertain. But as a disruptive technology of network, SDN has become a new growth point of IT and network industry. New network industry chain is forming, which will bring about great influence on network hardware and software and network architecture. The technology roadmap that used to be closed to the Internet will certainly change in the future, and the architecture of the network system will become more flexible to support increasingly rich web applications. Network equipment providers, network operators and Internet service providers are paying close attention to the wave of technological revolution brought by SDN. SDN will be an important component and core representative of the network in the future.

References

1. Xiaojin Tang. *Application of SDN and NFV in 5G Mobile Communication Network Architecture* (Mobile Information, Issue no.4, 2018)
2. Chaokun Zhang, Yong Cui, Heyi Tang, Jianping Wu. *Research Progress of Software Defined Networking* (Journal of Software, Issue no.1, 2015)
3. Shunmiao Zhang, Fumin Zou. *Research Review on Software Defined Networking* (Computer Application Research, August 2013)

Research on Student Management Model of Higher Vocational Colleges Based on Cloud Platform

Xu Yang[1,a]

[1]*Tianjin Bohai Vocational Technical College, 300402, Tianjin, P.R. China*

Abstract. This paper analyzes the current situation of higher vocational students and the problems existing in the management of higher vocational students, and puts forward the idea of making use of cloud computing technology to innovate the management of higher vocational students, that is, to construct an interactive system based on the educational cloud platform. To realize the interaction between teachers and students. The construction of student management model based on cloud platform is the requirement of information construction of student management and the reform of talent training mode in higher vocational colleges.

1 The connotation of student management in higher vocational colleges

Student management is a general term for planning, organizing, coordinating and controlling students' learning and activities outside school. It is the process that the school administrator organizes and guides the students to carry out various kinds of education according to the educational standard, aim, plan and organization, so as to promote the students' all-round development and accomplish the task of training professional talents more effectively.

The management of students in higher vocational colleges is an important part of school management, which includes the daily management of students, the ideological and political education of students, the cultivation of good behavior of students and so on. The level of student management is directly related to the normal operation of the school teaching order, and plays an important role in the realization of the goal of talent cultivation in vocational colleges and in promoting the growth of students. On the one hand, compared with ordinary colleges and universities, the quality of students in higher vocational colleges is poor. Students' knowledge base, learning ability, learning habits, learning attitude and enthusiasm have a big gap compared with ordinary colleges and universities. On the other hand, the goal of talents training in higher vocational colleges is quite high. The decision of the State Council on speeding up the Development of Modern Vocational Education (Guofa [2014] 19) clearly points out that vocational education should train hundreds of millions of high-quality workers and technical and skilled personnel.

2 Overview of the educational cloud platform

2.1 Basic definition of educational cloud platform

The educational cloud is the first professional education platform to apply cloud computing technology to the field of education. Cloud computing assisted education is a new subject which intersects computer and education. It mainly uses its own powerful computing power to assist all kinds of education, teaching activities, exploring the application law of fusion with mainstream learning theory. It provides powerful resource sharing for education and teaching, and design and management of all kinds of teaching. The whole quality education cloud platform structure is mainly realized with cloud computing as the framework, centralized hosting and providing platform, resources sharing and abandoning the isolated island of information, taking the school education community as the existing education network, and upgrading the campus network for the non-website. Schools provide a new generation of education network, campus network, class network. The education cloud platform realizes the Internet, telecommunication network, radio and television network cross-platform use and mobile short message support for Unicom, telecommunications, mobile network coverage.

2.2 Basic functions of educational cloud platform

The educational cloud platform offers many useful features, such as cloud-based collaboration and interaction, online forums, online documentation,

Wikiblog, and so on. Under the guidance of counselors and teachers, under the environment of educational cloud platform, students can independently cooperate to create columns such as class resources, class dynamics, class announcements, class photo albums, class compositions and class competitions, etc.. Using these columns to carry out related activities can effectively narrow the distance between class students and teachers, students and students, and further enhance the cohesion of the class.

Education blogs facilitate students to learn, discuss, communicate and progress with each other; they also allow students to fully demonstrate their personality and express their views in blogs or Weibo so that their parents can pay attention to their children's growth at any time. And cultivate the student has the thought, is good at and dares to express the ability, promotes the student to grow healthily.

3 The connotation of student management model in higher vocational colleges based on cloud platform

Management is a system engineering, the essence of management is service. With higher vocational colleges hardware conditions continue to improve, transformation of cultivating mode in the development of education information and talents, the traditional mode of thinking and mode of student management has a serious impact on the students management in higher vocational colleges, the overall level of service, hindered the process of information construction and application of higher vocational colleges the level of student management mode in higher vocational colleges. Based on cloud platform is based on cloud network platform, with the help of information technology, through multiple parallel collaborative work management system, student management departments, for students to provide convenient, efficient service, real time for students, working mode, comprehensive management type. The construction of the model takes the student perspective as the starting point, deconstructs the existing work pattern divided by the student management department, and then according to the common and individual characteristics of the various work tasks, takes the business process as the main line.

4 The significance of implementing student management model based on cloud platform in higher vocational colleges

4.1 The important contents of the Construction of Educational Informatization in higher Vocational Colleges

The Ministry of Education's "Education Informatization Development Plan 2011-2020" points out that education informatization should be placed in the strategic position of supporting and leading the modernization of education. Accelerating the construction of vocational education informatization has gradually become the consensus of vocational colleges and universities. A few days ago, driven by the tide of educational informatization, the informational education and teaching reform in higher vocational colleges, like the development of fire and tea, changed the traditional learning model, broke the restrictions of time and space, and met the needs and autonomy of students. Flexible learning requirements, meet the needs of ubiquitous learning, teaching efficiency and teaching quality has been greatly improved. Higher vocational college student management as an important part of school education and teaching, compared with the application of information technology in education and teaching management, there is still a big gap in the level of informatization construction of student management in leaving colleges and universities, although some information products have been used.

4.2 The need of Educational and Teaching Reform in higher Vocational Colleges

At present, the higher occupation education in our country is to expand the size change of epitaxial objective mode for development to enhance the quality of the core connotation type development model. In order to adapt to this change, higher vocational colleges by insisting on open education, deepening cooperation, such as modern apprentice system, such as the alternation of the combination of talent training mode came into being, enrich the content of school enterprise cooperation, deepen the reform of higher occupation education, has injected new vitality into the occupation education. Selection and orientation of talent training mode, breaking the administrative class construction in Higher Vocational Colleges of the traditional teaching mode and learning mode, which requires the internal organization management in higher vocational colleges, The flexible teaching and learning mode also brings new challenges to the management of students in higher vocational colleges.

5 The strategy of constructing student management model based on cloud platform in higher vocational colleges

5.1 Strengthen the consciousness of Service and change the way of work

Service is the essence of student management. Since the late 1990s, the connotation of student work in colleges and universities has changed greatly. Besides emphasizing the functions of education and management, the functions of guiding and serving students have been emphasized. The concept of student affairs management, such as "student-oriented" and "one-stop service", has gradually formed. The two basic contents of "student service" and "student development" have become the main connotations of student affairs.

Built to serve as the main working mode of the student management work platform, must put down the focus of the work, in-depth understanding of the status of the students as the starting point, to promote the all-round development of students as the ultimate goal of the work, highlight the dominant position of students, understand students seeking reasonable litigation. At the same time, the use of management platform for students to give full play to students' self management ability and strengthen students' autonomous management. We must make it clear that the transformation of student management work, is not a simple leap, not reinvent the wheel, but with improved inheritance.

5.2 Integrate work tasks and build management platform

The construction of student management platform is the practical environment and important foundation of constructing student management model based on cloud platform in higher vocational colleges. The traditional student management mode has low information level, or each management system is relatively independent, and the efficiency of student management work is low, which can not better reflect the basic purpose of student service. According to the practice of student management in higher vocational colleges under the background of educational information construction, a student management platform based on cloud platform is built to ensure the systematization, comprehensiveness and immediacy of student management, and to improve the quality of service to students.

5.3 Optimize management team and improve service capability

The student management team in higher vocational colleges is mainly centered on the student work department, the admissions and employment department, the League committee, the security department and the student work office of the departments, including counselors, class teachers, professional teachers, etc.. Jointly carry out ideological and political education to students, daily management education work. There are many problems in traditional student management, such as single way, long working cycle, disordered procedure, low efficiency and so on. The student management model based on cloud platform is implemented with the help of open network platform, which has the characteristics of strong comprehensiveness, timeliness and standardization. To build a team with outstanding ability is to ensure higher vocational education. A key content of the efficient operation of the student management model based on the cloud platform.

5.4 Innovating the working Mechanism and improving the efficiency of Management

The construction and operation of student management mode based on cloud platform has changed the traditional student management mode. The student management model of higher vocational colleges based on cloud platform requires innovative management mechanism, communication mechanism, cooperation mechanism, docking mechanism and incentive mechanism to meet the needs of the whole student management and service work. To continuously promote the healthy development of student management.

6 Conclusion

To sum up, there are still many problems in the management of students in higher vocational colleges, which brings great challenges to the management of students in higher vocational colleges. In view of this, students' managers in higher vocational colleges should apply modern information technology to student management, which can not only help students build up their confidence in learning, but also do a good job of student management.

Educational informatization is a means, not an end. The construction of student management model based on cloud platform through information technology is the requirement of higher vocational college student management information construction, which has strong practicality and popularization value. Due to the late start of information construction in higher vocational colleges, there are still many deficiencies in the practice of this model, which need to be constantly explored and perfected.

References

1. Cao Yang. Study on the difficulties and Countermeasures of strengthening Student Management in higher Vocational Colleges [J]. Journal of Beijing Labor and Security Vocational College.
2. Dai Haiqun, Tao Wei. A probe into the work of Class Teachers in higher Vocational Colleges [J]. Science and Technology Information Development and economy.
3. Chen Zhibin. Discussion on Student work in higher Vocational Colleges [J]. China Adult Education (2009 / 23).
4. Luo Zheng. A brief talk on the present situation and Countermeasures of Student Management in higher Vocational Colleges [J]. Journal of Tianjin Institute of Finance and Trade Management.

Research on Urban Logistics Competitiveness in Fujian Province Based on Factor Analysis and Cluster Analysis

Hongmao Wei[1]

Fujian Polytechnic of Information Technology, Fuzhou City, Fujian Province, China

Abstract: As an important province in the southeast coastal area, Fujian is composed of 9 cities. Due to various economic, political and geographical influences, the logistics development of these cities is uneven. Based on the analysis of the factors affecting the competitiveness of urban logistics, this paper establishes the evaluation index system of urban logistics competitiveness. Factor analysis is used to evaluate the logistics competitiveness index of each city in Fujian Province, and the comprehensive score and ranking of the logistics competitiveness of each city are obtained. Cluster analysis is used to divide 9 cities in Fujian into 4 categories, and the reasons for the results are analyzed.

Keywords: Fujian province; Urban logistics; Competitiveness; Factor analysis; Cluster analysis.

1 The competitiveness of urban logistics

1.1 The connotation of the competitiveness of urban logistics

Urban logistics refers to the dynamic process of serving the needs of urban economic development, the physical flow of goods within the city, the collection and distribution of goods between the city and the outside region, and the clearance of urban waste. The competitiveness of urban logistics refers to the competitive ability of urban logistics industry to compete for logistics resources, to occupy logistics market, to expand logistics power and to gain momentum of growth.

1.2 Factors affecting the competitiveness of urban logistics

As the factors affecting the competitiveness of urban logistics have not been clearly defined at home and abroad, based on field research and relevant literature, the factors of urban logistics competitiveness with high recognition degree are summarized and compared. The influencing factors can be divided into five categories, namely, the scale of urban logistics, the current logistics resources of logistics, the demand for urban logistics, the level of urban macroeconomic development, and the level of urban informatization and talents.

1.2.1 Urban logistics scale

The scale of urban logistics is a standard to measure the development of urban logistics industry, and is one of the important factors to evaluate the competitiveness of a city's logistics. The scale of urban logistics can also be measured by the total quantity of goods, turnover, express delivery business and the added value of the logistics industry. The total quantity of goods shows that the number of logistics industry work and the turnover of goods comprehensively reflect the total amount and distance of transportation, and the volume of express delivery can also reflect the development degree of urban logistics industry and the added value of logistics industry reflects the value created by the logistics industry.

1.2.2 Urban logistics resources

Urban logistics resources are the necessary guarantee to maintain the normal operation of the urban logistics industry, and also the basis of a city's logistics competitiveness. The total amount of investment, employees, miles of logistics (kilometers, railways), the number of vehicles, ships and other tools, the number of logistics enterprises, the number of logistics parks and so on can all be called the logistics resources of a city.

1.2.3 Urban logistics demand

Logistics demand is a kind of derivative demand. There is a strong correlation between urban logistics demand and urban economy, and it has a great influence on the competitiveness of urban logistics. The total volume of imports and exports and the total retail sales of social

[1]Fund project: Supported by Program for New Century Excellent Talents in Fujian Province University.
Wei Hongmao (1979-), Male, Zhouning, Fujian, Master, Associate Professor, Research direction: Research on Regional Logistics

consumer goods reflect the logistics demand of a city from the side.

1.2.4 Urban macroeconomic development level

The development of urban logistics is closely related to the development of urban economy. Only the prosperity of urban economy can promote and improve the development level of urban logistics. With the improvement of urban economy, the logistics transportation between various industries will increase, thus promoting the development of logistics industry. Therefore, the economy is the key material guarantee for the development of logistics industry and the upgrading of urban logistics competitiveness. We can see the current situation of a city's economic development through its GDP, GDP growth rate and consumption level.

1.2.5 Urban informationization and talent level

In the "Internet +" era, the development of urban logistics industry can not be separated from the support of information technology, as well as excellent management concepts and mature operation technology. Modern logistics requires excellent management and technical talents in all aspects. It needs to be able to control the complete logistics process, with professional knowledge theory and new talents with a highly strategic vision. Talents are the high-quality resources for competition. The more talented people are, the stronger their competitiveness. Therefore, the urban logistics industry can strengthen the talent reserve resources to improve the economic competitiveness of urban logistics.

2 Evaluation index system of urban logistics competitiveness

Improving and perfecting the evaluation index system of urban logistics competitiveness has the important significance of enhancing self-awareness, optimization and upgrading. According to the reasons that affect the competitiveness of urban logistics, the evaluation system of urban logistics competitiveness is established (Table 1).

Table 1 The index system of urban logistics competitiveness

First level index	Second level index
Urban logistics scale	X_1 Total volume of goods (ten thousand tons)
Urban logistics resources	X_2 Total investment in transportation, storage and post industry (100 million yuan), X_3 Logistics mileage (kilometer), X_4 A-level logistics enterprises (one)
Urban logistics demand	X_5 Added value of transportation, storage and post industry, X_6 Total retail sales of social consumer goods (10000 yuan)
Urban macroeconomic development level	X_7 GDP (100 million yuan)
Urban logistics informationization and talent level	X_8 number of students in logistics majors in ordinary universities (person)

3 Research on urban logistics competitiveness in Fujian province

3.1 Research cities and data sources

Fujian province is located in the southeast of China, the shore of the East China Sea, the east facing the sea, the Taiwan province across the sea, the Pearl River Delta and the Yangtze River Delta connecting Guangdong province in the southwest, Jiangxi Province on the west, Lishui and Wenzhou in the northeast of Zhejiang province. Fujian province is the second largest coastal region in China, with a length of 3,752 kilometers, making it very convenient to go to sea. It can be seen that the development area and transportation network of Fujian Province have great advantages. It can be said that it is one of the provinces with superior logistics conditions and is also an important province under the "One Belt, One Road" strategy. This paper mainly analyzes nine cities in Fuzhou and Xiamen, the main cities in Fujian Province. The basic data (Table 2) is mostly derived from the 2017 China Urban Statistical Yearbook, with individual data from other sources. For example, the data of X_4 is the number of logistics enterprises above grade A in each city of Fujian province. The data are from the official website of Fujian Provincial Department of Commerce as at the end of 2017. The data of X8 are the number of students majoring in logistics in colleges and universities in Fujian. Data are collected from the school enrollment prospectus in recent years, so all data sources are reliable, and the results are also available.

3.2 Factor analysis

3.2.1 Factor index analysis

The software SPSS19 is used for factor index analysis. The main operation is to process the data according to the standard and eliminate the different dimensions.

3.2.2 Adaptive test

The KMO test is used to check the partial correlation between variables. The KMO value that can carry out factor analysis is between 0.5-0.9. Once the scope is exceeded, the result will be affected. After the adaptive test, the correlation between variables is found in this paper, and the KMO value is within the range of 0.5-0.9. Therefore, factor analysis can be continued. In addition, through Bartlett's spherical test, it is found that the Sig value is 0. In the test standard, if the Sig value is less than 0.05, it means that there is a correlation between the variables of the test, then the Sig value of this test is 0, which proves that there is a kinship between the variables, so the factor can be analyzed.

3.2.3 Factor analysis result

The first 2 factors are extracted by using the extraction principle with the characteristic value greater than 1, and the cumulative variance is 87.835%. It is proved that these 2 factors contain most of the index information, and the factor extraction effect is very good.

Table 3-2 The rotated component matrix [a]

	Component	
	1	2
GDP (100 million yuan)	.974	-.130
Total amount of goods (ten thousand tons)	.948	.246
Number of students in ordinary universities (person)	.908	.154
Added value of transportation, storage and post industry (ten thousand yuan)	.905	-.025
Total fixed assets investment (100 million yuan)	.903	.404
The number of logistics enterprises (one)	.794	.478
Total retail sales of social consumer goods (ten thousand yuan)	.785	.058
Road mileage (kilometer)	-.028	-.988

It can be seen from the rotated component matrix (Table 3-2) that the first factor has a large load on the 7 variables of GDP, total amount of goods, number of students in ordinary universities, added value of transportation, storage and post industry, total fixed asset investment, number of logistics enterprises and total retail value of social consumer goods. The second factor has a large load on the road mileage variable.

Table 3-3 Component score coefficient matrix

	Component	
	1	2
Total amount of goods (ten thousand tons) X_1	.161	.053
Total fixed assets investment (100 million yuan) X_2	.128	.183
Road mileage (kilometer) X_3	.139	-.769
The number of logistics enterprises (one) X_4	.095	.257
Added value of transportation, storage and post industry (ten thousand yuan) X_5	.191	-.152
Total retail sales of social consumer goods (ten thousand yuan) X_6	.154	-.069
GDP (100 million yuan) X_7	.221	-.245
Number of students in ordinary universities (person) X_8	.166	-.012

Based on the table above, the scores for each factor are calculated as follows:

$F1=0.161X_1+0.128X_2+......+0.166X_8$

$F2=0.053X_1+0.183X_2+......-0.012X_8$

According to the principal factor variance contribution rate after the table rotation, the principal component synthesis model of each common factor weight is constructed, and then the comprehensive score of urban logistics competitiveness is obtained:

$Z=0.79F1+0.210F2$

By substituting the values of F1 and F2 into the above formula, a comprehensive score of urban logistics competitiveness can be obtained.

3.3 Cluster Analysis

3.3.1 Clustering method

According to the comprehensive score of urban logistics competitiveness, the logistics competitiveness of nine cities in Fujian Province is divided into four categories, which are very strong, strong, general and weak.

3.3.2 Cluster analysis result

Table 4 Cluster analysis result

Category	City
Very strong	Fuzhou, Xiamen, Quanzhou
Strong	Zhangzhou
General	Putian, Sanming, Longyan
Weak	Nanping, Ningde

The first category is cities with very strong logistics competitiveness - Fuzhou, Xiamen and Quanzhou. It can be seen that the first factor scores of the above three cities also rank in the top three. Their common features include developed urban economy, high income and consumption level.

From Table 3-4, it can be seen that Fuzhou Logistics has the strongest competitiveness, with a score of 1.29, of which the first main factor score is 1.67, which is much higher than other cities, which is the first reason for Fuzhou to rank first.

The second category is Zhangzhou, a city with strong logistics competitiveness. It can be seen that the scores of the first factor and the second factor in Zhangzhou are also relatively advanced, and the urban economic level, income and consumption level are relatively high. Therefore, from the point of view of logistics demand, the logistics demand in Zhangzhou is also relatively vigorous, which leads to the development of its logistics industry, and makes its logistics competitiveness stronger.

The third category is Putian, Sanming and Longyan, which are generally competitive in logistics. It can be seen that Putian's second factor score is second, the urban road mileage has a high contribution, indicating that Putian has the potential to develop the logistics industry, but the economic aspect is relatively weak. People's living standards limit the demand for logistics, and the business is not as developed as Quanzhou, because the competitiveness of the logistics is general.

The fourth category is cities with weak logistics competitiveness - Nanping and Ningde. It can be seen that Ningde's second factor score is third, but the first factor score is ninth, indicating that the city's economic ability is poor, and the logistics facilities are not perfect. The location in the southwest is not enough, the resources are less, and the economic base level is also low.

3.4 Conclusion

This paper compares the logistics competitiveness of nine big cities in Fujian Province and obtains the ranking of the competitiveness of each city. These rankings are consistent with the official rankings of Fujian Province, proving that the eight index as a reference for the evaluation system is correct. In addition, the logistics competitiveness of 9 cities is divided into 4 categories by clustering method. The specific conditions are listed in Table 4. Among them, the most competitive cities are Xiamen, Quanzhou and Fuzhou. The weakest logistics competitiveness is Nanping and Ningde.

The conclusion of data analysis combined with the collected information is as follows:

3.4.1 The competitiveness of urban logistics is greatly affected by the location, and the space is "high in the southeast and low in the northwest"

Fujian has a long coastline and many important cities have obvious coastal advantages. In addition, these cities are located in the developed coastal areas with better economic foundation, perfect infrastructure construction, advanced information technology, goods storage, packaging, transport, loading and unloading equipment. Especially, the coastal logistics port scale is increasing, greatly improving the competitiveness of Fujian's urban logistics. At present, the volume of goods transported through Fujian port accounts for 90% in the province and 85% in China (container), of which Fuzhou and Xiamen are one of the most important port logistics foundations in China.

3.4.2 Urban economy is the basis of logistics competitiveness

The economy is an important material support for the development of logistics, and logistics is an indispensable part of economic development. Fujian Province's economic development is fast and stable, and the province's GDP has maintained a sustained high development in recent years, laying a solid foundation for the development of the province's logistics industry. Fuzhou and Xiamen are benefiting from the rapid development of the economy and become the most competitive cities in the province. Economic development will inevitably lead to the improvement of urban living standards. People's pursuit of material will lead to a strong demand for logistics, and demand will drive development. By giving investment support to the logistics industry and cultivating relevant professionals, the development of the entire industry will be promoted, and the competitiveness of logistics will be continuously strengthened.

3.4.3 The leading role of regional leading enterprises has provided development experience for enterprises of all sizes

In the past twenty years, Fujian province has seen a number of leading enterprises in the logistics industry. These enterprises have summed up a set of experience in developing and expanding the logistics industry in terms of total output value, enterprise scale and operation. Relevant small enterprises can learn from the experience of these enterprises, copy their models and improve their own ability to develop logistics. At present, Fujian Province has a number of leading enterprises in the logistics field, and some are famous throughout the country's logistics industry, such as Shenghui Fujian Logistics Company, Fujian Rongtai Logistics Company, Fujian Transportation Group Co., Ltd. and Xiamen Port, etc. Some are state-owned enterprises, some are private enterprises, and have strong logistics competitiveness both inside and outside the province. Through the data in Table 2, it can be seen intuitively that the number of logistics enterprises above grade A in each city. The competitiveness of a city's logistics is also greatly dependent on a leading role of leading enterprises, driving the development of the entire industry, forming a strong competitive position, matching the number of logistics with economic development, and promoting the promotion of logistics competitiveness.

References

1. Tan Guanyin, Zuo Zeping. *The Dynamic Comparison of the City Logistics Competitiveness in the Economic Zone of West Taiwan Strait* [J]. Economic Geography, 2012, 32(3): 107-113.
2. National Bureau of Statistics. City Social and Economic Investigation Division. *2017 China City Statistical Yearbook* [M]. Beijing: China Statistics Press, 2017.
3. Chen Ping. *Analysis of the Development of Modern Logistics* Industry *in Xiamen*[J]. Logistics Science and Technology, 2014, (2): 62-67.
4. Wei Jigang, Zhao Fujun. *"One Belt, One Road" Construction and New Opportunities for China's International Logistics* [J]. China Logistics & Purchasing, 2015 (23): 68-69.
5. Ye Yan. Status *Analysis Logistics Industry Fujian Province Speeding up Its Development* [J]. Value Engineering, 2014, 36: 112-118.
6. Zhang Ling. *Cluster Analysis and Evaluation of Logistics* Competitivity *of Cities in Shandong Province* [J]. Logistics Technology, 2014, 33(9): 286-289.
7. Yang Yanping, Liu Hui. *On the Spatial Difference and Functional* Orientation *of Urban Logistics Competitiveness in Henan Province* [J]. Journal of Henan University of Technology, 2016, 12(4): 47-56.

Table 2 Index data of 9 cities in Fujian Province in 2016

	Total amount of goods (ten thousand tons)	Total fixed assets investment (100 million yuan)	Road mileage (kilometer)	The number of logistics enterprises above A level (one)	Added value of transportation, storage and post industry (ten thousand yuan)	Total retail sales of social consumer goods (ten thousand yuan)	GDP (100 million yuan)	Number of students in logistics majors in ordinary universities (person)
Fuzhou	25494.54	487.26	11408	53	2525898	37631418	6197.64	3240
Xiamen	27108.27	500.08	2197	88	2833197	12834596	3784.27	1260
Putian	5464.79	271.58	6388	15	676149	6231302	1823.43	135
Sanming	9288.39	234.82	14915	11	1090700	4806339	1860.82	180
Quanzhou	24593.15	414.53	17526	85	4206504	10980568	6646.63	1575
Zhangzhou	9345.41	282.17	12200	21	1759655	8755936	3125.35	315
Nanping	3410.98	140.6	15622	7	513980	5566788	1459.79	315
Longyan	8281.18	186.17	14314	14	1110874	7290015	1895.67	135
Ningde	4450.94	160.84	11569	11	774893	5123472	1623.11	135

Table 3-1 interpretation of total variance

Component	Initial eigenvalue			Extraction of load square sum			Sum of squared rotational loads		
	Total	Percentage of variance	Cumulative %	Total	Percentage of variance	Cumulative %	Total	Percentage of variance	Cumulative %
1	5.803	72.544	72.544	5.803	72.544	72.544	5.553	69.415	69.415
2	1.223	15.292	87.835	1.223	15.292	87.835	1.474	18.420	87.835
3	.817	10.214	98.049						
4	.108	1.352	99.401						
5	.030	.379	99.780						
6	.015	.188	99.968						
7	.002	.028	99.996						
8	.000	.004	100.000						

Table 3-4 Urban logistics competitiveness and rankings

City	F1	Ranking	F2	Ranking	Urban logistics competitiveness	Ranking
Fuzhou	1.67	1	-0.13	4	1.29	1
Xiamen	0.73	3	2.19	1	1.03	2
Putian	-0.86	8	0.93	2	-0.49	5
Sanming	-0.52	5	-0.47	6	-0.51	6
Quanzhou	1.38	2	-1.20	9	0.84	3
Zhangzhou	-0.14	4	-0.14	5	-0.14	4
Nanping	-0.81	7	-0.63	8	-0.77	9
Longyan	-0.58	6	-0.51	7	-0.57	7
Ningde	-0.87	9	-0.02	3	-0.69	8

Design and Realization of Online Teaching Platform Based on WebPlus in Medical University

Qinglian Yu[1,a], Tao Qi[2]

[1] *Modern Education Technology Center, Qiqihar Medical University, Qiqihar, China*
[2] *Qiqihar No. 6 Middle School, Qiqihar, China*

Abstract. Online teaching platform is a teaching method that advocates the guidance of teachers and focuses on students. The traditional teaching mode can't meet the education mode in the information age, the position and function of teaching platform and teaching resources in the teaching activities of teachers and students are becoming more and more obvious. Based on the management platform of the website group, this paper builds a online teaching platform conforming to the teaching characteristics of medical colleges, aiming at completing the intellectualization of the teaching platform and effectiveness of the design of teaching resources, stimulating students' enthusiasm for learning and improving teachers' teaching quality.

Keywords: Website group; teaching platform; teaching resources

1 The introduction

With the rapid development of computer and network technology, the application of online teaching are more and more common, the traditional single PPT courseware has been unable to meet the current form of teaching, education workers in colleges and universities must follow the time development pace, update teaching ideas, always be prepared to accept the new knowledge [1], online teaching platform arises at the historic moment. The online teaching platform is more and more popular among teachers and students because of its rich content, vivid image and strong interaction [2]. Medical colleges and universities teachers' computer level is limited, medical teaching experiments of video and image is more, based on the individual design of online teaching course sections of a single or design for more words, content rich and vivid enough, practicality is not strong, so that caused the cost a lot of manpower material resources to create the online teaching of course utilization rate is not high, resource sharing is difficult, not reached the reasonable use of resources, not convenient students' learning and teachers' teaching. According to the teaching characteristics of medical colleges and universities, this paper constructs the online teaching platform in line with the teaching rules of medical colleges and universities. The design of online teaching platform should reflect modern education theory, reflect advanced education thought [3-4], and also improve the teaching quality and students' learning skills [5]. Due to the fast update speed of computer technology and the high cost of education input, the research and development of network teaching platform requires a large amount of manpower, material resources and time [6], which should be saved as much as possible in the construction process. It is of great significance to establish a unified online teaching platform, and it is also of great importance to meet the teaching needs of teachers in medical colleges and the call for students to learn independently. Especially, it is particularly important in the context of education industry's continuous deepening of informatization construction.

2 Technical framework of WebPlus

WebPlus is mainly a platform tool for express delivery to build an information portal website. This platform tool can conveniently integrate structured and unstructured information data and various application systems, and can display the information of the website portal. The functions of online teaching platform are realized by the functional components of the application background, and the personalized online teaching platform is constructed by using the platform. This platform covers teachers' personal basic situation, teaching courses, key and difficult explanation, classroom exercises, homework after class, online answering, interaction between teachers and students and other rich teaching resources. Network teaching platform is not only a teaching platform, but also a platform for teacher-student communication [7].

2.1 Simplified editing in background

WebPlus offers a visual online article editing tool that is as easy to edit as Word. WebPlus editors can also insert, upload various document attachments, and even directly

[a] Corresponding author: yuqinglian@qmu.edu.cn

insert media files. Edit the layout as shown below.

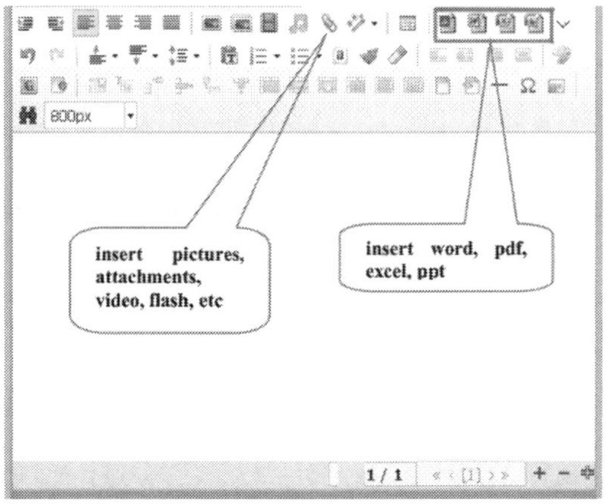

Figure 1. Visual background editing

2.2 Quick release and revision

WebPlus provides quick and easy ways to build websites, such as wizard and copy. All templates are simple Html files or fragments. Users can make them by themselves and have low requirements for professional skills. Html editing tools such as FrontPage, Dreamweaver and even Word can be used to complete them. There is no executable code in the template, and a rich and colorful display interface can be configured without writing the code, which not only ensures the system security but also reduces the difficulty of learning and making. Administrators can add as many templates to a website as they like, binding color styles, composition structures, and information content to each column within each template. The process of making and adjusting the new template does not affect the normal operation of the original configuration of the website. When the adjustment is satisfied and no mistake is made, the new template can be officially used to modify the whole website in an instant.

3. Design personalized online teaching platform by application of WebPlus

The purpose of developing online teaching platform is to meet the needs of teachers and students in the era of rapid information development, so that education teaching activities can achieve better results. On the one hand, it is more convenient for teachers to teach; on the other hand, the needs of students to learn independently can meet. In terms of functional design, the platform must take teaching as the first priority and insist on student-centered design. The main process of conventional teaching should be reflected in the online teaching platform, including the following aspects [8]: course design and release, resource download, online test, homework, performance query, teacher-student interaction, etc. In general, the function integration of the online learning platform is easy to design as a function module. According to the requirements of the platform, it mainly covers the function module before teaching, the module in specific teaching and the after-school guidance module after teaching, as shown in the figure below.

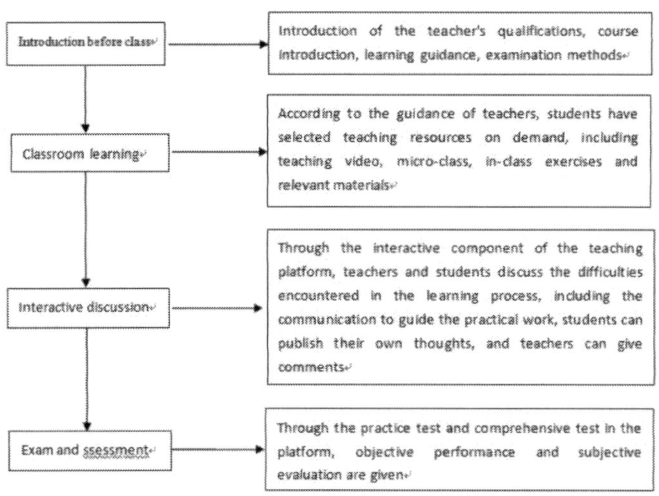

Figure 2. Basic modules of the teaching platform

3.1 Function design before teaching

The pre-teaching functional modules mainly include the personal introduction, course introduction, course design and release and other related management functions. This functional module is mainly about information display. Students have a preliminary understanding of the teachers through their personal education, scientific research achievements, professional titles and other aspects, which is convenient for students to choose courses. The teacher also carries out the content release work such as course design, specific chapter layout, course explanation and analysis, etc., and the students' pre-class and after-class review can also be operated through this platform.

3.2 Function demonstration in teaching

The online teaching function in the teaching platform is the main part of the whole platform. This paper wants to establish is a personalized and customized teaching platform in line with the teaching in medical colleges, the teaching courses on the platform are divided into theoretical teaching and experimental teaching. In the specific teaching process, it is divided into PPT course explanation, video demonstration, micro class demonstration of key and difficult knowledge, and individual analysis of teaching images. The whole platform involves a lot of contents in the teaching process, and it is not a single video that can explain a medical course clearly. Each course needs to be customized and refined gradually in the process of application.

PPT courseware added to the teaching platform requires large contrast between background color and font color, clear font size, convincing illustrations in courseware without copyright disputes, reasonable insertion of video format that can be normally played. As a new teaching method, micro class teaching uses information technology to make use of fragmented time in accordance with cognitive laws to learn certain knowledge points. The length of micro class is 5-8 minutes commonly, the longest should not exceed 10 minutes. Micro class is mainly to highlight the teaching of certain knowledge points in classroom teaching (such as key points, difficult points and doubtful points in teaching), which is a complete presentation of knowledge points. The difference between micro class and traditional video teaching lies in the length of time, but it also belongs to the category of video teaching. The processing of video here adopts the streaming server, which has high technical requirements for the system. The system must have an efficient server engine built in and apply multi-thread and multi-concurrent flow processing technology, which can meet the demand of multiple users to watch the teaching video at the same time. Video format needs to adopt current most advanced standards, and should be compatible with various current popular media formats, as far as possible to reduce the requirements of computer configuration, without additional software installation, convenient promotion and application.

The examination of teaching effect needs to be carried out through the test method. According to the teaching content and teaching requirements, the online test questions can be designed, and the question types can be selected, filled in, answered simply, and the case analysis, etc. Teachers can set questions in sections or in the whole course. Specific questions can be divided into different levels of difficulty. Students can master knowledge step by step. The objective questions are automatically graded by the system, while the subjective questions are reviewed and given online by the teacher, and the students' scores of this course are automatically synthesized and generated by the system.

3.3 After-class counseling function

The design of function module mainly reflected on the interactive capabilities, teachers can according to the requirement of the curriculum content arrangement of various practice teaching and plan, students can independently according to the requirements of teachers' practice study, within the prescribed period of time to upload to learn as a result, teachers timely according to the results of the student's study gives comments and grades, complete the teaching interaction.

Online Answering questions is also an interactive communication, students can interact with teachers via the Internet with the key points and difficulties of what they have learned. Teachers are required to respond to students' doubts in a timely and rapid manner, so as to improve students' interest and efficiency in learning, and at the same time, effectively improve the use efficiency of online teaching platforms and promote their healthy development.

4 Conclusion

In the field of modern education, education teaching mode has been changed in higher medical colleges and universities. The application of online teaching platform promotes and reform the existing teaching mode, enriches teaching methods and teaching approaches, provides students with personalized development space, improves teaching quality and promotes the development of the discipline. As a rapidly developing teaching form, network teaching platform has been increasingly valued in the current information-based education environment, so as to effectively promote the healthy and orderly development and management of education teaching functions.

Acknowledgement

This work was supported by guidance project of the science and technology bureau of Qiqihar, Heilongjiang Province under grant No.GYZD-2017010.

References

1. Mian Wang. Design and implementation of network teaching platform of computer network technology course based on CLAROLINE [J]. Computer products and circulation,2017(7):25.
2. Qingjie Ma. Design and implementation of computer network teaching platform [J]. Information and computers, 2018(9):79-81.
3. Fang Li, Xianbin Yan. Adaptive research on "combination of teachers and students" in the view of constructivism [J]. Journal of langfang normal university (social science edition), 2012,(2): 115-117.

4. Jianjuan Shao. Practical research on carrying out teaching mode reform in the construction of secondary vocational reform and development model school [J]. Scientific Chinese, 2014, (11): 187.
5. Silius,T.K..The Usefulness of Web-Based Learning Environments.[EB/OL]. http://matwww.ee.tut.fi/arvo/liitteet/usefulness_of_web.pdf, 2011-3-4/2011-4-6.
6. Kai Chen, Hanbing Wang, Huiyu Liu, et al. Design and implementation of computer network theory teaching support platform [J]. Journal of electrical and electronic teaching,2017,39(3):105-109.
7. Kenan Yu. Analysis on the design and implementation of computer network teaching platform [J]. Computer fan,2017,(3):139-140.
8. Meina Xiao. Impact of cloud computing on teaching [J]. Information and computers, 2015,(21) : 58-59.

Design and Implementation of 3D Effect Web Page Based on JavaScript Technology

Huiyou Sun[1], Shuangyuan Li[1a], Mingqian Jia[1]

[1] *Jilin Institute of Chemical Technology, 45 Chengde Street, Longtan District, Jilin City, Jilin Province,China*

Abstract. With the development of Internet technology, people's production and life are greatly influenced. Web design is widely used in Internet world. Web design and user experience are inseparable. In the pursuit of webpage layout and aesthetics, but also to add user interaction functions, Dynamic effects technology based on JavaScript can achieve user interaction requirements. The perfect combination of JavaScript dynamic effects and interactive features is the best way to achieve webpage effects. This paper expounds the application method of JavaScript, and studies the special effect application of JavaScript technology in webpages through examples.
Keywords: JavaScript; 3D effect; Web page technology

JavaScript is a literal, universal, prototype-based, object-oriented scripting language. The design principle is to provide code that can be inserted into different applications without taking up operating system and network resources. JavaScript has the following features and advantages: explanatory scripting language, simple development environment, note pad can be used to write code, good security and dynamic, cross-platform, and strong expansibility.

In this paper, the features of JavaScript technology are demonstrated and analyzed through examples. The application of JavaScript technology in the Web can design many personalized dynamic Web page effects. This paper expounds its design idea and provides the realization method of web 3D effects. The JavaScript effect technology is applied to web design, and its performance and design effect are analyzed in detail.

1 Understand the Basics of JavaScript

How JavaScript is used (direct mode and referential mode)

```
<script type="application/javaScript">
<!—
function myFunction() {
document.getElementById("myPar").innerHTML="Hell
o World";
}
var mychar ="This is a javaScript! Use direct insert! "
document.write(mychar+"<br/>")
//-javaScript finish-->
</script>
<div id="myPar"></div>
```

The direct method is implemented by means of a pair of tags <script> direct mode</script> directly, and changes and adjusts the page by means of HTML writing rules and javaScript operation rules. When you need to make changes to the page, simply write the rules in the pair of labels. Of course, you can add a pair of tags, and writing rules in this tag is also an effective method[1]. (find the right pair of script tags for strict advice)

<script type= "application/javaScript"> this is the W3C's new standard for browser identification javaScript coding, which is interpreted by the browser by calling the corresponding interpreter[2].

It is important to note: embedded script tags in the XHTML document (for example the PHP documentation), if in the absence of references to external files, should add the cdata statement in the script, cdata will tell the browser the document does not use XML parser for text data parsing, avoid is greater than and less than operators cause the browser to parse error[3].

End of "//-JavaScript": the role of the double slash in the JavaScript language and <!---> is the same in the HTML language. It's called an annotation symbol. It's used to annotate and hide unrunning text. Document.write () function indicates to the corresponding information in parentheses in the output to a window, var is to declare a variable, sometimes not, the statement can also be used to code the rigorous and unnecessary trouble typically statement, because a lot of time in a javaScript document more than one or two variables, more conducive to the handling of each variable is clear statement. Note that <script></script> this pair of tags is not fixed and can be included in anywhere of the labels <head> < / head > or < body > </body>. There are two common conventions. One is to add a pair of tags under the code of the plate. The other is to write the script tag directly at the beginning and end of the document body, regardless of the plate position[4].

[a] Shuangyuan Li: lsy@jlict.edu.cn

```
function myFunction() {
document.getElementById("myPar").innerHTML="Hell
o World";
}
```

This is a custom javaScript function that tells the browser to execute the getElementByld () function in the entire web document object model, locate the web element whose id value is myPar, and add the HTML element "Hello World!" to it. In the later research of 3D effects technology, this method of dynamically adding HTML to elements is applied.

```
<script src="url" type="text/javaScript"></script>
```

The example above is the basic format of javaScript reference way, through the same way of external links with CSS will all javaScript code written in a javaScript source file (general with js file extension), and by importing the language to import the entire source files to the index of javaScript on the page in the change, this approach can improve the utilization rate of the program code.

The URL represents the address that needs to be imported into the program file to find the program file through the address solution program. Again, such statements can be placed in the head or body of an HTML document, but in general we usually place such files in the first place. When the web page is opened, the first thing the web page does is to load the content, and such files can be put in the first place, which can be first loaded, and then start to display the content of the home page, so as to avoid the phenomenon of page crash when the web page loads[5].

Assuming that you want to achieve the effect of the example in "direct insert mode", you can first create a JavaScript source file named "JavaScript. Js", which reads as follows:

Document write(" this is JavaScript! Use the direct insert method!");

You can call the program on a web page like this: <scriptsrc="javaScript.js"type="text/javaScript "></script >, then you can achieve the same effect in the direct way.

You can also make the version of javaScript when importing files at the same time, such as: <script SRC ="javaScript.js"type="text/javaScript;Version=4.18"></s cript>, which tells the troubleshooter and maintainer that this is version 4.18, 4 is the basic version number, and .18 is the small version number.

Note: anything in the script tag that specifies the SRC attribute is ignored.

2 Web 3D Implementation

In the first part of this article, I introduced the basic application of JavaScript, and learned that JavaScript can realize simple user interaction and increase user experience. Here's an example of how JavaScript can be used in web effects.

Web 3D animation can attract the interest of visitors. What if the 3D effect is achieved through JavaScript technology? Detailed implementation methods are listed below.

```
<!DOCTYPE html PUBLIC "-//W3C//DTD XHTML 1.0
Transitional//EN" >
<html>
<head>
<meta http-equiv="Content-Type" content="text/html;
charset=utf-8" />
<title> Effect of 3D navigation </title>
</head>
<body>
<style type="text/css">
body{background:black}
.point{position:absolute;height:80px;}
</style>
<script>
var r=200,dv=0.01,w=100,x=400;y=100,pn=8; //r is
radius, dv is offset, w is width of picture, x is Menu
abscissa, y is menu ordinates, pn is number of menu
pictures
var pi=Math.PI,d=pi/2;
var pd=Math.asin(w/2/r),ed=pi*2/pn,sm;//pd is the
inverse sine of each picture
function goR(){
var o=document.getElementById('imground');
var arrimg=o.getElementsByTagName('img');
for (var n=0;n<arrimg.length;n++){
arrimg[n].onmouseout=function(){sm=setInterval('round
Move()',50);} // Move the mouse away from the menu
arrimg[n].onmouseover=function(){clearInterval(sm)} //
Mouse over the menu to stop the rotation
arrimg[n].onmousedown=function(){dv=dv*2} // Click on
the menu to speed up the transition
}
sm=setInterval('roundMove()',50);
}
function roundMove(){
var v=document.getElementById('imground');
var arrimg=v.getElementsByTagName('img');
var o,ta,strFilter;
for (var n=1;n<=pn;n++){
o=arrimg[n-1];
ta=Math.sin(d+ed*n);// Gets the sine of the current offset
strFilter='';
if (ta<0){// The sine value corresponds to negative radians,
where the picture rotates to the back of the circle
o.style.left=Math.cos(d+ed*n-pd)*r+x+'px'; // Passes in
the abscissa of the current picture movement
}
else{// When the image rotates to the front of the circle
o.style.left=Math.cos(d+ed*n+pd)*r+x+'px';// Passes in
the abscissa of the current picture movement
}
o.style.top=ta*10+5+y+'px'; // Passes in the vertical
coordinate of the current image movement
o.style.width=Math.abs(Math.cos(d+ed*n+pd)-
Math.cos(d+ed*n-pd))*r+'px';
o.style.zIndex=parseInt(ta*10);
if (o.style.zIndex<0){// Flip the image as it rotates to the
back positionstrFilter='FlipH(enabled:true)';
}
else{ // Displays the front of the image as it rotates to the
front
```

```
strFilter='FlipH(enabled:false)';
}
if (ta<0){
ta=(ta+1)*80+20;
}else{
ta=100;
}
strFilter=strFilter+'        alpha(opacity='+ta+')';        //
Transparent effect (for IE)
<img class="point" src="images/300.jpg"/>
<img class="point" src="images/400.jpg"/>
<img class="point" src="images/500.jpg"/>
<img class="point" src="images/600.jpg"/>
<img class="point" src="images/700.jpg"/>
<img class="point" src="images/800.jpg"/>
</div>
<script language="javaScript">goR();</script>
</body>
</html>
```

3 Summarize

JavaScript as a dynamic type and weak type of scripting language translation type, its browser based operations, support the distributed computing, and functions are performed on the client, do not need a specific environment for development, any JavaScript plain text editor can edit text, cross-platform, which can realize multiple platforms to share code, also reduce the network transmission, will be part of the information submitted data verification and validation on the client.

The use of special effects, as a demonstration method of JavaScript in the layout process, is to satisfy users' demands through dynamic display with the most intuitive

```
o.style.opacity=ta/100; // Transparent effect (for non-IE)
o.style.filter=strFilter; // Add filter effects to menu images
}
d+=dv; // Increase offset
}
</script>
<div id="imground">
<img class="point" src="images/100.jpg"/>
<img class="point" src="images/200.jpg"/>
```

visual impact through a series of editing and design techniques, such as picture composition and coordinate and point painting, under the condition of language features based on JavaScript.

References

1. Y. Cao, J. Wang, JavaScript Programming Analysis, Science & Technology Association Forum (the semimonthly), **5**, 62 (2009).
2. Y. Zhang, Exploration of Integrated Application of Javascript And Java Language in Dynamic Web Design, University Education, **8(1)**, 63-64 (2012).
3. J.S. Zheng, M. Jiang, Research on a Web Layout Method Based on DIV+CSS+JavaScript, Computer Knowledge and Skills, **17**, 1556-1558 (2008).
4. S.W. Ping, Y.Y. Pan, X.J. Zhang, X.R. Du, Development of a Lightweight Animation Engine Based on HTML5 and JavaScript, Computer technology and development, **23(12)**, 5-10 (2013).
5. S.Y. Pang, Discussion on the Improvement of JavaScript Code Efficiency in Web Page Loading, China Academic Journal Electronic Publishing, Digital Technology & Application, **07**, 232 (2017).

Information Service System for Internet of Vehicles

Xue Xing[1,a], Chenyang Liu[1]

[1]*College of Information and Control Engineering, Jilin Institute of Chemical Technology, 132022, Jilin, China*

Abstract. This system is an Android mobile phone information service system for internet of vehicles. The information service system has four types of functions, including a login registration function, an information search function, a location function, and an information query function. The connection between cars and cars is gradually evolving into Internet of Vehicles from the traditional vehicle self-organizing network. The need for real-time service information for vehicles has also followed. Therefore, the research mainly designed an information service system for users of vehicles.

1 Introduction

With the development of the new era of the Internet of Things, more and more cars are gradually evolving into a car network from the traditional vehicle self-organizing network, and the demand for real-time information services for vehicles has also followed, so the development of a vehicle-oriented user Android mobile phone information service system is very necessary. The ideal goal of the Internet of Vehicles is to achieve a deep integration of people, vehicles, goods and environment, reduce social costs, improve traffic efficiency, and improve urban service levels. The Internet of Vehicles also includes vehicle telematics, a service for electronic data exchange with connected vehicles for remote diagnostics and location-based provisioning, on-demand navigation and audio-visual entertainment. The focus of the car network is the integration of people and vehicles, the car is an extension of human capabilities, and people are the expansion of vehicle intelligence [1].

2 Related technologies

Android is a software platform and operating system based on Linux kernel, which has several outstanding advantages. Android is a development platform and a completely free smartphone platform. The system is developed by Google, and has a complete range of search, weather forecast, Google Talk, map, Gmail, etc. Application has the unparalleled advantages of other systems.

The system uses SQLite as the database platform, and SQLite is a lightweight, cross-platform relational database. Support most of the functions in SQL92 standard, including views, transactions, triggers, etc. The core engine of SQLite does not rely on third-party software and does not need to be "installed" to use it, so it can be deployed more easily. All information in its database, such as tables, views, triggers, etc., is contained in a file. This file can be copied to other directories or other machines without affecting the use [2].

3 System overview

3.1 Feasibility analysis

The system runs on an Android phone and uses Android Studio to develop based on the Java language. The system uses the embedded lightweight database SQLite in the database. The system calls the Internet Information Service Interface. The overall structure is modular, the code structure is standardized, and the system has extremely high versatility, good scalability and strong maintainability [3]. In the current development process of the system, the existing manpower, material resources and technology can be fully developed. The mobile phone information service system is technically feasible.

The system development tool is Android Studio, which is a free and open source Android development integration environment. The database used by this system is the free embedded lightweight database SQLite. The Internet service function interface used in this system does not need to pay fees, and does not require excessive capital investment in the development process. Based on the market share of Android mobile devices, promotion and user use are relatively easy. Therefore, the mobile phone information service system is economically feasible.

3.2 Feasibility analysis

As a portal for the mobile phone information service system, the main functions of the login registration

[a] Corresponding author: patricia_xx@126.com

module can be divided into two types: registration and login. The system divides the registration and login functions into two pages, the user registration page and the user login page.

The information search function needs to be divided into the following five specific functions. VIN frame number search vehicle detailed information, brand car search brand under the detailed car name, DTC fault code search fault location description and solution suggestions, city weather search function return weather details and violations search to return detailed vehicle violation information.

The positioning function needs the positioning function to be an important function of the mobile phone information service system. This function is mainly implemented by using the positioning function provided by the high-tech map open platform, including the current position of the owner of the locomotive, the path planning of the person's workshop, and regional location function of the high incidence of violations.

The information query function needs, the information query class function is an auxiliary function of the mobile phone service system. The function is mainly divided into two specific functions. After the oil price inquiry in the province and the city, the oil price and the vehicle limit inquiry function return the limit line specific information.

3.3 System design

The information service system can be structurally divided into two aspects: user registration and system service functions. Users register and store their accounts and passwords in the local SQLite database. When they log in, they query the database and judge whether the user can log in successfully according to whether there is user information in the database. All kinds of services provided by the system are implemented by calling the Internet service API, sending requests through mobile phones, receiving return parameters and displaying the return results in the mobile interface [4].

As a whole, the functions of the system are mainly searched and returned by the Internet through calling the Internet interface and uploading parameters. According to the returned parameters, the mobile information service system carries out format conversion and display in the user's mobile phone interface. This is the main way to realize the mobile phone application. In programming, each module is basically composed of four main parts (except positioning function), namely uploading parameters, returning parameters, page activity and page layout. Location function design is relatively special, which is mainly developed by using SDK, an open platform of AMAP. Its design and implementation methods need to refer to the official documents of AMAP. The sub-function of passenger-vehicle path planning under positioning function is also based on AMAP. The function of passenger-vehicle path planning needs not only the current coordinates of the owner, but also in principle. Vehicle position coordinates need to be uploaded by vehicles, but because the development conditions do not meet the conditions of real-time upload of vehicle coordinates, so the second step is to use the way of simulation vehicle coordinates, that is, the coordinates of vehicles are fixed, through the way of real-time coordinates of owners and fixed coordinates of virtual vehicles, the coordinates of people and vehicles are obtained. Through the path planning function of AMAP, the path planning of human workshop is realized [5].

4 Detailed system

4.1 Login registration function

The login interface identifies whether the input username and password are registered users. The system's username and password are stored in the user Info table of the device's local database SQLite. The information in the database table is read during login, and the user can be judged whether the user can login to the system or not according to the information [6]. After successful login, users jump to the main interface of the system function. The interface mainly provides nine buttons, including VIN frame number, brand car system, DTC fault code, vehicle location, weather forecast, today's oil price, illegal search, illegal high-incidence area and tail number limit.

The main function of the registration interface is to manage the security of the system. First of all, it is necessary to determine whether the user has entered the required information. The user name and password of the system are stored in the user Info table of the device local database SQLite. When registering, the correct user account password is written into the database.

4.2 Information search function

Information search includes VIN frame number search function, brand car system search function, DTC fault code search function, weather forecast search function and illegal search function.

VIN frame number search function is mainly through the user input 17-bit VIN frame number in the functional interface, click the "search" button, the system calls the Internet VIN frame number query service interface, upload request parameters, and according to the return parameters, display the returned JSON data on the mobile screen. When the user did not enter the 17-bit VIN frame number and clicked the "Search" button, the system popped up the prompt "Please enter the VIN code".

The interface address is http://getVIN.api.juhe.cn/CarManagerServer/getVINFormat.

Support format: JSON

Request: get

Users input the name of the car brand to be searched in the functional interface, click the "search" button, and the system uploads the request parameters by calling the Internet car search service interface. According to the return parameters, the returned JSON data is displayed on the mobile screen, and the search results are arranged in tabular form. When the user does not enter the name of

https://doi.org/10.1051/itmconf/20192502005

the automobile brand and clicks the "Search" button, the system pops up the prompt "Please enter the automobile brand".

Interface address: http://op.juhe.cn/onebox/car/brand
Support format: JSON
Request mode: http get

The main function of the DTC fault code search function is to return the vehicle fault name represented by the fault code according to the DTC vehicle fault code input by the user, and provide the corresponding fault resolution suggestions. The function design is mainly to input the vehicle DTC fault code through the user interface, click the search button, and upload parameters through API. According to user input vehicle DTC fault code, vehicle fault is searched, and information including fault location, fault description, impact and solution suggestion is returned.

Interface address:
http://getDTC.api.juhe.cn/CarManagerServer/getDTC
Support format: JSON
Request: Post

The weather forecast search function searches the current city's weather forecast according to the user's input city name, and returns detailed information including the current city, today's weather, today's temperature, wind direction, clothing index, clothing suggestion, ultraviolet intensity, car washing index, travel index, morning exercise index, etc. Through calling the Internet weather forecast service interface, uploading request parameters, and according to the return parameters, the returned JSON data is displayed on the mobile screen. When the user does not enter the city name to search for the weather and clicks the "Search" button, the system pops up the prompt "Please enter the city name".

Interface address: http://v.juhe.cn/weather/index
Support format: json/xml
Request: get

Violation search function, mainly according to the user input city code, license plate number and engine number, searches for vehicle violation information, returns the date, place, behaviour, code, penalty, and whether to deal with the detailed vehicle violation information. The system calls the Internet illegal search service interface, uploads request parameters, and displays the returned JSON data on the mobile screen according to the return parameters. When the user does not enter the city code and clicks the "Search" button, it prompts "Please enter the city name"; when the user does not enter the license plate number and clicks the "Search" button, it prompts "Please enter the license plate number"; when the user does not enter the VIN frame number and clicks the "Search" button, it prompts "Please enter the VIN frame number".

Interface address: http://v.juhe.cn/wz/citys
Support format: json/xml/jsonp
Request mode: get post

4.3 Positioning function

Vehicle positioning function, mainly through the user in the functional interface click the "vehicle positioning" button to locate the owner's current location, this function is realized through the development of Android positioning SDK provided by AMAP, through its positioning API to obtain positioning results, reverse geocoding (address text description) and geographic fence functions.

The function of path planning in human workshop is to locate the current coordinates of the owner and the uploaded coordinates of the vehicle. Through the location of the human workshop, the shortest and most convenient path between two points can be intelligently planned.

To achieve this function, first we need to complete the display of map and location blue dots, and then realizes the function of walking path planning. Walk Route Overlay can be used to draw the walking road map layer, including the starting and ending points and turning points, according to the data of starting and ending points and walking routes. In addition, you can customize the icon of the end point and the turning point.

To display maps, prior to using the map SDK, the relevant permissions need to be set in the Android Manifest. XML file to ensure that the map function can be used properly.

The first step is to configure the Android Manifest. XML file and declare the permissions required by the map SDK (including its search function):

<!-- allow the program to open the network socket > >
<uses-permission android:name=
"android.permission.INTERNET" / >
<!-- allow the program to set the write permissions of the built-in SD card > >
<uses-permission android:name=
"android.permission.WRITE_EXTERNAL_STORAGE"
/ >
<!-- allow programs to get network status > >
<uses-permission android:name=
"android.permission.ACCESS_NETWORK_STATE" / >
<!- allowing programs to access WiFi network information >
<uses-permission android:name=
"android.permission.ACCESS_WIFI_STATE" / >
<!-- allowing the program to read and write cell phone status and identity >
<uses-permission android:name=
"android.permission.READ_PHONE_STATE" / >
<!-- allow programs to access CellID or WiFi hotspots to get a rough location > >
<uses-permission android:name=
"android.permission.ACCESS_COARSE_LOCATION"
/ >

Then, set up the AMAP Key, add the following contents into the application tag:

<meta-data android:name= "com.amap.api.v2.apikey" android:value= "key" >
// developer's key

The second step is to add a map development kit to the project.

Step 1: add the so file, create a new jniLibs directory in the src/main/ directory, and put the file in it. Using default configuration, there is no need to modify build.gradle. Create the folder jniLibs in the main directory and copy the armeabi folder of the downloaded file into this directory.

Step 2: put the jar package in the LIBS directory. For each jar file, right-click - select Add As Library and import it into the project. Or use the menu bar to select File ->Project Structure->Modules-> Dependencies. Click on the green plus sign to select File dependency. Then select the jar package you want to add.

The third step is to display the map. The "AMap" class is the controller class for the map and is used to manipulate the map. The tasks it carries include: map layer switching (such as satellite maps, night maps), changing map states (map rotation angle, pitch angle, center point coordinates, and zoom level), adding marker markers (Marker), drawing geometry (Polyline, Polygon, Circle) and various types of event monitoring (clicks, gestures, etc.), "AMap" is the most important core class of the Map SDK, and many operations rely on it. After the MapView object has been initialized, construct an "AMap" object. Define a map view:

MapView = (MapView) findViewById (R.id.map);
MapView.onCreate (savedInstanceState);

This method needs to be overwritten. The virtual machine needs to preserve the current state of map rendering in many cases.

Initialize map controller object:
AMap aMap;
If (aMap = = null) {
AMap = mapView.getMap ();}

The blue dot is displayed, and the blue dot refers to the function of displaying the current location point after entering the map. Since version 5.0.0 of Android Map SDK, it is not necessary to rely on Android to locate SDK. Map SDK and location SDK need to be introduced into the project before version 5.0.0.

Walk Route Overlay can be used to draw the road map layer, including the starting and ending points and turning points, according to the data of the starting and ending points and walking routes. In addition, you can customize the icon of the end point and the turning point.

4.4 Information query function

Users click on the "today's oil price" button in the main function interface. The system uploads the request parameters by calling the Internet oil price query service interface. According to the return parameters, the returned JSON data is displayed on the mobile screen. It shows the local oil price of the day of the provincial and municipal names, 92#, 95#, 98# three kinds of gasoline and 0# diesel oil.

Interface address: http://apis.juhe.cn/cnoil/oil_city
Support format: json/xml
Request: get/post
Request example:
http://apis.juhe.cn/cnoil/oil_city?key=APPKEY
JSON returns data:

{"city": "Beijing",
"b90": "Jing 89: 6.02",
"b93": "Beijing 92: 6.44",
"b97": "Jing 95: 6.85",
"b0": "6.07"}

The user clicks the "tail number limit line" button on the main function interface. The system uploads the request parameters by calling the Internet tail number limit service interface, and displays the returned JSON data on the mobile phone screen according to the return parameters. Returns the year, month, day, week, and city of the limit at the time of the query, and returns specific information including the time limit, the restricted area, the penalty, other instructions, and whether or not the line is restricted today.

5 Conclusion

The information service system adopts the principle of software engineering, and completes the system development through requirements analysis, overall design and detailed design. The entire information service system has clear processes and comprehensive functions. The system mainly uses the combination of Android and SQLite technology, by calling the Internet service platform interface. Combining the service functions related to the owner's car, the system's practicality and ease of use are greatly enhanced. This system is a mobile phone information service system developed for car network users.

The main modules of the system are relatively simple to update in the future, using a lightweight SQLite database. The system also has the advantages of friendly interface, convenient operation, high efficiency and good safety. I believe that this information service system for car network users is indispensable information service software that helps car owners manage their cars in daily life and master vehicle information in real time.

References

1. J. Wan, J. Liu, Z. Shao, A.V. Vasilakos, M. Imran, K. Zhou, Sensors (Switzerland) 16 (2016).
2. I. de la Iglesia, U. Hernandez-Jayo, E. Osaba, R. Carballedo, Sensors (Switzerland) 17 (2017).
3. C. Fernandez, M.A. Vicente, M.M. Galotto, M. Martinez-Rach, A. Pomares, (2017).
4. D. Octeau, D. Luchaup, S. Jha, P. McDaniel, IEEE T SOFTWARE ENG 42 (2016) 999-1014.
5. P. Zhang, W. Zhang, S. Niu, Z. Huang, Beijing Youdian Daxue Xuebao/Journal of Beijing University of Posts and Telecommunications 38 (2015) 21-25.
6. Y. Zheng, S. Kell, L. Bulej, H. Sun, W. Binder, IEEE SOFTWARE 33 (2016) 55-63.

Design and Implementation of Welding Robot Based on PLC

Litao Wang

Shaanxi Polytechnic Institute, Xianyang Shaanxi 712000 China

Abstract. With the development of the revolutionary tide of new technology, our production scale is gradually expanding. Manual production has been unable to meet the requirements of industrial production. In order to improve production efficiency and welding quality, we developed a welding robot. Because it has the characteristics of high production efficiency, stable welding quality and large practical demand. It is developing most rapidly. With the development of PLC technology, we gradually apply it to the development of welding robot. Its advantages of good ductility, low cost and convenient maintenance can bring great value to industrial production.

1 Introduction

The promotion of science and technology and the requirement of industrial production on science and technology level influence and promote each other. The scale of production required by human society is gradually expanding. Most modern enterprises expand production scale through mass production. The larger the scale of production, the finer the division of labor. Each type of worker performs only a few actions, which are often monotonous and repetitive. These operations can be achieved through mechanical structures [1]. In addition, the efficiency and quality of manual operation are affected by human responsibility, technical level and other factors. It is difficult to guarantee the quality of production completely and produce higher waste products. Some processes cannot be achieved by hand. Manual production cannot meet the requirements of industrial production. Aiming at this phenomenon, a welding robot was invented. They can be used to complete production tasks in harsh environments, improve welding quality and improve production efficiency. How to improve production efficiency and welding quality, the solution of new technology is to develop welding robot [2]. It doesn't worry about the work environment, and it may save physical labor. However, welding robot has very low requirements for operation technology and can shorten the cycle.

The design of robot control system is the most important part of industrial robot [3] design. However, there are a variety of robot control systems [4]. Although the performance of its dedicated controller is very comprehensive, its price is relatively high. Along with the PLC development and the technical consummation, how to select and own control system is the key of this topic. We should combine the economic benefits of the enterprise and use P LC as the controller of the robot to ensure the stability and reliability of the product.

2 Welding Robot

Welding robot [5] has been updated for several generations with the development of technology, but the basic components of welding robot are basically unchanged. It mainly has two parts, one is the free movement of the body, the other is driven by some mechanical welding equipment. If take arc welding robot as an example, its main components are control cabinet, welding power supply, wire feeder, teaching programmer and welding gun. The control system is mainly divided into two categories: one is non-servo control system [6], which has a general accuracy and low price; Second, servo control system [7] has high precision and high price.

The non-servo control system is a pre-programmed motion track, and then the system controls the motion axis according to the given program for continuous motion. At the end of the motion, it doesn't care if it's in place. Usually, it mainly needs to control a movement according to the feedback signals of various detection switches. This control method is simple and mainly suitable for robot systems with fixed trajectory and simple motion program.

Servo control [8] is a kind of control method commonly used in robots. Sensors are used to detect movement and collect information such as position and speed of components. Then, it sends the detection results to the corresponding control system, and finally the system continuously corrects its motion trajectory according to the feedback data. And then finally it detects if the motion is in place. This kind of method is more complex, but its positioning accuracy is higher and its application is more extensive.

Figure 1 shows the servo control system. The servo control system has a very high control precision, the system USES a variety of sensors to continuously track the precise position of the joint and other parameters, the detected data feedback to the controller to form a closed-loop servo system. However, under the control of the server, the position and speed of each joint are controlled by the corresponding program. The internal program debugging is more flexible, the system can quickly complete complex operations. At present, servo control system is basically used in most high-performance robots.

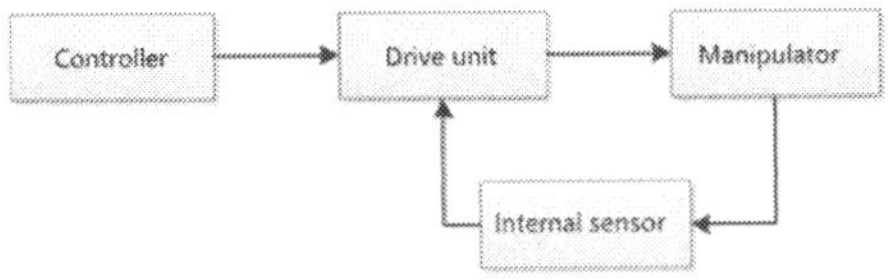

Figure 1. Closed-loop servo system

3 PLC control system

The control system can act as the brain of the robot and determine the movement of the robot. Robot control system has many forms, and its advantages and disadvantages are different. Robots generally need to have strong computing power. PLC is used as the controller to connect the wire in a simple and easy programming way, which can directly use special instructions to complete the multi-axis control of the robot. One of the characteristics of PLC is PLC as a controller without complicated circuit design. It assigns values directly to the terminals and then connects them for control. The robot controller usually takes the microprocessor as the center, and USES tools such as motion trajectory design, programming software and control algorithm to achieve accurate motion control. Usually, in the control process, the acceleration, specific speed, position and other parameters of the detection element are fed back in time according to the results, and finally the relevant instructions are adjusted to achieve this.

The classical servo control system has many forms. According to the analysis of the control theory, the system can be divided into five parts: the controlled object, the controller, the link to perform the work, the comparison and the test. The parameters controlled by the system are carried out through the controlled object, usually including velocity, displacement and torque. The execution work link sends out a series of signals according to the controller, converts the corresponding control instructions into specific actual mechanical movements according to the requirements, and finally drives the actuator to work. Usually the actuator is usually a motor or manipulator, etc. The controller control loop is PID. It is necessary to efficiently convert the output deviation signal and control each actuator according to the requirements of the instruction, so as to complete the corresponding steps. The comparison link is to detect the data and feed it back to the system, then compare it with the system signal, and calculate the error according to the comparison data. It is necessary to continuously measure the output data between the systems, and then change the required data into a device in the comparison link. At this time, the link is usually the sensor and the transformation loop.

Robot operations are generally reproduced through real-time programming, as shown in figure 2. According to the position of the robot and the surrounding environment, the operation flow and the corresponding movement path of a certain robot are set. According to its functions, it is divided into four parts: basic functions and parameters Number setting, teaching and other functions.

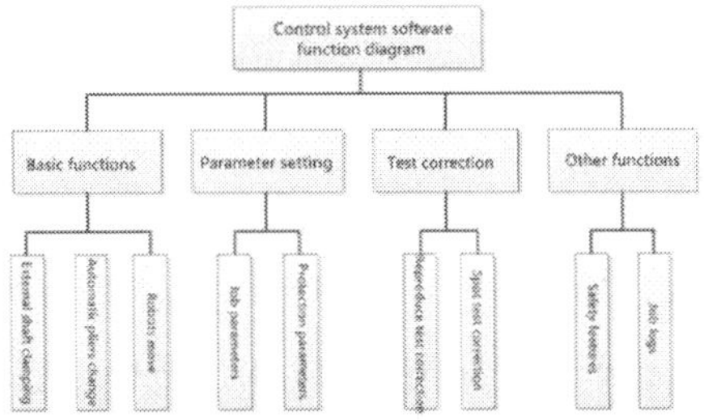

Figure 2. Control system function diagram of welding robot

The parameter setting here includes operation parameters and protection parameters. Because robot programming requires real-time performance, real-time detection of safety signals is required. PLC has many interfaces and modules, generally used in industrial control field of control system. PLC built-in many programming languages, according to the specific task can be faster to write a program. These programs can be debugged on the computer, but also can be stored directly in the PLC internal, improve the executability and extensibility, and then easier to achieve process control. PLC can also be used as industrial control computer, its hardware structure and microcomputer similar.

4 Robot control

The driving device of the robot is an electric motor, which then pushes the motion between the joints to be executed. Therefore, the robot needs to have unique requirements for the motor, including low moment of inertia and high starting torque. The motor of end-effector is required to be as small as possible in order to reduce its moment of inertia and reduce the difficulty of the system. To ensure high speed response and reliability is the key factor of motor selection. The motor control of joint drive is to set the trajectory and determine the key position points, as shown in FIG. 3. The steps are as follows:

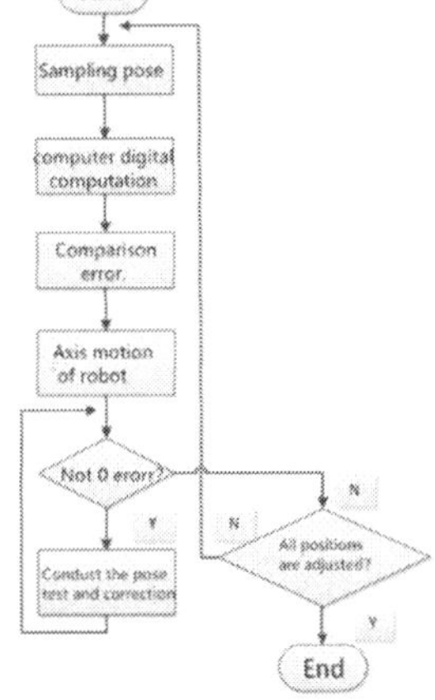

Figure 3. Control flow chart

Firstly, the sensor signal at the joint position can judge the position of the end-effector, and the sensor signal can be transmitted to the main computer, and then transformed, and finally the pose data can be obtained.

Secondly, the main computer can solve inverse kinematics, solve the vector of each joint, and then store it.

Once again, the positions of the joints and the actual positions are compared, the deviation signals are obtained, and the motor is automatically accelerated and decelerated according to the deviation size, so as to ensure that the deviation is small.

As the robot moves, various parameters are generated and recorded, which can provide the basis for adjusting the motion at any time.

Then, when the deviation signal is close to zero, the robot will stop. At this point, it means that the robot has reached the position of instruction and will prepare and send out the next pose information. The robot will continue to repeat the above steps.

5 Conclusion

Under the revolutionary tide of new technology, many foreign developed countries apply robot technology in large quantities. Welding robot is an important part of industrial robot. Welding is a high precision but heavy labor, so the manufacture of welding robot can liberate the labor force, promote the development of industrial robots. It has been widely used in more and more enterprises.

References

1. Chen haichu, Cao Quan, Xiong Genliang, Yang Piao, Sun Junlong. Design and implementation of programmable welding robot teaching system [J]. Hot processing technology, 2016, 45 (19): 179-182.
2. Li Zhiqiang, Guo Guangling, Fan Ding, Shi Yu. Arc welding robot with NC welding displacement machine teaching system [J]. The design and implementation of manufacturing technology and machine tool, 2004 (8): 61-61.
3. He Xingxing, Zhang Yixin. Use SOLIDWORKS for welding robot design and simulation [J]. Journal of CAD/CAM and manufacturing information, 2014 (12): 47-49.
4. Yuan Junfeng, Yi Guochun, Xu Suexin, Geng Yunxiang, Zhang Hongjian. Design and implementation of automatic welding robot workstations for security doors in housing [J]. Automation of manufacturing industry, 2014, 36 (21): 146-148.
5. Liu Shengpeng, Ye Hua, Wang Dan. Design and implementation of safety controller for industrial welding robot [J]. Industrial control computer, 2009, 22 (10): 13-14.
6. Huang Shouning, Jiang Chaoning, Dai Jianshu. Design and implementation of welding robot controller based on S3C2440 [J]. Manufacturing automation, 2009, 31 (09): 169-171.
7. Zhang Yang, Wang Xuanyin, Liu Songguo. Design and implementation of embedded teaching system for welding robot [J]. Modular machine tool and automation processing technology, 2007 (03): 1-3+7.
8. Jin Yunxiang, Jiang Lipei, Zou Yong, Chen Haiyang, Sun Yaling, Xu Feng. Design and implementation of interactive control system for pipeline welding robot [J]. Journal of Beijing university of petroleum and chemical technology, 2006 (01): 24-27.

Design and Implementation of Energy Saving Management System Based on Data Mining

Yuan Yuan

Xinjiang University Science and Technology College, Xinjiang 843000, China

Abstract. With the acceleration of urbanization, various items have generated a large amount of energy consumption on the basis of intelligent control, which has aroused widespread concern. Energy conservation has become an important direction of society. Colleges and universities are an integral part of society and a large energy consumer. Therefore, energy conservation management in colleges and universities is an important content. At the same time, designing energy-saving management systems in colleges and universities can not only meet the needs of energy-saving supervision in colleges and universities, but also deepen the significance of building a resource-saving concept into students. Through the construction of energy-saving management, it can realize the supervision of campus energy consumption, and further provide reliable data support and effective solutions for the school's energy-saving management level.

1 Introduction

With the development of economy, environmental problems are becoming more and more prominent. Recently, although economic construction has achieved fruitful results in various aspects, it has sacrificed resources and environment. Energy has become a key factor affecting global economic development. Energy conservation and emission reduction have become the requirements of social development. More and more governments and organizations are spontaneously carrying out the work of energy conservation and emission reduction [1]. The energy consumption of colleges and universities also occupies a certain proportion. It is quite urgent to establish the energy saving system in colleges and universities. The design is based on the campus and can be extended to other public buildings. With the increase of urban energy consumption [2], the energy quantity of colleges and universities also increases year by year. However, domestic colleges and universities lack scientific management in energy use. Energy conservation systems vary widely among institutions. It is of great significance to build an applicable supervision system for campus energy conservation. Colleges and universities are places to train constructors. By building an energy conservation supervision system, we can shape people's awareness of energy conservation, which is also meaningful for the future.

At present is an information age, the general trend throughout the world every corner. While the impact of the Internet on the human way of life, at the same time, the technological leap also affects the way people think. Therefore, the campus energy conservation management system [4] also needs to be in line with The Times from the perspective of development, and its process needs to be informatization and digitalization.

The system mainly adopts B/ s-based digital energy saving platform, which has strong expansibility and compatibility. At the same time, the server side can support popular databases, and energy-saving management monitoring points can be established in campus, buildings, floors and rooms [5]. Power, water and gas can also be monitored through wired or wireless equipment, and real-time monitoring, transmission and analysis can also be carried out. Figure 1 shows the principle of B/S system.

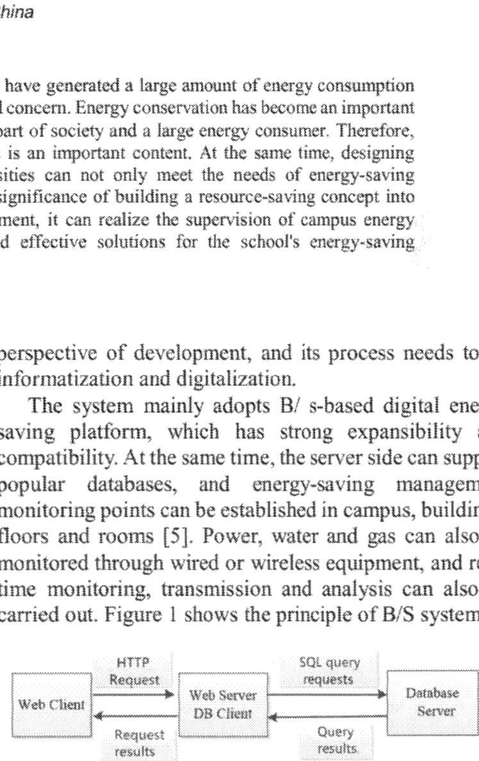

Figure 1. Principle of B/S system

2 Data mining

Data mining is a technical process of identifying unknown and useful knowledge from massive application data [6]. As an interdisciplinary subject, data mining involves many subjects, such as machine learning, database, etc. With the development of informatization, data mining has been paid more and more attention. Data mining [7] mainly solves the problem that the amount of human data processing increases sharply. It can help people according to some technical means to obtain useful knowledge for themselves. Generally, the steps of data mining are as follows: first, data cleaning is to process the given data. Its main purpose is to clear the noise in the data, but also can correct the wrong data; Secondly, data integration [7] can be regarded as a process of inductive integration. It often uses the database technology to integrate multiple data into a consistent data for storage; Again, data conversion. Data conversion takes relevant data out of the database [8] and converts the data into a form suitable for mining through some operations; Then you move on to data mining, which is the core step. We need to use the mining model [9] to extract some data patterns based on the data prepared in the early stage; Then comes the model evaluation, which is usually a combination of the result evaluation and analysis, and the feasibility of the result can be judged according to the standards and materials. Finally, knowledge representation, usually presenting data results to users in a popular way [10].

The system is controlled by computer, campus communication technology and other traditional equipment systems. It can carry out automatic control to complete the work of energy saving control and management of buildings and facilities in the unit area, so as to achieve the goal of energy saving. This energy saving management system mainly designs the system from the supervision aspect. Its main process is to collect information and then provides guidance. At the same time, the data result is usually the result of calculation and processing of energy saving business, including some data statistics. Each of the different data often takes the cell as the measurement point data, and the calculation node of energy saving management based on data mining is shown in figure 2.

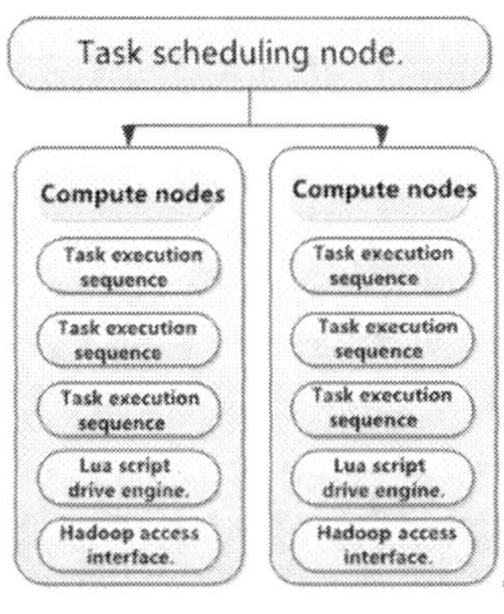

Figure 2. Calculation node of energy saving management

3 Regulatory model

Traditional energy conservation supervision system usually sets a closed value inside the system when conducting supervision. In order for this system to compare the energy consumption collected with the closed value data, a pre-set index value is usually required. However, there are many problems with this solution: for example, it is difficult to determine the data of a closed value. It is too high or too low to have some impact on the system of energy conservation supervision. This makes it less effective to regulate. Different seasons and different building structures will also hinder the supervision. Our processing method is generally static analysis of historical data first. The results we get are usually not monitored in real time. As a result, the energy consumption supervision system is lagging behind. Therefore, we propose a new regulatory model. This model is based on data mining technology to monitor the energy consumption of buildings. This model can be monitored in real time. Firstly, the building energy consumption pattern is identified and the data is saved to match the previous building energy consumption pattern. Then we analyze the results of pattern matching to determine whether there is abnormal energy consumption, and then determine whether the energy consumption is normal. FIG. 3 shows the flow chart of building energy consumption supervision.

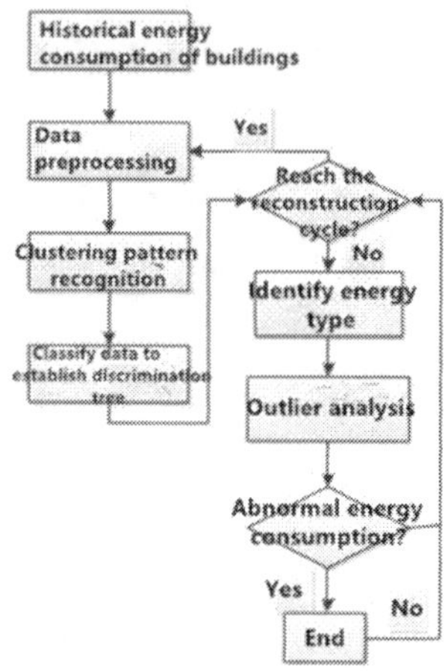

Figure 3. Flow chart of building energy consumption supervision

The main purpose of energy consumption regulation is to improve the accuracy of regulation. Firstly, we should excavate the energy consumption of the monitored buildings. Since the patterns corresponding to the energy consumption of buildings usually change with the characteristics of buildings, the results of pattern recognition of buildings need to be reset and judged. The condition must be satisfied before we can recognize the pattern again. The specific steps are as follows:

First of all, the historical energy consumption value of the pretreatment building in the system platform can be generally treated in accordance with the requirements put forward to specify the energy consumption characteristics of the system, such as the time usually involves every minute, every second, every day, every month, etc., while the average energy consumption, low energy consumption and so on are usually considered in the characteristics.

Secondly, after pre-processing, the mode of building historical data value in the platform needs to be recognized again, and then the established energy consumption mode of the building is obtained. Finally, the judgment tree of energy consumption mode is constructed based on the recognition results.

Thirdly, according to some cases of newly introduced building energy consumption values, the energy consumption of newly collected building energy consumption data can be identified and analyzed with the corresponding patterns in historical data. At the same time, the current outlier can be determined according to the judgment results. If not, it means that the energy consumption of the buildings collected at present is normal.

Fourthly, if the alarm platform of a particular building has a continuous alarm over a long period of time, it can be concluded that the building has reached the model reconstruction cycle.

Finally, if building energy consumption pattern recognition just meets the pre-set pattern conditions, it is necessary to repeat the previous process of building energy consumption pattern recognition and the process of building energy consumption pattern judgment conditions, so as to obtain new building patterns and judgment conditions, otherwise it will be under supervision all the time.

4 Conclusion

Since entering the 21st century, the lack of energy and resources in China has been accelerating. Energy conservation and emission reduction have gradually become research hotspots. Research based on energy conservation management becomes very necessary. This paper takes colleges and universities as the research object, studies the supervision platform, especially the energy consumption of buildings, and hopes to be helpful for the follow-up work.

References

1. Hu Jie, Meixue. Study on energy conservation and emission reduction control system based on big data technology [J]. Qinghai social science, 2014 (06): 75-79+177.
2. Yang Changqing. Data collection and management of energy saving and emission reduction control system under big data technology [J]. Automation and instrumentation, 2017 (11): 185-186+190.
3. Wang Qixiang, Zhou Chunlei, Sun Zuozhu. Research on distributed computing framework of energy saving and emission reduction monitoring system based on big data platform [J]. Science and technology communication, 2016, 8 (01): 108-109+178.
4. Qi Juan. "big data" helps traffic pollution control and emission reduction -- establishment of the first traffic energy conservation and emission reduction laboratory in Beijing, Tianjin and Hebei [J]. World of transportation managers, 2015 (21): 42-44.
5. Fu Juanjuan, Lin Guolong. Energy saving and emission reduction measures for port shipping industry in the era of big data [J]. Transportation enterprise management, 2017, 32 (03): 4-6.
6. Qiu Haiping. Intelligent heat grid promotes heat supply enterprises to achieve energy saving and emission reduction [J]. Energy saving and environmental protection, 2017 (10): 64-66.
7. Wang Qixiang. Data collection and management of energy conservation and emission reduction control system under big data technology [J]. Science and technology wind, 2018 (32): 84.
8. Hu Lianghao. Research on the application of energy consumption supervision model based on data mining in the campus energy conservation supervision platform [D]. Anhui university, 2016.
9. Zhu Baiqing, Lu Haixing, Li Dongbo. Design and development of forging production scheduling system for energy saving and emission reduction [J]. Machinery design and manufacturing, 2013, 11: 35-38
10. Li Dan. China tower energy management system supports the development of base station energy saving and emission reduction based on Internet of things and big data technology [A]. Communication power committee of Chinese communication society.

Thinking on the Planning and Design of Environmental Landscape in Qiang Region

Jundong Ye

School of Art, Aba Teachers College, Wenchuan, China

Abstract. Based on the analysis of the design of environmental landscape architecture in Qiangzhai Style, it is proposed that the design of landscape architecture should be based on computer-aided design technology. Landscape architecture design integrates many disciplines, and any good building usually includes two aspects of internal and external space design. The design idea is the premise of deciding whether the Qiang landscape architecture design can be done well or not. It needs more understanding of the Qiang architecture, culture and art to do the related design well. Cultural creativity is also an important part of the strategy of Rural Revitalization and the construction of characteristic villages in Qiang nationality areas.

1 Introduction

Qiang is a minority nationality with a long history in China. Now it mainly lives in Aba, Sichuan Province. At present, rural areas in Qiang nationality area are generally developing economy vigorously, and various rural tourism and farmhouse pleasure are rising. Researchers should pay attention to the strategy of rural revitalization and the construction of characteristic villages in Qiang nationality area. A resident of a Qiang village in Western Sichuan has developed a landscape architecture project which integrates catering, leisure and sightseeing. It mainly constructs a landscape architecture with Chinese style and Qiang architectural style. The first floor is catering, and the second and third floors are accommodation. In front of the house, a narrow and winding garden yard was built, in which several pavilions with some Chinese garden style and artificial landscape pools were built, and a lot of greening was done. On the roof of the main landscape building and at the gate of the courtyard, the villager put up a sign called "Qiang Village Style" and held a number of Qiang style dances. The guests ate a lively scene of roasting whole sheep, which caused many people to watch. However, over the years, not many visitors have come to the " Qiang Village Style " for recreation or sightseeing. On an occasional occasion, the author learns that the villager first found a local well-known artist to realize his idea, design drawings, that is, several hand-painted effect drawings, and then the villagers found people engaged in construction to complete the construction. The first impression of this landscape architecture is not very much like Qiang architecture, especially the lack of Qiang culture elements in interior decoration. The whole indoor and outdoor environment design makes people feel less beautiful, not attractive, and the use function of the building is not considered. To do a good job in the planning and design of environmental landscape in Qiang nationality area, designers should think from many aspects.

2 Make full use of computer aided design technology

With the rapid development of computer science and technology, computer-aided technology for environmental landscape planning and design is becoming more and more advanced. Geographic Information System (GIS) and Virtual Reality (VR) have become important technologies in landscape planning and design. CAD, 3DMAX, SKETCHUP, VARY, ENSCAPE, LUMION, PHOTOSHOP, VR virtual reality technology and GIS geographic information system have become the technologies widely used in landscape design. The earliest computer aided design technology and platform used in graphic drawing technology is CAD, which has been widely used in urban planning, architectural design and industrial design, and also in landscape design, bringing new ideas and concepts to designers. The advantage of CAD is that the drawing is accurate. Now, it is mainly used for drawing detailed construction drawings, and also for three-dimensional modeling and performance. Compared with traditional hand-drawn design, it can better use the design intentions in actual construction, avoid the similarities of landscape design schemes, and faster than traditional manual drawing. In addition, the modeling and rendering software, as well as other software continue to bring forth new field of vision and progress. Landscape planning and design has achieved the convergence of science and aesthetics, and has become a comprehensive and systematic design discipline. [1] Therefore, in order to do a good job of landscape planning and design in Qiang nationality area, designers should make full use of computer-aided design technology, in order to have a brilliant design plan and satisfactory performance.

3 Landscape architecture and design in Qiang Nationality Area

3.1 Traditional landscape architecture of Qiang Nationality

The Qiang people generally live in their stockades. Their traditional buildings are stone and stone towers, and some of them are built entirely from loess clay. There are three or four stories in a blockhouse. The traditional stone blockhouse of the Qiang nationality has an inclination angle of about 10 degrees. The walls inside the house are vertical, and the walls outside the house are gradually contracting from bottom to top, forming a narrow trapezoid on the width below and above. The whole building is similar to the overlay bucket. The main building materials are stone, clay and wood. The wall structure receives a lot of points in the construction technology. Qiang architecture also includes temples, bridges, trestles, official villages, workshops and so on. From the beginning to the end of traditional Qiang architecture construction, there are no drawings and brackets, and no suspension layouts, all based on superb skills and experience. [2] In addition, the buildings are not made of reinforced concrete, but local materials. Some buildings did not collapse in the earthquake, and still stand erect to maintain the original landscape. Qiang people's Shicheng dwelling houses, the blockhouse is a continuation of the style of dry railings. [3] Traditional Qiang architecture shows a simple and natural image, forming a unique and spectacular landscape.

3.2 Comprehensive environmental discipline

Landscape architecture is a combination of natural and artificial elements through art and science. Apart from house buildings, flower racks, doors, wooden floors, grape racks, pavilions, corridors, platforms, rockeries, pools, fences, waterscapes, fountains, lawns, swing roads are the contents of landscape architecture. Landscape architecture design is similar to landscape design and environmental design, but with different names, its content is very extensive. Landscape architecture design is also landscape design. In addition to the so-called gardening, greening and gardening, it also includes the planning, management and utilization of ecological land and the development of territorial landscape, which is a comprehensive environmental discipline. Landscape Architecture Design is a multi-disciplinary design field which integrates architecture, gardening, planning and other disciplines. Landscape architecture usually appears in scenic spots, parks, squares and other landscape sites, or it has the function of landscape marking itself. It can be said that it is a landscape, but also has the role of landscape. Landscape architecture differs from ordinary architecture in that it combines environment with culture and pays attention to them.

4 Qiang's interior furnishings and interior and exterior environment design

4.1 Qiang Interior Furnishings

Qiang watchtower indoor bottom keep the cattle and lay asde farming tools; the middle floor has bedrooms, storage rooms, fire ponds, Guozhuang and shrines, respectively, for people to live in the floor; the upper floor for the Qiang "Baishi God" and grain storage; the roof of the house is a platform, mainly used for sunning food, while entertainment and leisure use. The Qiang people's interior furnishings have been influenced by the Han people. The interior reflects some characteristics of the Han people's interior. However, there are fire ponds in every family's house, and shrines such as "the God of corner" and "the master of heaven and earth". Walking into the interior of the landscape architecture of "Qiang village amorous feelings", we can see the windows, doors and indoor room doors which are the neoclassical traditional style in the Han nationality area of China. There is no cultural connotation related to Qiang nationality in the interior. It's just that the appearance of the landscape architecture has a little something to do with the Qiang style, but it's a little simple. Although the interior furnishing design of "Qiang village amorous feelings" landscape architecture does not necessarily follow the traditional Qiang interior design, but it can not be in the interior furnishing or decoration without any Qiang style characteristics.

4.2 Interior environment design

Indoor and outdoor environment design is an integral part of landscape architecture design. Usually, a good building contains two basic contents interior and outdoor space design. An indoor space environment will have different effects after completion, which is caused by the different styles of interior architectural design schemes. Most experts believe that the interior design is actually the interior space environment design, is the deepening of architectural design, is the interior work, study, life and other necessary environmental space for the composition of the desired design. Generally speaking, interior decoration are only the work and means to realize the partial design of interior environment design.

Interior environment design involves furniture furnishing, texture and performance of decoration materials, arts and crafts, greening, gardening and other art fields, and it is a new subject with strong comprehensiveness. It is closely related to architecture, structural engineering, ergonomics, architectural physiology, sociology, building materials, psychology, folklore and other disciplines. Therefore, the interior environment design not only considers the problems of the ceiling, the ground and the wall of the building space, but also uses interdisciplinary knowledge to construct the space environment comprehensively in all directions and at many levels. Such as the use of knowledge of plane composition, three-dimensional composition and spatial composition, as well as the principles and material means of light and shadow, reflection and color change, illusion, etc. to change the size and scale of space, different psychological feelings, create the required style and environmental atmosphere.

4.3 Outdoor environment design

The external environment of the building is a reflection of the technology and art of a nation and an era, and also a true portrayal of the residents' life style, ideology and values. This kind of reflection of cultural regionality, epochality and comprehensiveness is incomparable to any other environment or individual thing. This is because the external environment of the building contains more human impressions reflecting culture, and new content is added every moment. The external environment of group buildings is often a symbol of a city, a region, or even a nation or a national culture. [4] For example, Walian Residence, designed by Malaysian Chinese architects in 1982, has a 15-metre-high atrium with three-storey roof and projecting air windows, which can be ventilated from front to back. Deep eaves make people live in a pleasant environment with good ventilation and no sunshine. Part of the atrium is built above the pool. There is a swimming pool above the pool, just above the surface of the water. The inclined wall beside it makes the water in the pool pour into the lower pool like a waterfall. The wood structure of Walian residential houses is very delicate, which represents the modern buildings with local interest that had begun to be popular at that time. This style is especially popular in tourist hotels. [5] In fact, this building is a landscape building.

From this, we can see that indoor and outdoor environmental design is an integral part of landscape architecture design, which is an important component of landscape architecture design. If the landscape architecture of villages in Qiang area develops economy, without excellent interior and exterior environment design, the landscape architecture will be eclipsed, will not be noticeable and loved by people.

5 How to design landscape architecture of Qiang Nationality

5.1 Design ideas decide design

How to do a good job in Qiang Landscape Architecture Design is actually decided by the design idea. The ideas mentioned here are mainly the professional knowledge acquired and the comprehensive thinking ability formed by the relevant knowledge of traditional Qiang culture. Without abundant professional knowledge, no matter how good the idea is, it will be difficult to achieve good wishes, so people will not like the final landscape architecture and its environment. Environmental planning, implication, concept, theme, form, space, streamline, aesthetic, artistic conception, material, color and so on should be considered in the design thought. Landscape architecture can also be said to be architectural landscape, which belongs to the category of landscape planning and design. Modern landscape planning and design is a subject specialty which faces to life, is close to life and is very popular. But this does not mean that the threshold of discipline specialty is popular and secular. On the contrary, for the personnel engaged in this subject specialty, to fulfill their mission of discipline specialty, the need is comprehensive. Scientific knowledge, profound life experience and touching artistic imagination. [6] Architectural Design of Individual or Group Design

References

1. Liu Haiyuan. Application of Computer Aided Technology in Landscape Architecture Planning and Design: Taking Xinghua Park in Gaocheng District as an example [D]. Hebei University of Economics and Trade, 2018:8.
2. Jiang Bin, Zhang Yuan. Research on the Protection and Development of Traditional Culture of Qiang [J]. Journal of Southwest Minzu University (Humanities and Social Sciences Edition), 2009(4):20.
3. Zhang Ben. Study on the Artistic Arts of Qiang ethnic group [M]. Beijing: Tsinghua University Press, 2013:137.
4. Qian Jian, Song Lei. Design of the external environment of the building [M]. Shanghai: Tongji University Press, 2001:12-13.
5. Luo Xiaomo. History of Modern Foreign Architecture [M]. Beijing: China Construction Industry Press, 2004:294-295.
6. Xu Qing. Landscape Design Science [M]. Shanghai: Tongji University Press, 2014: 65, 67.
7. Xu Qing. Landscape Design Science [M]. Shanghai: Tongji University Press, 2014: 65, 67.
8. Zhang Huihui. Research on Public Art Design in Tourist Attractions of Qiang --- Using Buwa Village as An Example [D]. Southwest Jiaotong University, 2012.

On Intellectual Property Right Protection of Hyperlinks Infringement in China

Zehua Feng [a]

Doctoral Candidate of Graduate School and School of Marxism, Chinese Academy of Social Sciences, 102488 Beijing, China

Abstract. Hyperlink technology is an important technology for the dissemination of information in era of internet. With the rapid development of the network economy, various types of hyperlink technology are applied more frequently. Website operators also pay more attention to the ownership of their own network information resources and the protection of commercial interests. From the point of view of the protection of hyperlink technology, it has been regarded as an intellectual property right. Therefore, starting from different types of hyperlink technology and combining with the existing Copyright Law, Trademark Law and Anti-Unfair Competition Law, this paper reiterates the principles and standards of liability fixation for hyperlink infringement, which can provide countermeasures for website operators to resolve related infringement disputes.

1 The nature of the hyperlink behavior and the reasons for the dispute

Generally speaking, hyperlink technology refers to the information acquisition technology that can be freely accessed between different pages and columns by means of text, graphics, instructions and other media, and can establish links between different parts of the same page or between different pages. In European and American societies, hyperlink technology has been regarded as an intellectual property right.

1.1 Types of hyperlinks

According to the web links technology, hyperlinks can be classified into three types.

First, normal web links. In general, hyperlinks are normal links. The normal links can be divided into homepage links and paging links (it also known as deep links) according to the subjective purpose and linking mode of the linker. As the name implies, in the home page links, the builder of web links is guiding the website visitors (hereinafter referred to as visitors) to the home page of other websites, and its address bar still retains the original website, its legal risk is low. The deep links discussed in the intellectual property field refer to the way that the builder of web links bypasses the home page of the website and goes directly to the interface they want to use (usually the secondary pages of the website), and still displays the builder's address in the bar of the page, which will undoubtedly mislead visitors and make them unable to distinguish. This situation causes the confusion that who is the originator of website content, which affect the interests of original website operators.

Second, embedded web links. In the embedded links, the builder of web links displays the contents of the linked pages in his own pages through web links and the page address bar displays the builder's website address, so that visitors cannot perceive the contents of the pages from other pages [1].

Third, visual frame links [2]. Embedded and framed links also belong to their branches. In essence, they belong to a kind of embedded links. The technical feature of embedded links is that the windows of the linked websites are divided into several small windows (In other words, it can display multiple websites at the same time). Visitors cannot distinguish the real address of the pages they browse.

The above three types of hyperlinks are prone to causing legal disputes, especially in the form of deep links, the practice of skipping the permission of operator of the chained websites is equal to forcibly setting ticket fee points at the entrance of private gardens without the authorization of its owner in the real world to seek benefits. However, many commercial interests in the real world are not directly reflected by the number of clicks.

1.2 Causes of disputes easily by hyperlink Technology

Generally speaking, the owner of the website sued the person who had created web links without permission, mainly for three reasons. First, the most important source of revenue in website is advertising. In the Internet world, advertising revenue is directly depended on the number of visitors and clicks. builder of web links intentionally adopt the technology of hyperlink to skip the real websites (domain names) of the linked pages, which will

[a] Corresponding author: maofengren@163.com

lead to a direct reduction in the number of visits to the original websites and advertising clicks as well as directly affect their revenue. Secondly, some websites often use reverse counterfeiting when setting up links-to keep their own domain names on the original websites to mislead visitors, so that they have the illusion that the fake web pages is the real one. If the fake website gets bad evaluation, these negative contents can be added to the original website, damaging its goodwill. For example, a non-governmental IELTS training organization, in order to promote its credibility, links many parts of its website to the pages of the IELTS official website without permission or license. If the organization is not well managed and its reputation is impaired, it will also affect the credibility of the IELTS training center. Thirdly, unlawfully setting up hyperlinks without consent by the owner of web sites is obviously full of commercial hostility, suspicion of unfair competition by hitchhiking and infringement of the original owner's right.

In short, many websites in order to enhance their influence, often with a considerable number of websites exchange links. For one thing, visitors can clearly see the changes of domain name by clicking on the link column. Naturally, there will be no confusion about the ownership of the content in the website. For another, this way of exchanging friendship links is to get the consent of both web page owners, which is naturally different from the complex legal consequences caused by unauthorized use. The intellectual property disputes caused by hyperlinks discussed in this paper mainly focus on the way of deep links, such as those who set up hyperlinks without the consent of website owner, bypassing the home page of original websites, but still retain their own domain name or deliberately hitchhiking behavior.

2 Empirical analysis: the principle of imputation for hyperlinks Infringement

Academics and practitioners have basically formed a consensus on the principle of liability for hyperlink infringement [3]. The following two typical cases reflect this consensus.

2.1 Copyright infringement case of Beijing seven Color Rainbow Advertising Co., Ltd. v. Zhejiang Taobao Network Co., Ltd

In 2011, in the case of copyright dispute between Beijing Seven Color Rainbow Advertising Co., Ltd. (hereinafter referred to as Rainbow) and Zhejiang Taobao Network Co., Ltd. (hereinafter referred to as Taobao), the defendant, Taobao website, such as "Taobao Portal, Women, Flower Marriage", and it contains 18 pictures of the Rainbow's claims. In the meantime, the IP address bar of the web page that appears after clicking on that column is "http://taobao.onlylady.com", as well as the words "copyright2003-2009, copyright TAOBAO.COM" are displayed below these pages. The plaintiff, Rainbow Company, decided that Taobao had infringed upon its work by disseminating it without its permission, so it sued the court. Taobao's defense is that it only links the page content of the third-party website by means of iframe (i.e. embedded links), in other words, its page content is provided by the third-party website, and it also disconnects the corresponding links after the lawsuit. Therefore, the court should use the "Safe Harbor Rules" to determine that Taobao does not constitute infringement. The court held that the defendant Taobao had the right to decide the content, columns and sections of the web pages involved. Therefore, Taobao Company should be responsible for the legitimacy of the content of the website to review the obligation, and it should be responsible for the tort.

In this case, the court interpreted the legal nature of iframe links in detail, further affirming the qualitative basis of the "User Standard Theory". The exceptions to the "Safe Harbor Rules" and the subjective fault of the defendant (builder of web links) are classically expounded: Safe Harbor Rules is subjectively only applicable to the network service intermediaries who are not aware of the infringement facts in the dissemination of works. In the process of providing storage space, search service and link service, network service middlemen may not refer to the Safe Harbor Rules if their purpose is to use the works of the copyright owner to pursue certain commercial interests, such as click volume and promotion of related products. In the process of providing storage space or search service or link service, the intermediary shall provide relevant network services and shall not apply "Safe Harbor Rules" if they know that the infringement of copyright has occurred or should know that the infringement of copyright may occur.

Looking back on the judgment of this case, although the court ruled out the application of the "Safe Harbor Rules" by the "User Standard Theory", the judgment basis of the defendant's legal liability is still inseparable from the subjective malignant conviction of the defendant. In other words, the defendant has a complete decision on the contents, columns, sections and other settings of the web pages involved. The act of setting the plaintiff's address as his own web site does not meet the requirements of subjective ignorance or should be known, and is sufficient to presume that he has subjective malice. The defendant take the name of web links as a cover, using iframe's link mode, in fact this plagiarism cannot be justified.

2.2 Infringement case of Shenzhen Qvod Technology CO., LTD. for Information transmission right

The plaintiff, China Film Co., Ltd. (Hereinafter referred to as China Film) claimed that the function of the software from the company of Shenzhen Kuaibo Technologies Co., Ltd. (Hereinafter referred to as Kuaibo) infringed on the right to disseminate the information of its work in Internet, so it filed a lawsuit in court. The plaintiff claims that keywords (such as movie "I do") are typed into the software search box of the defendant's Player software would direct to a third-party search site, which displays the search results for all the resources and is a complete video of the film involved. At the same time, the above search results can be linked to the film broadcasting site. The film copyright is owned by the Chinese Film Company but not licensed.

After investigation, the court held that although the defendant's claim of search engine integration did not link to infringing works, it directed the users to a third-party search site, which not only limited the search object to specific types of documents, but also limited the search scope to specific sites. Therefore, it can be concluded that the defendant and the linking web sites jointly implemented the search. So the defendant has subjective fault for linking infringement works involved. Finally, the court ordered the defendant to stop the infringement and compensate the plaintiff for the loss.

Unlike the previous case, Kuaibo in this case has not taken the technology of visual frame link to take possession of the content of the linked website. However, the search link service provided by Kuaibo also exists in the situation of knowing or should know subjectively without the consent of the linked website. Although the Kuaibo and third-party search websites provided link search freely, it did not conceal the domain name of China Film. Subjectively, their behavior of skipping the home page of China Film and reaching the website of a film directly does not rule out its desire for film viewers to think that this part of the film is all their intentions. Therefore, Kuaibo is still liable for its own faults, including subjectively unauthorized use and prudently scrutinized obligations.

3 Regulation of hyperlink behavior in intellectual property law

The infringement caused by hyperlink technology needs to be discussed in two aspects. First, the direct infringement of other people's copyright, in other words, it acts that directly hinder copyright owners from exercising the rights of copy, distribution, adaptation and dissemination in Internet, which are becoming more and more rare in practice (the builder of web links often affect the dissemination effect interests of the original website when the third-party websites are involved). Second, through the assistance, connivance and joint participation of third-party websites, the right to disseminate information on the Internet has been infringed [4], just like the second cases mentioned above. In practice, the defendant (the builder of web links) often invokes subjective unknowns (when a third party website involved) and the "Safe Harbor Rules" to defend the infringement accusations. Then how do the various departments of the legal system for intellectual property judge the infringement?

3.1. Copyright law protection is still the best choice although there are some deficiencies

Through deep links, the information and materials of the original website may not necessarily be stored on the server of the builder of web links, because the builder usually provides a guide but does not directly copy the contents of the original website. Therefore, it is difficult to define that this act infringes the owners' copyright to reproduce and distribute. Although the Copyright Law stipulates the right to disseminate information on the Internet, it does not specify the form of infringement.

As a special law of the Copyright Law, Article 23 of the Regulations on the Protection of the Right to Information Dissemination in Internet(RPRIDI) stipulates that Internet service providers afford search or link services for the customers, after receiving notice from the obligee, disconnect the linkages of works, performances, audio and video recordings that are infringed upon by the provisions of this Regulation, it shall not be liable for compensation. However, those who know or should be aware of the infringement of the works, performances, audio-visual recordings that are linked to original websites shall bear joint liability for their tort. This regulation directly establishes the imputation principle of linking service provider, but the first half of the provisions undoubtedly give the builder of web links the opportunity to take advantage of its loophole. Videlicet, after the builder has completed the malice behavior of infringement and seized the interests, there is still the opportunity to prove that he or she is subjectively unknowing or objectively disconnecting the link in order to weasel out of obligation. Since the predication of subjective fault will directly determine the liability of tort, the criteria for judging the subjective intent of the builder of web links is also particularly important. Article 23 clarifies that although builders who known or ought to be known their infringement is still liable, the criteria of "know" and "ought to know" are not clearly defined, which is difficult to realize in judicial practice and easily leads to excessive discretion of the court. It is possible to overload the responsibility of the builders or even make the rights of the owner of original websites damaged without relief.

3.2 Other protection: the coverage is not wide and the connection between the articles is unbalance

Article 36, paragraph 3 of the Tort Liability Law in China stipulates that if a network service provider knows that customers has infringed upon others' civil rights and interests by using the network service and has not taken necessary measures, it shall bear joint liabilities with its customers. As a law with general regulation, the Tort Liability Law does not adopt the same criteria of "know" or "ought to know" as RPRIDI, so its burden of proof for potential infringers can be said to be looser. Some scholars advocate using the Trademark Law to protect domain names and regulate hyperlinks. However, the essence of a trademark is to help consumers differentiate between various goods or services, while a domain name is the address where a network user enters the cyberspace to enjoy different products or services. As a kind of network technology, the characteristics and functions of hyperlinks cannot be exactly equal to domain names. Therefore, we do not advocate this means of protection [5].

Within the existing legal framework of China, the Anti-Unfair Competition Law is regarded as a powerful supplement to the Copyright Law and the Trademark Law. Undoubtedly, the act of setting up deep links without permission does have some benefits for the owners of original websites, but the act of retaining its original domain name without authorization may mislead visitors into the illusion that the web page they browsing belongs to the original website, whose behavior has met the requirements of confusion in legal practices. However, the Anti-Unfair Competition Law is mainly used to regulate commercial competition. The competition between linked websites is not obvious in real life. This has fallen into the strange circle of regarding hyperlinks as trademarked domain names, and the scope of protection is not comprehensive. On the contrary, under the premise that RPRIDI has made clear the attitude towards the link behavior, it is more appropriate for the behavior of hyperlink technology to be regulated by special regulations.

4 The fault determination standard to the builders of web links: a unified evaluation path of subjective and objective views

As for the fault determination standard of the builders of web links, we must take the interests of the builders of web links and the owners of original websites into account at the same time, seeking a unified standard in the balance of interests and relief. According to the four elements (i.e. subject elements, subjective elements, non-intervention elements and assistance relief elements) established by the "Safe Harbor Rules", we can easily find that the subjective fault of the builders is often inseparable from other objective criteria. In other words, when judging whether the builders is subjectively "fault" (i.e. whether he knows or should know that his actions are illegal), we can discuss it in two situations. First, in the absence of third-party website intervention, we can determine that the builders have subjective intention if the linking website is used to avoid the original websites or tampered with the domain name. Of course, the builders positively cooperate with the act of cutting links after the event, still being reserved the opportunity of exemption from liability for the link setting behaviors. Secondly, when third-party websites are involved, it is difficult for judges to decide whether the builders has subjective intent on the link behavior. Coupled with the exemption of the "Safe Harbor Rules", the interests of the original websites may not be protected. At this time, we need subjective evaluation standard, identifying the fault of the builders. If the builders does not edit, store or modify the linking services provided by the third party websites in any form, and any evidences to prove that he or she knows the ownership of the contents of the original websites, it is not appropriate to identify his or her subjective fault, in case the alienation of the principle of "Fault Liability" to the principle of "Fault Promotion", thereby improperly aggravates the burden of proof of the builders. The development of hyperlink technology undoubtedly provides great convenience for the replication and dissemination of Internet information. The hyperlink technology from one page to another page should be able to build a convenient bridge between customers and linked pages and is conducive to the development of the Internet information industry.

5 Conclusion

Faced with more and more infringement disputes of network hyperlink, the legal systems also needs to respond to them in a timely manner. The comprehensive protection system centered on RPRIDI has not yet fully clarified the basis for the liability of unauthorized behaviors in hyperlink. We can adhere to the unified evaluation mechanism of subjective and objective standards on this basis, handling all kinds of disputes in judicial practice, so as to balance the interests of all parties in hyperlink relations. The protection from copyright law is still the most effective and appropriate means to regulate the legal relationship involved in the behaviors of hyperlinks. Nevertheless, we must clarify the judgment principles of "Subjective Fault" of the builders if we want to guide the judicial work in practice more effectively.

References

1. Li Zhuo, Probe into the Infringement of Intellectual Property Rights on Hyperlinks on the Internet, Intelligence Journal, p.71, No.5, Vol.23 (2004).
2. Jiao Wenming, Legal Regulations on Hyperlink Infringement, Journal of Nanjing University (Philosophy, Humanities and Social Sciences), p.128, No.5, Vol.38(2001).
3. He Xiaobing, Legal Issues on Infringement of Internet Links, Science and Technology and Law, p.694, No.4, Vol. 92(2011).
4. Zheng Chengsi, Intellectual Property Literature, Beijing: China University of Political Science and Law press, pp. 174-176(1999).
5. Xu Songlin, Criminal Regulations on Deep Linking Behavior of Video Search Websites. Intellectual Property Rights. pp.26-31, No. 11, Vol.28(2014).

Review of Performance Pay at County Level Public Hospitals

Shuwei Gu [1], Qiuying Yue [1], Xiaowen Wan [1,a]

[1]*School of Economics and Management, Jiangxi University of Traditional Chinese Medicine, China*

Abstract. Performance pay in county-level public hospitals is an important part of the reform of public hospitals, which largely determines the success or failure of the reform of public hospitals. This paper reviews the concept of performance pay, the recognition of hospitals and staff, the main performance pay model, current situation, design principles and ideas in County-level Public hospitals, and provides some reference for future research and reform direction of performance pay in County-level Public hospitals.

In 2015, the General Office of the State Council "opinions on the implementation of comprehensive reform of county-level public hospitals" put forward that "the salary level of medical staff should be reasonably determined... Perfecting the performance pay system, hospitals distribute their income independently through scientific performance appraisal, so as to achieve more work, more merit and better remuneration[1]. The promulgation of relevant policies and regulations provides a good external environment for the reform of personnel compensation system in County-level Public hospitals. Based on a systematic review of the status quo of performance pay in county-level public hospitals in various regions, this paper analyzed and summarized the problems existing in the pay system, and put forward an optimization plan for the reform of performance pay system in County-level Public hospitals.

1 Data and methods

In this paper, CNKI and Wanfang database are used as data sources to search for "county public hospitals" by advanced retrieval method, which contains different keywords, including "performance", "salary", "income", "treatment", "wage", "personnel distribution system", "satisfaction" and "incentive". Theme is used to accurately search for "county public hospitals". Search time is up to 2018.3.15. After reading the literature topics and abstracts, 68 valid literatures were found.

2 Research status of performance pay in county public hospitals

2.1 Definition of concept

Performance pay originated from Taylor's differential piecework system, which is a kind of salary system that links the employee's salary with the assessment results. Domestic scholars have also made some explorations. Yuan Zheng[2] believes that performance pay is composed of basic and rewarding performance pay, the former is determined by Social Security Departments and the Ministry of Finance according to objective factors such as local economic development level and post responsibilities, while the latter is linked to individual workload and contribution. Hou Tiantian[3] pointed out that performance pay mainly reflects the actual performance and contribution of employees, and hospitals can distribute independently under the guidance of national policies. Huang Jinzao[4] believes that performance pay is a reward based on the overall results of employee performance appraisal. Generally speaking, it is essentially a salary system based on the results of performance appraisal of employees.

2.2 Hospital and staff awareness

Performance pay can play an incentive role for medical staff and improve work efficiency, but to a large extent, it depends on the correct understanding of medical staff. Li Xiaorui[5] surveyed 52 county-level public hospitals in a province and found that 34 hospitals had not yet carried out performance appraisal, accounting for 40% of the total number of county-level public hospitals in the province. From the hospitals that have implemented the performance pay scheme, staff in different positions have different perceptions of performance pay. Yu Xiaobo[6] found that, in the investigation of county-level public hospitals in Zibo, the recognition of performance pay by clinical medical staff was the highest and that of administrative departments was the lowest. The intensity of clinical front-line work is strong, so there will be some emphasis on performance pay plan. Performance pay is higher than that of other departments, and recognition is correspondingly increased.

[a] Corresponding author: 645479278@qq.com

2.3 Main mode

2.3.1 Equalitarianism model

The equalitarianism mode refers to the distribution way directly according to the number of departments. The income gap under this mode can be neglected, similar to the "big pot rice" in the planned economy period, which is common in County-level Public hospitals, such as individual departments of Zhangqiu Traditional Chinese Medicine Hospital [7]. The egalitarianism mode has hurt the enthusiasm of medical staff, and is not conducive to the long-term development of hospitals in the end[8].

2.3.2 Balance of payments model

Balance of revenue and expenditure model is commonly used in modern hospitals, such as the total performance accounting of Yudu People's Hospital[9]. Performance pay is based on Department income and expenditure reduction, and then a certain amount of total performance pay is extracted according to the proportion, and then it is redistributed by the department interior[10]. This model links medical staff with hospital interests and helps hospitals save expenses[8-9], but it may also lead medical staff to pursue economic interests one-sidedly while ignoring basic ethics, increase income by prescribing more prescriptions and excessive medical treatment or reduce necessary consumables to reduce expenditure, which is contrary to public welfare characteristics[11-13].

2.3.3 Workload performance model

Workload performance model refers to a model based on setting different business scoring criteria according to risk difficulty, working time, labor intensity and other factors of different departments, and making more accurate evaluation of workload of medical staff in different departments by using unified scoring coefficient[9]. It is common in the stage of hospital business development, such as the internal personal performance pay accounting in the Department of Yudu County People's Hospital and the performance allocation scheme implemented by a county-level public hospital in Shanghai in 2015. This model effectively solves the problem of one-sided pursuit of economic indicators and low work enthusiasm, which is conducive to the fairness within the hospital.

2.3.4 Comprehensive performance mode

The comprehensive performance model is mainly a distribution model based on comprehensive consideration of workload, professional technology, post title and other factors. It can integrate all kinds of comprehensive factors into the distribution plan of performance pay, which is more systematic and comprehensive. But there are also some drawbacks, such as the difficulty in quantifying some factors, leading to standard deviation and unfair. Hospital should consider carefully when formulating allocation criteria and consult with departments to avoid negative idle work caused by mistaken decision-making.

2.4 Satisfaction study

According to the survey on the satisfaction degree of performance pay in county public hospitals, the satisfaction degree of most medical staff to performance pay distribution is very low. Pan Min[17] sampled the county-level public hospitals in Chengdu and Panzhihua, and found that the average of salary and performance dimensions of different departments were less than 3 points (total 5 points). Mo Xinxinxin[18] surveyed 3 sample counties in Guangxi and found that the comparison of remuneration and workload was one of the most unsatisfactory items. Feng Xiqiu[19] found that one of the main reasons is unfair, and the performance pay of departments with "good efficiency" will be higher, and the gap between different hospitals is large.

2.5 Operational performance study

At present, the medical staff in county public hospitals are not satisfied with the performance pay distribution scheme, which is also due to the existing problems in the distribution mode to varying degrees. There are three main problems:

Firstly, Performance pay assessment is too concerned about economic indicators[20]. Fully embodies the public welfare is the characteristics of public hospitals, public hospitals at the county level are no exception. However, many public hospitals pay too much attention to economic benefits and neglect social responsibility for their development. Li Xiaorui found that in some hospitals which have carried out performance appraisal, the performance pay of some hospitals still stays on the bill of lading, which seriously deviates from the concept of "patient-centered" service and increases the burden of patients' medical expenses[5].

Secondly, the gap between departments is too small. Only when we have a certain gap can we really play an incentive role. However, the phenomenon of egalitarianism and "big pot" in county public hospitals is common. Pang Jialing found that the performance pay gap is too small, and there is no difference between doing more and doing less, which is one of the reasons for dissatisfaction [21].

Thirdly, Medical staff's pay is out of proportion to their income. Payment in proportion to income can reflect fairness, but the performance distribution of county-level public hospitals can not reflect it well. The different volume of business and workload caused by some objective factors among hospitals will also lead to external unfairness[4]. In hospitals, unreasonable design of performance pay system, inadequate distribution according to work and inadequate consideration of actual working ability are also major reasons[22].

2.6 Design principles and ideas

"More work, more pay, better pay" provides the general principle for the performance remuneration system of county-level public hospitals. Based on this principle, Shishi City allocates performance according to comprehensive indicators and tilts to the clinical front line[23]; Danyang People's Hospital determines remuneration[24] according to the principles of clinical>Medical Technology>Assistant and functional departments, and according to factors such as quality and quantity of work; Liuyang People's Hospital of Hunan Province determines to the clinical front line, medical quality and key posts. Business backbone and management and efficiency tilt principle[25]. In the long run, "More work, more pay, better pay" will become the general principle of performance pay reform in the future, and realize the transformation from policy to reality.

3 Evaluation and prospect

As an important part of the reform of public hospitals, the performance pay of county-level public hospitals is of great importance. However, at present, there are few special studies on performance pay in county public hospitals, most of which are mentioned incidentally in the study of compiling or the whole salary system, or about the overall study of public hospitals, but not to county public hospitals. As a part of public hospitals, county-level public hospitals also have some personality factors in their performance pay. Therefore, it is necessary to study the performance pay of county-level public hospitals rather than incorporate it into the study of public hospitals. In addition, the existing studies are mostly focused on case studies or general issues, but lack of systematic review. The research on systematic review needs to be enriched and excavated.

References

1. Website of Department of System Reform. Opinions on Implementing Comprehensive Reform of county public hospitals [EB/OL]. (2014-03-26) [2014-04-04]. http://www.nhfpc.gov.cn/tigs/s3581/201404/9204caf 25546 eb875274ba77499e04.shtml.
2. Yuan Zheng. Research on the reform of personnel system and distribution system in public hospitals [J]. Cooperative economy and science and technology, 16(2013).
3. Hou Tiantian. Study on Influencing Factors of doctors'salary in county public hospitals based on job value [D]. Qingdao University, (2015).
4. golden kitchen. Discussion on salary reform of county public hospitals under the new health care reform [J]. contemporary accounting, 04(2016).
5. Li Xiaorui, Yu Runji. Investigation and analysis of the implementation of performance appraisal system in county-level public hospitals [J]. Health Economic Research, 06(2016).
6. Investigation and analysis of performance pay of employees in county-level public hospitals of Yu Xiaobo, Tian Liqi, Wang Wei. Zibo [J]. Qilu Medical Journal, 30(2015).
7. Zhugeli. Study on the process and effect evaluation of comprehensive reform of county-level public hospitals in Shandong Province [D]. Shandong University, (2017).
8. Zhang Deyu. Research on Performance Wage Distribution Method of County Public Hospital Based on Budget Proportion Method [D]. Nanhua University, (2016).
9. Deng Dasong, Liu Zhenyu. Probe into the Performance Pay Management System of County Public Hospital Based on RBRVS --- Take Yudu County People's Hospital of Jiangxi Province as an example [J]. Journal of Jiangxi University of Finance and Economics, 06(2017).
10. Yin Yanling, Xu Bing and Yang Yan. Discussing the Hospital Bonus Allocation System Based on Workload [J]. Hospital Management Forum, 30(2013).
11. Zhong Wei. Discussion on the transformation of performance reform system in county public hospitals, [J]. enterprise research, 10(2014).
12. Lu Xuemei. A Brief Talk on the Design of Performance Wage Reform in county public hospitals [J]. Finance and Economics (Academic Edition), 23(2016).
13. Jiang Zhengqiang. Research on performance management of Taizhou H county hospital [D]. Jiangxi University of Finance and Economics, (2016).
14. Hu Qiongwei. Research on the positive incentive mechanism of a public hospital in Shanghai [D]. Shandong University, (2015).
15. Jiang Zongshun. Reflections on the guiding system of performance pay distribution in hospitals [J]. Hospital Management of China, 33(2013).
16. Zhao Shasha. Discussion on Performance Wage Distribution in Public Medical Institutions [J]. Primary Health Care in China, 27(2013).
17. Pan Min, Huang Maojuan, Zhang Mei. Survey and Suggestions on Occupational Evaluation of Medical Staff in County-level Public Hospitals from the Perspective of Pay Equity [J]. Jiangsu Health Career Management, 27(2016).
18. Moxinxinxin, Feng Qiming, Luo Hongye, Luoping, Chen He, Gao Hongda, Li Yangfeng, Zhangjuan. Analysis of job satisfaction and its influencing factors of medical staff in county-level public hospitals of Guangxi [J]. Modern Chinese Doctors, 53(2015).
19. Feng Xiqiu. Survey and analysis of staff satisfaction with county-level public hospital reform in Anhui Province [D]. Anhui Medical University, (2014).
20. Yang Qunhui. Research on Performance Management of Hospital Organization Based on PDCA Closed Loop [J]. Modern Hospital, 17(2017).
21. Pang Jialing, Wu Weimin, Yang Xiuling, Jiang Shuai and Fan Li. Investigation and analysis of satisfaction of medical staff after the reform of County-level public hospitals [J]. Health Economic Research, 08(2014).
22. Qin Yongfang. New model of personnel compensation system and performance management in county-level public hospitals [J]. China Hospital, 19(2015).

https://doi.org/10.1051/itmconf/20192503002

23. Sui Ping. Research on the establishment and management of county public hospitals [D]. Shandong University, 2017.
24. Zhou Lijian, Lin Yijin. Actively promote the comprehensive reform of county-level public hospitals by taking the opportunity of grade hospital evaluation [J]. Modern Hospital, 16(2016).
25. Deng Zongwei. Practice of economic management and performance distribution in county-level public hospitals under medical reform [J]. Journal of Chinese Medicine Management, 21(2013).

A Study on Construction of Brand Image for Cultural Tourism Based on Visual Grammar
--- Taking the Brand Image of "Mystery" of Xiangxi as an Example

Ying Liu

College of International Education, Jishou University, China

Abstract: With the deep integration development of culture and tourism, cultural tourism brand has become an important factor of core competitiveness. As the brand of cultural tourism of Xiangxi Tujia and Miao Autonomous Prefecture (hereafter referred to as Xiangxi), "Mystery" represents the core value of Xiangxi's culture and tourism. The publicity video of *Mysterious Xiangxi* becomes the important carrier of the "Mystery" brand, playing a vital role in the transmission of brand image. This paper illustrates and analyzes the constructing features of brand image of "Mystery" from dimensions of representation meaning, interactive meaning and composition meaning respectively based on visual grammar, and puts forward some suggestions on it combining with four factors of cultural brand image design.

Keywords: Visual grammar; Mystery; Xiangxi; brand image

1 Introduction

With the deep integration development of culture and tourism, tourists' expectations for tourism services and specialties are constantly becoming higher and higher, so effective tourism brands are crucial factors in the competition of culture and tourism industry. Tourism industry is a strategic pillar industry in Xiangxi. It sets "Mystery" as its cultural tourism brand, which just fits its cultural essence. Compared to other tourism orientation, the biggest competitive advantage is not just its rugged mountains and green waters, but also the ethnic culture, folk custom and mysterious culture. (Li, 2011) Besides clear position of the brand image, its effective communication is more important. The publicity video of *Mysterious Xiangxi* plays a vital role in spreading the brand of "Mystery" and attracting domestic and foreign tourists.

According to the previous study, most domestic researches focus on its communication strategies or marketing strategies. There are few studies on analyzing the brand image of ethic culture tourism from the perspective of social semiotics. How does *Mysterious Xiangxi* construct and spread brand of "Mystery"? This study takes the official publicity video of Xiangxi, *Mysterious Xiangxi* as an example, analyzes the constructing features of brand image of "Mystery" from dimensions of representation meaning, interactive meaning and composition meaning respectively based on visual grammar and puts forward some suggestions to improve the effectiveness of transmission of tourism brand and enhance the communication competence of local ethical culture.

2 Visual grammar

Visual grammar is to study the way how the people, places and things are depicted in the images, their relations with the viewers, and the way they are integrated into a meaningful whole. Kress and van Leeuwen's visual grammar provides the methodologies to interpret the meaning of image systematically. Its basic principle is to take Michael Halliday' social semiotic approach to analyze other semiotic resources like image, gesture, music and so on, to study the meaning "potential" and structure. These semiotic resources are viewed as inter-related meaning-making systems, which are used to construe social practice. Following Hodge and Kress (1988:1), everything in society and culture "can be seen as a form of communication". Halliday' model with its three functions sets a starting point for description of image because it works well as a source for thinking about all modes of representation." (Kress & van Leeuwen, 2006 [1996]) In recent years, scholars at home and abroad have conducted extensive research on the multimodal discourse analysis. The social semiotic approach to multimodal analysis construes the meaning of multiple semiotic resources such as language, gesture, proximity, gaze, music and so forth in order to establish the framework of multimodal symbolic semantics. According to the development and research of multimodal discourse analysis, it is not only a theoretical

Corresponding author: shizhe112000@163.com

research framework but also an important approach of discourse analysis.

3 Interpreting the brand image of "Mystery" from visual grammar

The data selected in this study is the official publicity video named *Mysterious Xiangxi* released by local government. It includes the introduction and four short episodes, "Green Xiangxi", "Cultural Xiangxi", "Open Xiangxi" and "Harmonious Xiangxi". The brand image of "Mystery" is constructed through the semiotic resources like images, words, music, sound, color, time and so on.

Semio-tics / Time		image	words	music	sound	colour
0—0′ 45″	Introduce-tion	√	√	√	√	√
0′ 48″—2′ 32″	"Green Xiangxi"	√	√	√	√	√
2′ 33″—4′ 45″	"Cultural Xiangxi"	√	√	√	√	√
4′ 46″—7′ 07″	"Open Xiangxi"	√	√	√	√	√
7′ 08″—8′ 35″	"Harmo-nious Xiangxi" and ending	√	√	√	√	√

The design of cultural tourism brand is composed by auditory factors, visual factors, factors of psychological perception and factors of comprehensive perception. These four factors constitute a complete image system of cultural tourism brand. (Zhang & Wang, 2011) How does *Mysterious Xiangxi* construct and spread brand of "Mystery"? How do the four factors of cultural tourism brand design work together? The following parts will analyze the constructing strategies of "Mystery" from dimensions of representation meaning, interactive meaning and composition meaning respectively based on visual grammar and cooperative effect of the four factors.

3.1 Representation meaning of "Mystery" in the *Mysterious XiangXi*

In the introduction of *Mysterious Xiangxi*, the implication of mystery is represented by analytical processes of the conceptual representation. The nine scenes show the rugged mountains and green water, ancient city, Aizhai Bridge and so on. This part summarizes the features of mysterious Xiangxi--a peaceful utopia and a well-known ecological and cultural park at home and abroad. To further illustrate mysterious image, the publicity video is divided into four episodes. In the episode of "Green Xiangxi", it is to introduce unique natural environment of Xiangxi, its abundant green agricultural products and eco-cultural tourism. There are thirty-five scenes in "Green Xiangxi" which can be divided into four parts. Part one presents Xiangxi's unique natural environment including primeval forests, Wetland park, You River and Wu River and so on (12 scenes). Part two introduces Xiangxi's ecological agriculture like by GuZhang Tea, BaoJing Golden Tea, kiwi fruit, Ponkan, JiuGui wine through action processes and reactional processes of narrative representation (six scenes). Part three informs the eco-cultural tourism like MengDong River, QiFeng Lake, Dong River, Wetlands Park and so on through analytic processes of narrative representation. Part four describes the dynamics behaviors of tourists like running, climbing, drawing in the forest and so on to demonstrate that tourists indulge in the beautiful scenery by action processes of narrative meaning.

Analysis of "Green Xiangxi"

representational meaning	analytical process	action process and reactional process	analytic process	action process
contents	natural environment	ecological agriculture	eco-cultural tourism	harmonious coexistence of human and nature
distribution of scene	12	6	9	4
percentage	41.9%	19.3%	29%	12.9%

In "Cultural Xiangxi", by action processes of narrative meaning, it introduces Xiangxi's long and mysterious history, culture of loving the family, loving the country and loving the world. By You River and Wu River which run through Xiangxi, it reviews the glorious history of the former great Qin Empire and Laosi Cheng. Then, by action processes of narrative meaning, it introduces the World Intangible Cultural Heritage, like Miao's Drum Dance, Miao Embroidery, Tujia Brocade, Laosi Cheng heritage site, the South Great Wall and so on. In addition, by action processes and reactional processes of narrative meaning, it is to convey humanistic spirit and folk culture vividly, making viewers experience personally feeling, like folk song of Miao, Maogusi dance of Tujia people, Chenhe High-pitched, Tujia Waving Dance and so on (18 scenes).

Analysis of "Cultural Xiangxi"

Representational meaning	Action process	Action process	Action process & reactional process
Contents	Great Qin empire and Laosi Cheng	World Intangible Cultural Heritage	Humanistic spirit and folk culture
Distribution of scene	16	12	27
Percentage	29%	21.8%	49%

In "Open Xiangxi", on the one hand, it depicts the development of transportation in Xiangxi and establishment of the open platform; on the other hand, it displays the development of tourism and culture industry mainly by action processes of narrative meaning in order to attract investment and cooperation.

Analysis of "Open Xiangxi"

Representational meaning	Action process	Action process
Contents	Transportation & tourism industry	Combination of cultural industry and tourism industry
Distribution of scene	16	50
Percentage	24.2%	75.8%

In "Harmonious Xiangxi", through action and reactional processes of narrative meaning, like smile, holding hands, toast, drinking, throwing caps and so on, these action and eye contact form the vectors, to expresses the harmony between Tujia and Miao minority and Han nationality, the harmony between tourists and local dwellers, reflecting Xiangxi's upward spiritual outlook. In addition, by the symbolic processes of the conceptual meaning, like light, lantern, fountain it indicates harmony and a better future for XiangXi.

Analysis of "Harmonious Xiangxi"

representational meaning	action process	reactional process	symbolic process
contents	upward spiritual outlook	harmony between tourists and local dwellers	light, lantern, fountain
distribution of scene	26	8	3
percentage	70.3%	21.6%	8.1%

In conclusion, the mysterious image of the publicity video *Mysterious Xiangxi* is mainly through action processes, reactional processes of narrative meaning and analytic processes of conceptual meaning. The mystery is mainly reflected by mysterious natural ecological environment and Nuo culture. Xiangxi's natural ecological environment is expressed by analytic processes of the conceptual meaning. It's mysterious humanistic spirit and folk culture is expressed by action processes and reactional processes of narrative meaning, making tourists experience the personal feelings. By the combination with movement and standstill, *Mysterious Xiangxi* weaves a delicate and mysterious scroll, compose a sweet and pleasant song and have a wonderful dream for the audience.

3.2 Interactive meaning of "Mystery" in the *Mysterious Xiangxi*

According to Kress & van Leeuwen, if the viewer is not object, but subject of the look, and the represented participant is the object of the viewer's dispassionate scrutiny. No contact is made. This image is called "Offer". (Kress & van Leeuwen, 2006 [1996]) In the video of 8′54″ minutes, there was seldom eye contact between the participants and the viewers, except the girl in the Miao dress staring at viewers at 4′15″ minutes and people in the video waving to the audience viewers. Even in the reactional processes of the narrative meaning, the focuses of the eye contact are not the viewer because it intends to create a sense of mystery and charisma of Xiangxi. What's more, in the video, the cultural celebrities, like ShenCong wen, HunagYong yu, and SongZu ying, they don't have direct eye contact with the viewers, deliberately creating mysterious and profound culture of XiangXi. According to the different perspectives of the scene, distant lens and panoramic picture take more part in the video, in order to introduce the overall image of Xiangxi and pay attention to macro and integrity. From a global perspective, the social distance is set between image participants and viewers to highlight the mystery. But in the introduction of specific intangible cultural heritage in XiangXi, like Miao items, Tujia brocade, Green agricultural products, close shots are used with the purpose to attract tourists and investors.

In order to take the viewer into the state of *mysterious XiangXi* and experience local culture and maintain equal relationship between participants and viewers, the angle is frontal and eye level. But in the episode of "Cultural XiangXi", low angles are used to review the history of XiangXi, like the Qin Empire, TuSi system and show respects for the heroes and the depth of history because "low angles generally give an impression of superiority and triumph". (Kress & van Leeuwen, 2006 [1996]) In terms of colour saturation, *Mysterious Xiangxi* has high modality and high color saturation. There are mainly distinctive colors like, red, blue and black of ethnic costumes and green Mountain and water in the video. On the contrary, in the retrospect of Qin dynasty between the 2′55″and 3′00″, color saturation is low because it recreates the scene by performance. In addition, the video pays attention to contextualization, like snowflakes in the scene of monument, water waves in the scene of clear water, fog in the scene of green and mountain in order to present high modality.

To analyze the *Mysterious Xiangxi* from the contact of the interactive meaning, it is mainly "offer" rather than "demand". From the perspective of social distance, it uses long shot in order to keep distant and mysterious. In addition, the angle is frontal and eye level, it involves the viewers and brings them intuitive and authentic experiences and feelings. Finally, through saturation and details, it highlights the authenticity of *Mysterious Xiangxi.*

3.3 Composition meaning of "Mystery" in the Mysterious Xiangxi

In *Mysterious Xiangxi*, key information is distributed in the center, where the titles and the names of scenic spots are placed in this video. From the layout of words and images in the video of *Mysterious Xiangxi*, the words are on the left, which are the given information but the images are on the right, which are the new information. According to the analysis from the perspective of salience, images are in the foreground with large size and words are in the background with small size. From the perspective of color saturation, the natural environment is mainly presented by the green and grey color. The humanistic society is mainly expressed by the color of red, blue, yellow and black which make the cold and warm colors complement each other, enable to display a colorful and dynamic picture of mysterious and dynamic Xiangxi.

In conclusion, the brand image of "Mystery" is mainly represented from three dimensions of visual grammar. First, in representational meaning, "Mystery" in the video of *Mysterious Xiangxi* is mainly represented by action processes of narrative meaning and analytical processes of conceptual meaning to display the mysterious natural ecological environment, green ecological products and folk culture. Second, "Mystery" between the viewers and the participants is mainly formed through long shot, high modality and high color saturation. Third, “Mystery” is expressed by combination of information value, salience and framing, from the center to the margin, highlighting the core scenic spots like Aizhai Bridge and intangible cultural heritage like Tujia’s Brocade in Xiangxi.

4 Conclusion

Based on the design of national culture tourism image, the publicity of *Mysterious Xiangxi* integrates factors of auditory, visual, psychological perception and comprehensive perception, paying special attention to visual elements and auditory elements, expressing the psychological perception factor through the folk festival culture, but there is still room for improvement in the presentation of comprehensive perception factors. For example, this video introduces the development of transportation and tourism industry, but it does not focus on the tourist service, transportation route, specialty food and local-style dwelling architectures.

According to the analysis of visual grammar and combining with four factors of cultural brand image design, this paper puts forward the following suggestions. First, optimize the representation of mysterious contents in *Mysterious Xiangxi*. It is suggested to increase and deepen the expression of the Nuo culture. It is necessary to precisely locate the mysterious culture in Xiangxi and find its core value and essence. The essence of the mysterious culture in Xiangxi is Nuo culture. It is necessary to further explore the creative design of Nuo culture, and reproduce the Nuo culture scientifically and innovatively while avoiding its sensitivity and feudalism. Second, strike the balance between the interaction and mystery with viewers. In the video of *Mysterious Xiangxi*, the interactive between the image and the viewer is limited. It is suggested to increase the interactive communication with the viewer because it can strengthen the psychological perception of tourists so as to better attract them. Third, strengthen the core elements of the mysterious brand. In addition to stressing the size and color of the core picture, the names of the core scenic spots can be highlighted to make the words and images more complementary.

In conclusion, to improve the communication validity of the mysterious brand image of Xiangxi, it is necessary not only to understand the cultural implication of the mysterious brand, but also to establish an effective multi-modal discourse coordination mechanism

Fund projects

1. Hunan Philosophy and Social Science Fund Western Project, China (15YBX048): “Multi-dimensional discourse analysis and its countermeasures of publicity and tourism promotion Xiangxi in the global context”

2. National social science foundation of JiShou University, China (16SKA015): “Study on the strategies of external publicity and tourism promotion in WuLing mountain areas from multimodal perspective”

References

1. Li Baishan. On Creative Design of Witchcraft Culture and Remodeling the Mysterious Tourism of West Hunan [J]. Journal of HuaiHua University, **6**, 4-5 (2012).
2. Hodge, Robert and Gunther Kress. *Social Semiotics*. Cambridge, UK: Polity Press in association with Basil Blackwell, Oxford, UK. (1988).
3. Kress, Gunther and Theo van Leeuwen. *Reading Images: The Grammar of Visual Design* (2 nd Edition). London: Routledge. [2006 (1996)].
4. Zhang Haiyan, Wang Zhongyun. Research of Establishing Ethnic Tourist Products Brand in Industrial Integration View [J]. Journal of Minzu University of China (Philosophy and Social Sciences Edition), **4**,17-23(2011).

Re-criticism of Geomantic Omen in Modern Design from the Perspective of Data Analysis

Qi Liu[1,a], Huagang Yang[2], and Yiwei Zhang[3]

[1]*Gold Mantis School of Architecture, Soochow University, No. 199 Ren Ai Road, Wu Zhong District, Jiangsu City, Suzhou Province, China*
[2]*Kunming University of Science and Technology, No. 727 Jingming South Road, Chenggong District, Kunming, Yunnan*
[3]*Ludong University, Room 232, No.49, Hongqi Mid-road 186, Zhifu District, Yantai, Shandong Province, China*

Abstract. Geomantic omen is both strange and familiar to the contemporary people. It is not only a part of the traditional Chinese culture, but also contains the contradictions and disputes in Chinese long history of thought, practice and theory. This article is based on the context of modern design, discuss the reason of the Geomantic omen cannot be the key factors of modern design from three perspectives, including research trend, discipline development, practice creation. Through the summary of data, typical cases, and geomantic theory, it is believed that modern geomantic research should be based on rational evaluation and theoretical research. Except that, geomancy can be study not only by using modern science and technology, but also through transcending the ideological level. Finally, the idea of the future development of geomantic is set up for the re-thinking and re-exploration of the contemporary research.

1 Trend analysis of overall research

1.1 Research trends in ancient times

Wang Qiheng, a famous expert on architectural geomantic omen theory in China, pointed out the scientific nature of geomantic omen and the value of contemporary research in his book "Research on geomantic omen theory". On the other hand, he also pointed out that geomantic omen research cannot get rid of the shackles and fetters of superstition. This view is also based on the historical background of the controversy. [1] Geomantic omen began to worship nature and spirit in the early period of human beings, and maintained consistency with the development of Chinese history. At the same time, geomantic omen embodied particularity. The whole development process of geomantic omen experienced a complex process from germination to maturity, from legend to life, from practice to theory, from fluctuation to stability and re-differentiation (Table 1).

Table 1. Setting Word's margins

Period	Definition	Features	Theory
Primitive society (budding period)	Number and sorcery	From primitive worship to fantasy.	Observing natural celestial phenomena
Shang and Zhou Dynasties (development period)	Choose capital and Divination	For capital building.	event must be divination first.
Qin, Han, Wei, Jin, southern and Northern Dynasties (maturity period)	Tombs and geomantic omen	Yin and Yang five lines appears.	Figure of the house
Tang, song and Yuan Dynasties (prosper)	Divination, Fangjia and geomantic omen	Gradually combining geomantic omen with religious architecture	The book of Mansion
Ming and Qing Dynasties (declining period)	geomantic omen	The genre is very complex and confusing.	Ten books in Yang Mansion
Contemporary (New exploration period)	geomantic omen	Gradually interdisciplinary with psychology and other subjects.	Chinese geomantic omen culture, etc.

The early geomantic omen is in the embryonic stage of development, and the initial intention comes from people's expectations for the improvement and beauty of life. In the Qin and Han Dynasties, with the unification of writing and currency, on the one hand, it promoted the scientific development of geomantic omen, on the other hand, it gradually breeds superstition. Historically, there has been a certain scale of criticism of geomantic omen since the Han Dynasty. In Lun Heng, Wang Chong, the representative of the Han Dynasty, criticizes the geomantic omen superstition of his time from the perspectives of residence, funeral system, life concept system and demonstration. [2] Touched the essence of superstition in geomantic omen.

https://doi.org/10.1051/itmconf/20192503004

1.2 Contemporary research trends

Nowadays, scholars such as Song Hong-xi have put forward the concept of contemporary natural geomancy while criticizing geomancy rationally. Objectively speaking, contemporary geomancy research has gradually abandoned the attitude of overpraise and overall criticism, showing a trend from perceptual judgment to rational research, and the exploration of this field has also been deepening. Starting from the theoretical research level, from the end of the Qing Dynasty to the present, the relevant theoretical books and documents are analysed by visual data (Table 2). It can be found that the contemporary development law of geomantic omen can be divided into three stages: before 2003, the development of geomantic omen tends to develop smoothly, while the development of geomantic omen in architecture or design is concerned. The domain has infiltrated, but there is no large-scale promotion and application. (Table 2)

Table 2. Visualized data analysis of geomantic omen Research

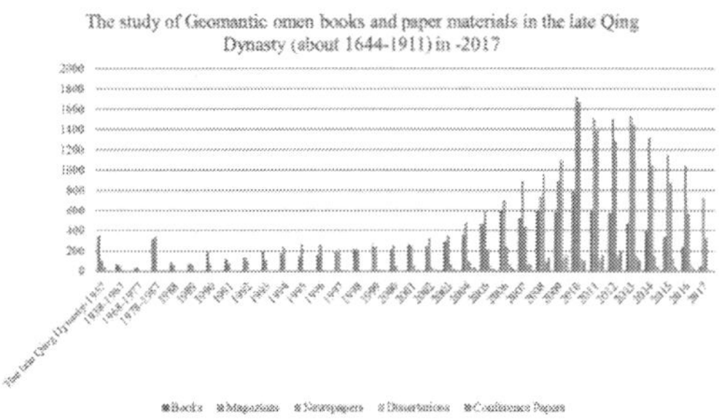

From 2003 to 2010, geomantic omen showed a rapid development trend, and the development of China's construction industry in this stage also showed a sustained growth trend, that is, in the context of the financial crisis in 2009, the national economy was in a downturn. During this period, the theory and viewpoints concerning the application of geomantic omen in the field of design were constantly enriched, and gradually began to dispel the single critical attitude towards geomantic omen in the past long period of time. Since 2010, the study of geomantic omen discipline has shown a trend of slow decline. The main reason is that discipline interdisciplinary and interdisciplinary research are constantly advancing in this period. This is the background of academic research in the process of blending and advancing natural science and geomantic omen, with the emergence of research platforms such as big data and *Internet* +. People have gradually changed their perspectives and methods of geomantic omen research, interpreting geomantic omen in a scientific, rational and logical way, discarding personal emotion and limitations, and conducting a rare but reasonable study. In today's unprecedented rapid development of science, geomantic omen discipline is still unable to get rid of the strange circle of superstition, there are also many phenomena that cannot be explained by science, which are closely related to people's activities and also incidental to contemporary social problems.

1.3 Overall research characteristics

First, the existing data show that there are a certain number of textual research books, literature, videos and network resources about geomantic omen theory and its application from the past to the present. However, from the overall content to the details of some principles, there is not a systematic combing, nor does it allow the public to form a common understanding. The same person in the same book has two meanings in the different Dynasty. [3] It is not only the change of content, but also the great misunderstanding of the original meaning. There are many absurd and mythical meanings in the explanation of the application of some geomantic omen principles.

Secondly, there are ambiguous explanations for a phenomenon, such as the grave pattern of "Xinshan B-direction and Xuchen". In *Geomantic omen Seventy-second Bureau*, it is considered that both the positive and the negative situation are evil, while in the *Essentials of Three-dimensional Geography*, it is considered that the bad luck should be combined with the water bureau. [4] Even its source, such as Guo Pu's *Funeral Books* in the Wei and Jin Dynasties, which has been inherited from ancient times, is not from Guo Pu himself, but from the Tang and Song Dynasties, but the real author has no way to verify. Nevertheless, even today's scholars who study geomancy regard Guo Pu as the author of Funeral Books without any textual research. Before the Wei and Jin Dynasties, the founders of geomancy pedigrees such as Zhu Xian Tao and Qing Wuzi were not legendary figures in historical records. It is not difficult to imagine that geomantic omen has some inaccuracies in theory, so the accuracy in many oral and personal teachings is even more difficult to grasp.

Third, some of the principles of geomantic omen language are too obscure, resulting in incoherence of learning or use. For example, many sentences of the *Ten Books of Yang Zhai* are written in classical Chinese. Because each person's interpretation ability is different, and the literal meaning of ancient Chinese characters should be interpreted in accordance with the corresponding context. At the same time, textual research on ancient texts is also required to prove the corresponding geomantic omen theory, therefore, it still causes misunderstanding deviation in varying degrees. Of course, this also reflects the inadequacy of the study of ancient Chinese literature in contemporary education. Because of the difficulties in understanding and understanding the traditional geomantic omen theory, it is difficult for us to form a complete geomantic omen concept when we understand and learn geomantic omen knowledge, and at the same time, it is impossible to promote its application.

2 Limitations of disciplinary development

Contemporary geomancy research is not systematic and rigorous. Some scholars have proposed that geomantic omen is a scientific summary, which embodies the wisdom of ancient Chinese philosophy, science and aesthetics, and has its own logical relationship. It is a natural part of traditional architectural theory. However, from the perspective of the research system of this discipline, there are some shortcomings, or the current research is not perfect and mature enough. From the late Qing Dynasty to 2017, this research compared the research data of geomantic omen with other subjects (Table 3& Table 4).

Table 3. Statistical tables for geomantic omen and other disciplines

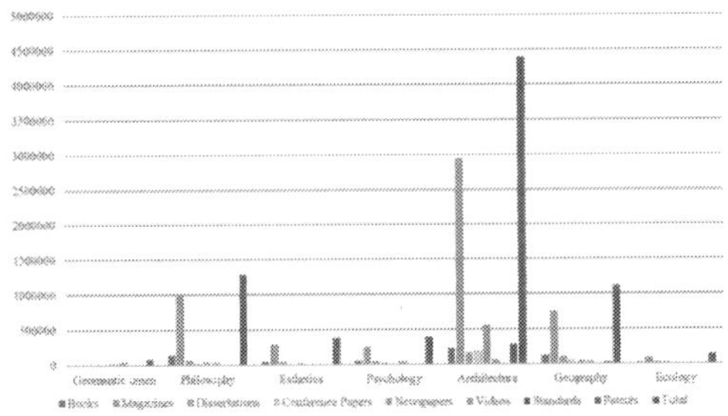

Table 4. Statistics of different types of subjects in the late Qing Dynasty (about 1644-1911) in -2017

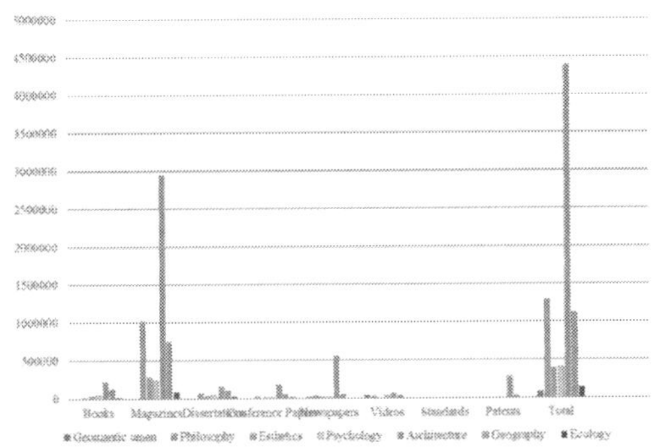

2.1 limitations of academic research

When geomantic omen compares with other disciplines or makes cross-disciplinary studies, the data are incomplete, and the interpretation of the past literature in modern and contemporary times is not deep enough. In addition, some geomantic practice experience and laws are difficult to verify accuracy through oral or personal teaching, literature and language, so that the perspective and knowledge obtained are one-sided. It is a meaningful, insightful and innovative research way to use the perspective of geomantic omen to interpret the discipline thoughts including philosophy and aesthetics. However, there are some limitations from the source of research subject resources, which are not accurate enough and easy to blur the concept.

2.2 limitations of knowledge dissemination

In the dissemination of subject knowledge, geomantic omen can be referred to by the public with little accurate information, which results in insufficient knowledge reserve at the understanding level. This is why in the long history of the past, the theory of geomantic omen has been either supportive or totally negative. Although people's attitude toward geomantic omen is more rational than in the past, the lack of basic data makes it difficult to break through the current situation. Therefore, the research of geomantic omen has been continuously supplementing, collecting, interpreting and analysing on the basis of predecessors. It still needs a process to transform obscure and difficult language into a mode of communication that can be universal to the public. From the point of view of data analysis, our existing research is also in the process.

2.3 limitations of inheritance and innovation

Based on the first two points, geomantic omen discipline needs to innovate and develop or has blind spots in combination with emerging science and technology, and it is also difficult to promote and intervene, whether in theory or in practice, which is also a dilemma that contemporary geomantic omen needs to break through. Chinese nature contains geomantic omen, emphasized in practice through technical means to target a realm of harmony is also present in architecture field. The living environment we are facing today has changed a lot. Besides environmental problems, social problems, ecological problems and resource problems, because of the richness of life dimension, we also need to face the addition and multiplication of all problems, which are far more complex than the problems that the geomantic omen view has to solve in the past. Although many of the natural concepts put forward by geomantic omen coincide with today's science, ideological exchanges are conducive to promoting exchanges and mutual promotion between the whole discipline and other disciplines. But it is not enough merely by thought. Ultimately, we must take the material environment of human settlement as the foothold. Therefore, at the level of practice and technology, geomantic omen still faces challenges.

3 Hysteresis of creative practice

3.1 hysteresis of ideas

Early *Zhou Li* • *Xia Gong Sima Xia* roughly described the principle and requirement that the method of selective settlement needs to observe the orientation and measure the land, which has preliminarily possessed scientific concepts and ideas. This reflects that the early concept of geomantic omen actually hoped to pass through practical experience and objective factual laws, but later development also separated the genre of metaphysics and superstition, which is an indisputable fact. Although today we should treat geomancy scientifically and rigorously and make use of geomancy, there are two important reasons why we still confine our creation to the circle. One is that we can't find a reasonable evaluation criterion to define geomantic omen; the other is that the rationality of geomantic omen used in modern design can't be judged in which aspects. Of course, we cannot say that these laws have no flexible scale, so as the basis for architectural creation is too rigid, but unreasonable content cannot be avoided or even boldly used through effective means, then it is not what we expect in the contemporary or future human settlements environment.

3.2 hysteresis of objective practice

Nowadays, we are familiar with many cases of geomantic omen in contemporary practice, such as the Bank of China Tower, Far East Finance Centre, Zhuge Bagua Village, etc. At the same time of these practical creations, theoretical advances are parallel. For example, *Geomantic Omen in American Cities*, written by Liang Xue, is a book that uses geomantic omen to analyse the planning and layout of American cities in a very detailed way. [5] His research also reveals that foreign scholars' research on Chinese geomantic omen and even the collection and collation of ancient books have not only stayed in the cognitive stage. At the same time, with the progress of globalization in China, a large number of foreign scholars have gradually shifted their attention to the deep exploration of geomantic omen with the deepening of the study of Chinese culture. It is precisely because such a hot spot is before us that we should take this opportunity to discuss the realistic significance and historical value of geomantic omen in the contemporary era. If we cannot explain this problem and see its essence clearly, we cannot advance our understanding of geomantic omen only by full of passion. If we talk about removing the superstitious part of geomantic omen, it will be pale and powerless to carry forward its scientific part.

3.3 hysteresis of technology

On the one hand, the combination of geomantic omen and modern design technology is difficult in technical path, on the other hand, it lags behind the expression of modern science and technology geomantic omen in practice. Since the 21st century, the field of architecture has realized the difficult establishment of non-linear models through BIM, Python, GIS and other software technologies, and even realized the transformation from virtual to reality through VR, AI and other emerging technologies, which is a very valuable breakthrough. Unfortunately, the combination of geomantic omen still stays in the collation and analysis of surface problems such as geomantic omen as a hot topic, whether geomantic omen has contemporary competitiveness or not, including this study can only be based on the modern literature and data of geomantic omen, for the combination, application and even promotion of geomantic omen in essence. The first phase is almost zero. In today's information explosion and ideological trend, it has also become a shackle for geomantic omen to break through at the ideological level.

4 Conclusion

At the present stage, based on the three levels of research trend, discipline development and creative practice, through certain data and combined with corresponding geomantic cases, it is considered that geomantic omen should not be considered as a key factor in modern design, but reasonable ideas and concepts in geomantic omen can be used to assist contemporary design, and attention should be paid to geomantic omen. There are three possible directions for geomantic omen's future development. One is found that it does not exist and is gradually dying out, just as human beings have assumed the ether as a substance. Another is geomantic omen has become an important discipline with its scientific value constantly rooted and flourished. The third may discover its scientific value for a period of time and be constantly excavated, but after a time zero point, the subject is disconnected from the real world's life needs, gradually declining and becoming a clear stream in the long history. However, science is not the only standard by which we measure the world. There are emotions, spirits and hopes. The time has come and we need to make choices.

References

1. Wang Qiheng, Research of Geomantic Omen Theory (Tianjin University Press, 2005).
2. Department of history, Peking University, Annotation of Lun Heng (Zhong Hua Book Company, 1979).
3. Song Hongxi, A thorough criticism of Geomantic Omen and eight houses Fengshui, Real Estate Information of China, 18 (2016).
4. He Xiaoxi, Exploring the Source of Geomantic Omen (Southeast University press, 1990).
5. Liang Xue, Geomantic Omen in American Cities (Liaoning Science and Technology Press,2004).
6. Song Hongxi, Inheriting natural geomantic omen and building beautiful China, China-Today Forum, 17(2013).

Preparation and Characterization of 1,2,3,4- Butane four Carboxylate Transition Metal Complexes

Kanglong Zhang, Xiaojin Qi

China University of Mining and Technology Yinchuan College

Abstract. 1,2,3,4- butane four carboxylic acidis（$Na_4C_8H_6O_8$）is mainly used to prepare photosensitive materials, medical polymer materials and functional polymer membrane materials.As a permanent finishing agent, 1,2,3,4-butane four carboxylic acid plays an irreplaceable role.In this paper, the preparation of metal complexes by the reaction of 1,2,3,4-butane tetracarboxylic acid tetrasodium salt（$Na_4C_8H_6O_8$）with transition metals is described. The composition and structure of the prepared metal complexes were characterized by infrared spectroscopy, thermogravimetric analysis and elemental analysis. At the same time, through the analysis of thermogravimetric curves, the order of thermal stability of metal complexes is (from large to small): $Co_2C_8H_6O_8{\cdot}2H_2O$ > $Cd_2C_8H_6O_8{\cdot}2H_2O$ > $Mn_2C_8H_6O_8{\cdot}2H_2O$ > $Ni_2C_8H_6O_8{\cdot}2H_2O$ > $Zn_2C_8H_6O_8{\cdot}2H_2O$ > $Zn_2C_8H_6O_8{\cdot}2H_2O$ > $Cu_2C_8H_6O_8{\cdot}2H_2O$.

Keywords: Transition metal complexes; thermogravimetric analysis; 1,2,3,4- butane four carboxylic acid; IR spectra

1,2,3,4-butane tetracarboxylic acid ($Na_4C_8H_6O_8$) is mainly used to prepare photosensitive materials, medical polymer materials and functional polymer membrane materials. As a permanent calendering agent, 1,2,3,4-butane tetracarboxylic acid has no formaldehyde in itself. Cotton and silk articles treated by it can obtain wrinkle resistance, solid shape and ironing-free properties. At present, the synthesis methods of 1,2,3,4-butane tetracarboxylic acid have been reported in China, but the literature on transition metal complexes of 1,2,3,4-butane tetracarboxylic acid is less. Therefore, this paper will further study and prepare metal complexes [1] Co, Cu, Ni, Mn, Zn, Cd and so on.

1 Experiment

1.1 Major reagents

(1) 1,2,3,4- butane four carboxylic acid ($Na_4C_8H_6O_8$).

(2) Two times distilled water.

(3) $NaOH$, $Cd(NO_3)_2{\cdot}4H_2O$ (the transition metal chlorides are all analytically pure).

1.2 Preparation of transition metal complexes of 1,2,3,4- butane four carboxylic acid with Cu as an example

In the preparation of copper, the first step is to weigh the amount of $H_4C_8H_6O_8$ molten water, add 30% $NaOH$ water solution while stirring, cool it, adjust the acidity and alkalinity to PH5-6, and concentrate the reaction solution. After cooling, the crystallization of 1,2,3,4- butane four carboxylic acid will be obtained. The white powder of $Na_4C_8H_6O_8$ was obtained by drying it at 90 C for 12 hours, and then it was put into a dryer for use. At this time, the quantitative $Na_4C_8H_6O_8$ is weighed and dissolved in water. After stirring and adding CuC_{12} to the aqueous solution, it should be noted that the mass ratio of CuC_{12} to $Na_4C_8H_6O_8$ is 2. It can be observed that a large number of blue precipitates are precipitated in the reaction solution, which is heated to 60-70 °C and stirred for 1 hour, and then cooled and filtered. Wash the precipitates with hot water for 3 times and remove the F in the precipitates. The blue precipitate $Cu_2C_8H_6O_8{\cdot}nH_2O$ was then dried at 75 ℃ for 12 hour. The preparation of other metal complexes is basically the same as that of Cu complexes, but Cd complexes are made by $Cd(NO_3)_2{\cdot}4H_2O$ and $Na_4C_8H_6O_8$ [2].

1.3 Using thermogravimetric analysis

In the analysis phase, the thermogravimetric analyzer (Pyris 1 TGA) produced by Perkin-Elmer is used. Use $M_2C_8H_6O_8{\cdot}nH_2O$, $Co_2C_8H_6O_8{\cdot}nH_2O$, $Ni_2C_8H_6O_8{\cdot}nH_2O$, $Cu_2C_8H_6O_8{\cdot}nH_2O$, $Zn_2C_8H_6O_8{\cdot}nH_2O$, $Cd_2C_8H_6O_8{\cdot}nH_2O$ to analyze and analyze the data. It can be observed that when the heating rate reaches 20°C per minute and the number of samples is 6 mg, when the temperature is between 30°C and 850, the flow rate of dry air is 20 ml per minute as the atmosphere.

1.4 Elemental analysis by infrared spectroscopy

In element analysis, the Fourier transform infrared spectrometer (Spectrum GX) produced by Perkin-Elmer Company and the DITGS detector are still used. After preparing the relevant testing instruments, we use KBr pressing method to test. At the same time, he found that the resolution of the spectrum was $4cm^{-1}$, and the range of this test was between $4000cm^{-1}$ and $400cm^{-1}$. The cumulative number of signals in the test scan is 64 times, the gain is 1, and the speed of OPD is 0.2cm per second [3] .

2 Experimental result

2.1 Determine the composition of 1,2,3,4- butane four carboxylic acid over metal complexes

Thermogravimetric analysis and elemental analysis can be used to verify the molecular formula of $Mn_2C_8H_6O_8$. The acquisition of $Mn_2C_8H_6O_8$ can be achieved by reacting M^{2+} with $(C_8H_6O_8)$. At the same time, according to the derivative thermogravimetric curves and thermogravimetric curves (as shown in Fig. 1 and Fig. 2), it is determined that the molecular formula of the final product is $Mn_2C_8H_6O_8{\cdot}nH_2O$.

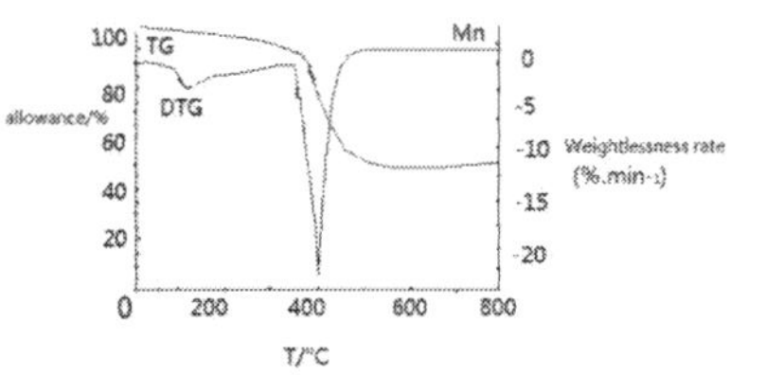

Figure 1. Derivative thermogravimetric curves.

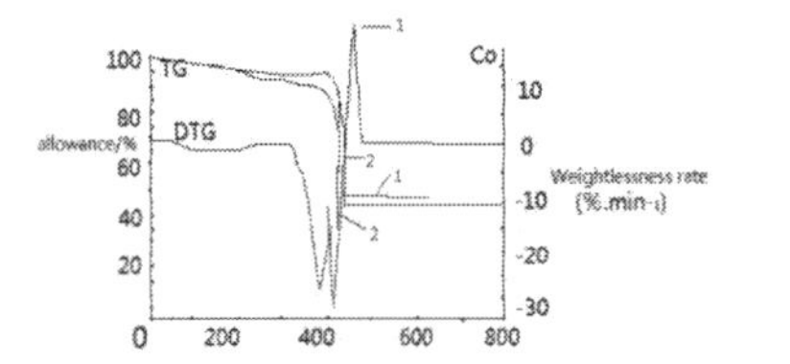

Figure 2. Thermogravimetric curves.

(1) The sample quality was 6302 mg, the experimental temperature range was 30°C to 850°C.

(2) The sample quality was 2028 mg, the experimental temperature range was 30°C to 650°C.

Through the observation of the icon, it can be found that the weight loss rate of crystalline water is when the thermogravimetric curve rises to the first stage. At the same time, the value of N can be further obtained based on this data. Under general experimental conditions, the products of thermal decomposition of the transition metal complexes are Cdo, CuO, ZnO, NiO, Co_3O_4, Mn_2O_3 and so on, in the range of temperature between 30 C and 850 C. At the same time, by analyzing the thermogravimetric data in the experiment (as shown in Table 1), it can be found that the mass fraction values of various complexes after thermal decomposition are basically consistent with the theoretical values, which further illustrates the correctness of the original formulation. Therefore, we can get the theoretical values of H% and C% according to the formulated chemical formula. After calculating the values, we can put the corresponding data into Table 2. Through the analysis of Table 2, we can conclude that the composition of the two elements (C and H) is basically the same as the formulated data. From this, we can see that the chemical formula of the complex is $M_2C_8H_6O_8{\cdot}nH_2O$, and the analysis results can thus be determined. Molecular formula for over metal complexes.

Table 1. Thermogravimetric data of complex in dynamic air atmosphere

Complex	Crystallized water		Residual mass fraction/%	Thermal decomposition of finaloxidation products
	Weightlessness rate/%	n	Measured value (calculated value)	
$Mn_2C_8H_6O_8{\cdot}nH_2O$	9. 13	2	42 38(42 00)	Mn_2O_3
$Co_2C_8H_6O_8{\cdot}nH_2O$	9. 20	2	42 25(41 80)	Co_3O_4
$Ni_2C_8H_6O_8{\cdot}nH_2O$	16. 84	4	35 32(35 60)	NiO
$Cu_2C_8H_6O_8{\cdot}nH_2O$	5. 02	1	42 60(42 40)	Cuo
$Zn_2C_8H_6O_8{\cdot}nH_2O$	9. 26	2	41 58(41 01)	Zno
$Cd_2C_8H_6O_8{\cdot}nH_2O$	7. 67	2	51 91(52 30)	CdO

Table 2. $M_2C_8H_6O_8{\cdot}nH_2O$ elemental analysis data

Complex	Colour	Elemental analysis, measured values (calculated values)/%	
		C	H
$Mn_2C_8H_6O_8{\cdot}2H_2O$	White	25 24(25 53)	2 76(2 68)
$Co_2C_8H_6O_8{\cdot}2H_2O$	Violet	24 69(25 00)	2 69(2 63)
$Ni_2C_8H_6O_8{\cdot}4H_2O$	Yellowish green	22 57(22 88)	3 43(3 36)
$Cu_2C_8H_6O_8{\cdot}H_2O$	Blue	25 20(25 59)	2 30(2 15)
$Zn_2C_8H_6O_8{\cdot}2H_2O$	White	24 08(24 17)	2 62(2 54)
$Cd_2C_8H_6O_8{\cdot}2H_2O$	White	19 21(19 55)	2 10(2 05)

2.2 Data analysis using infrared spectroscopy

Infrared spectra of 1,2,3,4-butane tetracarboxylic acid, 1,2,3,4-butane tetracarboxylic acid tetrasodium salt and their transition metal complexes were determined by infrared spectroscopy. The spectra of these three elements are shown in Table 2 (for transition metals, manganese is taken as an example, and the main characteristic peaks of A infrared spectra are shown in Table 3).

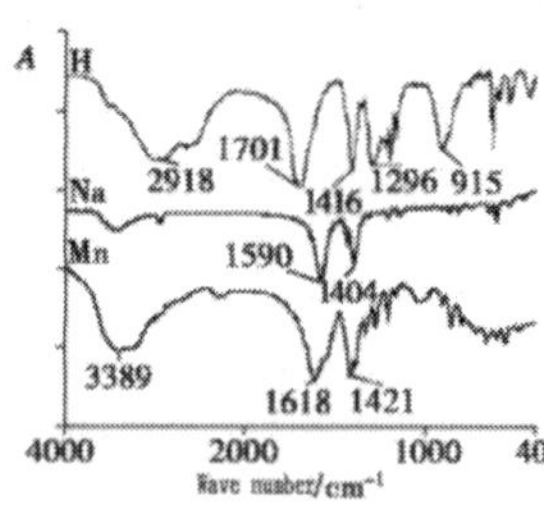

Figure 3. Infrared spectra comparison of 1,2,3,4- butane four carboxylic acid and four sodium salt and manganese complex.

Table 3. $M_2C_8H_6O_8 \cdot nH_2O$ main characteristic peaks of infrared spectra cm^{-1}

Complex	v_{OH}	$v_{as}(coo^-)$	$v_s(coo^-)$	v_{as}-v_s
$Na_4C_8H_6O_8$	3443	1590	1404	186
$Mn_2C_8H_6O_8 \cdot 2H_2O$	3389	1618	1421	197
$Co_2C_8H_6O_8 \cdot 2H_2O$	3390	1630	1419	211
$Ni_2C_8H_6O_8 \cdot 4H_2O$	3394	1631	1420	211
$Cu_2C_8H_6O_8 \cdot H_2O$	3447	1638	1434，1416	204，222
$Zn_2C_8H_6O_8 \cdot 2H_2O$	3379	1585	1423	162
$Cd_2C_8H_6O_8 \cdot 2H_2O$	3400	1578，1541	1434，1413	<186

In the infrared spectra of 1,2,3,4-butane tetracarboxylic acid ($Na_4C_8H_6O_8$), the C=O bond strong absorption peaks of -COOH are at $1701cm^{-1}$, and a pair of vibration coupling absorption peaks are at $1296cm^{-1}$ and $1416cm^{-1}$, respectively. At the same time, it can be further found that the out-of-plane angular variation of dimer carboxylic acid OH group caused wide peaks at $920cm^{-1}$ due to vibration. However, in the infrared spectra of 1,2,3,4-butanetetracarboxylic acid ($Na_4C_8H_6O_8$) and $M_2C_8H_6O_8 \cdot nH_2O$, the bond strength absorption peaks at $1701cm^{-1}$ disappeared completely, and the broad peaks of the out-of-plane angular vibration of the dimer carboxylic acid OH group also disappeared. Based on these data, it can be further concluded that the metal ions in the experimental reactions are fully compatible with - COOH, which leads to the disappearance of the C = O bond strong absorption peak of - COOH. This indicates that - COOH does not exist in $M_2C_8H_6O_8 \cdot nH_2O$, which is also consistent with the previous results of thermogravimetric analysis and elemental analysis [4]. You can see in Table 3, there is a strong absorption peak at $3447cm^{-1}$ to $3379cm^{-1}$ wide, this broad absorption peak is due to changes in peak water of crystallization -OH stretching vibration caused by the certain. The characteristics of carboxylate bands by metal ions and the carboxyl oxygen coordination mode play a great role, with ion carboxylate in metal according to figure four (coordination) three ways of coordination of [5].

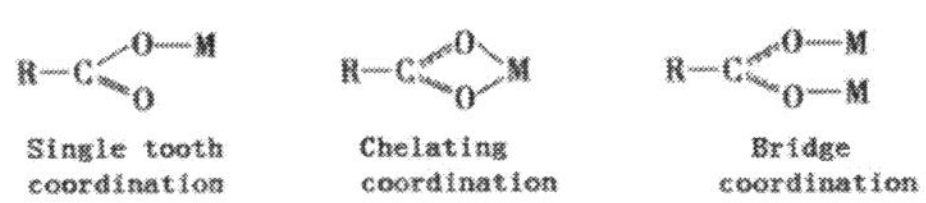

Figure 4. Coordination mode

It can be found that the size of $\Delta vcoo^-$ is the same as that of ions and ionic compounds in the three coordination modes. For example, in the single-tooth coordination mode, the $\Delta vcoo^-$ of compound itself is much larger than that of free ions; in the chelating coordination mode, the $\Delta vcoo^-$ of compound is much smaller than that of ionic compounds in the chelating coordination mode [6]. At the same time, we can see the values of $v_{as}(coo^-)$ and $v_s(coo^-)$ corresponding to $M_2C_8H_6O_8 \cdot nH_2O$ in the experiment. In order to further facilitate the experimental analysis of coordination methods, the table lists the effective data related to 1,2,3,4-butane tetracarboxylic acid ($Na_4C_8H_6O_8$), which serves as the basis for judging Δv. Taking $200cm^{-1}$ as the critical point for judging, a single-tooth coordination is greater than this value, and a double-tooth coordination is less than this value. At the same time, we can use $\Delta vcoo^-$ of sodium carboxylate and $\Delta vcoo^-$ of metal complex to judge and compare, so as to determine the form of coordination. According to the above experimental judgment basis, we can make further judgement. In the $Na_4C_8H_6O_8$ experiment of 1,2,3,4-butane tetracarboxylic acid, Co, Cu and Ni metal complexes were used as single-tooth coordination, Zn and Cd metal complexes were used as chelating coordination, and Mn metal complexes were used as bridge coordination. However, in the actual experiment, which of the three coordination modes should be used, we should also analyze and prove [7].

2.3 Data analysis using thermogravimetric analysis

Through the experimental thermogravimetric analysis, it can be concluded that the complexes of transition metals in 1,2,3,4-butane tetracarboxylic acid ($Na_4C_8H_6O_8$) experiment are different in the thermal decomposition process, which is caused by different transition metals. At the same time, we can further observe that there are two stages in the diagram of copper, Cd, Mn, Ni and Zn metal complexes: 1,2,3,4-butane tetracarboxylic acid ($Na_4C_8H_6O_8$). During the weightlessness stage, Co metal complexes began to gain weight in the third stage. Through experiments, we can know that CoO is produced during the thermal decomposition of $CO_2C_8H_6O_8 \cdot 2H_2O$ at a specific temperature, and CoO is oxidized to form Co_3O_4. At the same time, we can further find that there is a big difference between the predicted and measured values of CoO, which is due to the partial overlap between CoO and Co_2O_3 or Co_3O_4. From this we can speculate that in the whole thermal decomposition reaction, the changes experienced by the experimental substance are:

$Mn_2C_8H_6O_8 \cdot 2H_2O \rightarrow Mn_2C_8H_6O_8 \rightarrow Mn_2O_3$
$Co_2C_8H_6O_8 \cdot 2H_2O \rightarrow Co_2C_8H_6O_8 \rightarrow CoO \rightarrow Co_3O_4$
$Ni_2C_8H_6O_8 \cdot 2H_2O \rightarrow Ni_2C_8H_6O_8 \rightarrow NiO$
$Cu_2C_8H_6O_8 \cdot 2H_2O \rightarrow Cu_2C_8H_6O_8 \rightarrow CuO$
$Zn_2C_8H_6O_8 \cdot 2H_2O \rightarrow Zn_2C_8H_6O_8 \rightarrow ZnO$
$Cd_2C_8H_6O_8 \cdot 2H_2O \rightarrow Cd_2C_8H_6O_8 \rightarrow CdO$

At the same time, through the analysis of thermogravimetric curves, the order of thermal stability of metal complexes from large to small is obtained as follows: $Co_2C_8H_6O_8 \cdot 2H_2O$ > $Cd_2C_8H_6O_8 \cdot 2H_2O$ > $Mn_2C_8H_6O_8 \cdot 2H_2O$ > $Ni_2C_8H_6O_8 \cdot 2H_2O$ > $Zn_2C_8H_6O_8 \cdot 2H_2O$ > $Zn_2C_8H_6O_8 \cdot 2H_2O$ > $Cu_2C_8H_6O_8 \cdot 2H_2O$

3 Concluding remarks

In the experimental process, 1,2,3,4-butane tetracarboxylic acid tetrasodium salt ($Na_4C_8H_6O_8$) was prepared by reaction with excess metal salts. The composition and structure of the prepared metal complexes were characterized by infrared spectroscopy, thermogravimetric analysis and elemental analysis. At the same time, the thermal stability of the complex was studied by thermogravimetric analysis, and the order of thermal stability was obtained as follows: $Co_2C_8H_6O_8 \cdot 2H_2O$ > $Cd_2C_8H_6O_8 \cdot 2H_2O$ > $Mn_2C_8H_6O_8 \cdot 2H_2O$ > $Ni_2C_8H_6O_8 \cdot 2H_2O$ > $Zn_2C_8H_6O_8 \cdot 2H_2O$ > $Zn_2C_8H_6O_8 \cdot 2H_2O$ > $Cu_2C_8H_6O_8 \cdot 2H_2O$

References

1. Xiao Huifang, Yan Kelu, Ji Berlin. Application of sugar additives in wrinkle-resistant finishing of cotton fabric with 1,2,3,4-butane tetracarboxylic acid [J]. Journal of Textiles, 2018 (7): 89-94.
2. Preparation and characterization of transition metal complexes of Zhang Cheng, Zhang Lianhui, Jiang Heng, Gonghong and Wang Rui.1, 2, 3, 4-butane tetracarboxylic acid [J]. Chemical reagent, 2005 (02): 75-78.
3. Wang Licheng, Wang Jingyue, Yang Yuanyuan. Preparation of 1,2,3,4-butane tetracarboxylic acid [J/OL] by ozonation. Yunnan Chemical Industry: 1-5 [2018-10-13].
4. Xingjun Gao, Huan Zhang, Xianhong Wen, Bin Liu, Shouwen Jin, Daqi Wang. Structure of seven organic salts assembled from 2,6-diaminopyridine with monocarboxylic acids, dicarboxylic acids, and tetracarboxylic acids [J]. Journal of Molecular Structure, 2015, 1093.
5. Guo Zhengnan, Liu E, Wei Xi, Tang Qun, Li Huanlin. Synthesis, characterization and properties of metal-organic frameworks using 1,2,4,5-benzotetracarboxylic acid or 1,2,3,4-butane tetracarboxylic acid as ligands [J]. Journal of Inorganic Chemistry, 2016,32(01): 9-17.
6. Hao Wenbo, Yan Kelu, Chen Yongbang, Huang Jinxu. Antimicrobial/wrinkle-resistant composite finishing of cotton fabric with chitosan and butane tetracarboxylic acid [J]. Journal of Textiles, 2016, 37 (06): 95-100.
7. Wang Li, Jia Ru, Zhou Yonghua. Study on the reaction process of butane tetracarboxylic acid [J]. Acetaldehyde acetic acid chemical industry, 2016 (07): 14-15+22.

Analysis and Development Forecast of Water Resources in China

Ning E[1,a],

[1]*Basic teaching and research department of Harbin finance university Xiang fang district Harbin China*

Abstract. Based on the background of water shortage in Ningxia region, this paper studies the current situation and development prediction of water resources in China and establishes a regression analysis mode. Firstly, the current situation and major problems of water resources development and utilization in China were analyzed with Excel. Secondly, the regression model is established to predict the total national water consumption in 2020 and 2030, the results of the model prediction are compared with the national goals of 2020 and 2030. Finally, the ARIMA model was established by SPSS software to predict the time series and obtain the national and provincial water resource management and control and development trends in 2020 and 2030.

1 The introduction

In recent years, more people and less water and uneven spatial and temporal distribution of water resources are China's basic national conditions and water situation, the shortage of water resources, serious water pollution and deterioration of water ecology are very serious problems, which have become the main bottleneck of economic and social sustainable development. With the further development of industrialization and urbanization, the demand for water resources will continue to grow over a long period of time, the contradiction between supply and demand of water resources will be more acute, and the situation of water resources in China will be more serious.

2 The present situation of development and utilization of water resources in China and its main problems

According to the water resources bulletin 2012-2016, China's surface water resources and groundwater resources have little change each year, precipitation is greatly affected by other factors such as climate. See below.

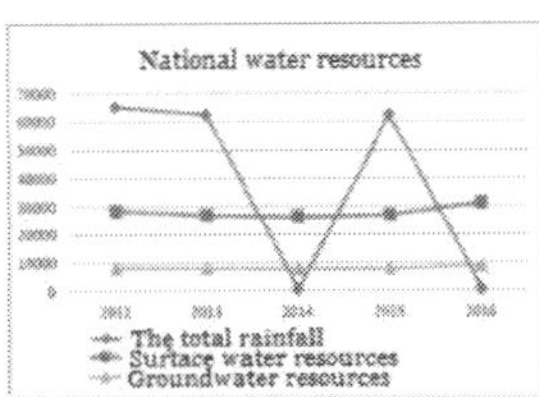

Figure 1. National water resources

The development and utilization of water resources situation in our country, from the national surface water exploitation and utilization of significantly more than the development and utilization of groundwater, mainly composed of surface water and groundwater is complementary, but different from the north-south geographical position, exploitation and utilization of six in the north area of surface water and groundwater development and utilization of a smaller gap was basically use at the same time, the status of exploitation and utilization of six in the south area of surface water and groundwater development and utilization of the gap is great, basic is in a state of only the surface water.

2.1 Use SPSS to process the data

Table 1. Anova

Model	Sum of squares	df	The mean square	F	Sig
Return to the	6874.884	1	6874.884	5.026	.111
Residual	4103.596	3	1367.865		
A total of	10978.480	4			

Conclusion R=0.791 regression model

$$Y = -26.220 + 6189.260 + \text{delta}$$

(The total value of allowance is not large, which is negligible in the range of allowable error.)

2.2 Compare the deviation with the target and make comparative analysis

According to the water resources bulletin of 2012-2016, use the regression function to predict water consumption in 2020 and 2030, the national water consumption in 2020 is 606.639.95 billion cubic meters, while that in 2030 is 602.521.7 billion cubic meters, which is quite different from the national target of 2020 and 2030, The predicted value is smaller than the target value, which indicates that the water consumption will be effectively controlled under the existing control measures.

3 Water consumption of ten thousand yuan of industrial added value

For industrial water use efficiency in different parts of the situation, in a study period, the region may be at an early stage, may also be a stage of development, gradually to the late stage of development, it is possible that the experience of development, early and late three times, so this article take the various types of mathematical curve model to fitting was carried out on the water consumption per ten thousand yuan of value-added by industry series.

3.1 Exponential model

In assuming the added value of industrial water consumption of ten thousand yuan a year relative change rate of linear change, then you can get a general solution, but for a specific area, single years of water consumption per ten thousand yuan of value-added by industry relative rate of change due to random variation is very big, can't fully satisfy the assumption, in this case, can use moving average or the geometric average method to analyze the sequence of potential change rule. According to the relative change speed sequence of water consumption per 10,000 yuan of industrial added value per year in anhui province, it can't reflect its law well. After the geometric average every four years, the sequence has a linear change trend.

3.2 Logistic model

In describing the biological growth rule, a Logistic model is commonly used to describe and the meanings of the model as follows: when the early growth of a species, because of the space and the food is enough, then the relative growth rate is a constant value of species, but as the number of biological development to a certain extent, with the competition between species makes biological development space and food source is not enough, so the relative growth rate will slow, eventually biomass to a certain limit. If the development of industrial water efficiency in a certain region has experienced three stages, including initial stage, development stage and later stage, the Logistic model can be shifted symmetrically, and the water consumption sequence of 10,000 yuan of industrial added value in this region can be fitted with the formula obtained by the transformation. The specific transformation results are as follows

$$P(t) = M' + \frac{P_0'}{1 + \frac{M'}{M' - P_0'} e^{kt}} \quad (1)$$

We take the derivative of this

$$\frac{dP}{dt} = -k(P - M)\left(1 - \frac{P - M}{P_0}\right) \quad (2)$$

It can be seen that the water consumption of ten thousand yuan of industrial added value decreased slowly in the initial stage, then the decline speed gradually increased, and finally slowed down, until reaching a certain stable lower limit.

3.3 Other functions

For the water consumption series of 10,000 yuan of industrial added value, the overall trend is downward, so other decline functions can also be used to try to fit the data series. From the actual data fitting, this paper recommends the following formula:

$$W(t) = \frac{a}{t^2 + b} \quad (3)$$

The decline trend of the water consumption of ten thousand yuan of industrial added value can be predicted by the annual average decline rate, which is expressed as

$$W_t = W_0(I - J)^t \quad (4)$$

The added value of ten thousand yuan of industrial water consumption forecast based on the ten thousand - 2010 water resources bulletin of the national and the provincial data of water consumption per ten thousand yuan of value-added by industry, and make use of national and provincial industrial production index, converts all water consumption per ten thousand yuan of value-added by industry in 2010, constant, using mathematical functions mentioned above, using the m atlab curve fitting toolbox curve f it - ting tool for curve fitting. Then, the water consumption of 10 thousand yuan of industrial added value in China and provinces was predicted by using the fitting function.

3.4 Forecast of water consumption per 10,000 yuan of industrial added value

Time series was used as the independent variable, water consumption of ten thousand industrial added value was used as the dependent variable, and 1997 was used as the first year for fitting, and the fitting result was expressed as

$$y = 288.3e^{-0.08275x} \quad (5)$$

Formula (5) is used to predict the water consumption of 10,000 yuan of industrial added value nationwide. The calculation result is 598 rn / 10,000 yuan, which is lower than the target value of 63 m / 10,000 yuan.

The same method was used to predict the wc per ten thousand yuan of industrial added value in all provinces in 2015. In the actual operation process, it was found that the wc per ten thousand yuan of industrial added value in Tibet autonomous region was not obvious.

4 Model evaluation and improvement

4.1 Model evaluation and improvement

This model USES ARIMA model to predict the development trend of water resources management and control, according to the official website to find the data can be predicted in 2020-2030 of ten thousand yuan GDP water consumption, actual irrigation water consumption per acre of arable land and water consumption per ten thousand yuan of value-added by industry development trend, thus the rationality of the results and precision is very high, and we only, it is concluded that the calculation results for data request is not high.

4.2 Disadvantages of the model

We use the time series model in the prediction. The time series analysis prediction method is to predict the future development based on the past trend of the country and provinces, and its premise is that the past of things will continue to the future. Need to point out that, f series forecasting method for outstanding between time series of short duration does not consider outside factors, so there is a defect prediction error, when faced with the outside world, great changes have taken place tend to have larger deviation, the effect of the time series prediction method for short-term earthquake prediction than the long-term forecast effect is good, we get the model also exist significant is not strong, so need to be improved.

Thank you

This paper is one of the periodical achievements of the Heilongjiang provincial youth academic backbone project, the dynamic model of measles infectious disease based on delay differential equation.

References

1. Xue Wei. SPSS based data analysis [M]. Beijing: Renmin university of China press, (2006: 107-121).
2. Han Zhonggeng. Mathematical modeling methods and their applications, Beijing: advanced education press, (2005).
3. Qin Xuhua. Technology innovation and application, discussion on improving utilization coefficient of irrigation water, issue (08, 2013).
4. Luo Bin. Research and application of a fast estimation method of software function scale based on linear regression analysis, university of national defense science and technology, (2013-05-01).

How to Construct Effective Consultation System for S&T Decision-making

Zijun Tang[1,a]

[1]*Office of Scientific Research Management Jishou University Jishou Hunan China*

Abstract. With the development of a new round of science and technology (S&T) revolution and industrial transformation in the world, the complexity of S&T decision-making is increasing. It not only needs the comprehensive participation of scientific, technological, economic, educational and other social factors but also an effective consultation system to guarantee. To build an effective consultation system for S&T decision-making, a lot of measures can be taken, such as establishing the system of the policy and regulation, perfecting the multi-mode operation system, constructing the support system of talent team, developing of multi-channel financing system, optimizing the system of social public participation and strengthening the system of interactive international cooperation.

1 Introduction

The consultation system of S&T decision-making is the inevitable result of scientific and technological progress and social development, and also the inherent requirement for government decision-making. As a result of the new round of scientific and technological revolution and industrial transformation, the complexity of science and technology strategy and policy making is increasing, and the comprehensive participation of scientific, technological, economic, educational and other social factors and various think tanks is needed. China also attaches great importance to the construction of the consultation system of S&T decision-making. In January 2015, *The Opinions on Strengthening the Construction of a New Think Tank with Chinese Characteristics*, issued by the Office of the CPC Central Committee and General Office of State Council, emphasized that "the consultation system of the decision-making is an important part of the construction of socialist democratic politics in China, and the new think tank with Chinese characteristics is an important content of the modernization of the national governance system and also an important part of the country's soft power "[1]. In September 2015, the Office of the CPC Central Committee and General Office of State Council issued *The Implementation Plan for Deepening the Reform of the Scientific and Technological System*, which called for "the establishment of a national consultation mechanism of innovation and S&T decision-making, the development of a good scientific and technological community and think tank to support innovation and S&T decision-making, the establishment of a national advisory committee of S&T decision-making" [2].On the May 30, 2016, General Secretary Xi Jinping stressed in his important speech *Striving to Build a World Science and Technology Power*, "We should speed up the establishment of mechanism of S&T decision-making to support administrative decision-making, strengthen the consultation system of S&T decision-making, and build a high level science and technology think tank to accelerate the institutionalization of major scientific and technological decisions "[3] February 2017, the CPC Central Committee passed the *Plan of the Construction Program of National Consultation System of S&T Decision-making*, pointed out to build a national consultation system and a think tank at the highest level of S&T decision-making. The Plan is a re-promotion of China's current consultation mechanism of S&T decision-making, marking the China's consultation of S&T decision-making is on the process of institutionalization and systematization. There are a lot of measures can be taken to construct the effective consultation system for S&T decision-making in China.

2 Improving the policy and regulation guarantee system

The smooth development of consultation of S&T decision-making is guaranteed by sound policies and regulations. Developed countries all regard the construction of perfect legal system as the key to promote the consultation of decision-making. The supporting policies and regulations of consultation of S&T decision-making in China are in the initial stage and need to be strengthened and improved in the following four aspects. The first is to incorporate consultation into the legal procedures for major decision-making of government departments, protect the legal status

[a] Corresponding author: zijuntang@163.com

of consulting bodies through relevant laws and regulations, and specify their power and responsibility relationship, expert selection, organizational structure and operation mode; Secondly, the status and role of different types of consultation bodies in decision-making should be clarified through legislation. In particular, the consultation procedures should be standardized and designed through specific legal provisions to ensure the relative independence of consultation bodies. Meanwhile, corresponding incentive measures should be formulated according to different consultation situations; Thirdly, establish the application and feedback system of important S&T decision-making consultation achievements, and strengthen the legal regulation of the formation, release and use of consultation reports. Fourthly, establish a supervision system and restriction mechanism for S&T decision-making consultation, and a public disclosure and hearing system for major decision-making matters, ensure the openness of all links and procedures of decision-making consultation, protect the right of supervision and information of the public, and promote the openness, transparency and fairness of decision-making consultation activities.

3 Perfecting the multi-mode operation system

It is a common direction for the development of consultation system of S&T decision-making in various countries to construct different and complementary consultation systems at different levels and of various types. It is a common practice in the international community to set up a committee with members spanning all fields, controlling the number of members and highlighting their representativeness. China has already established the construction plan of the national science and technology advisory committee, and it is necessary to further improve the operation mode of the institution. At the horizontal level, to promote the coordinated development of official advisory bodies and parastatal and civil advisory bodies, encourage the Government to purchase consultation services of S&T decision-making, support the development of market-oriented decision-making advisory bodies through corresponding policy measures, strengthen their financial support, and enhance the status and influence of civil decision-making advisory bodies, finally form a useful supplement to the official advisory body, make China's consultation of S&T decision-making to the direction of specialization. At the vertical level, there is a need for a multi-tiered and complementary advisory body layout, based on the hierarchical distribution of existing decision-making advisory bodies, from the national level, the sectoral level to the grass-roots level and social institutions. For example, in the case of high-level consultation on major political and diplomatic decisions, the national advisory committee on science and technology may make advisory recommendations on such decisions. When it comes to decision-making in the social and public fields, appropriate decision-making consultation bodies may be set up according to the local characteristics and actual conditions of various departments, institutions and regions. The perfect operation mechanism is the premise to ensure the decision-making level to grasp the relevant policy information accurately, timely and systematically, provide objective and reasonable scientific support for decision-making, and is also the key to test its effectiveness.

4 Constructing the support system of talent team

The high-quality S&T decision-making consultation needs the novelty, reliability and policy relevance of knowledge, which will inevitably put forward special requirements for the construction of talent team in decision-making consultation bodies. According to the present situation of decision-making consultation in China, it should be firstly focused on cultivating interdisciplinary knowledge talents and strengthening the ability of strategic research. In order to better cope with increasingly complex decision-making problems and enhance the effectiveness of decision-making suggestions, it is necessary to cultivate research talents with multi-disciplinary complementarity and cross-disciplinary advantages, and pay attention to the selection and training of talents in terms of professional depth, disciplinary breadth, scientific height and social perspective. Secondly, the evaluation and incentive mechanism of S&T decision consultation talents should be constructed through targeted measures. It will be formulated that unified and standardized evaluation standards for the employment, professional title assessment, moral character and ability and social contribution of talents, and take the social impact of the consultation recommendations as the core assessment indicators. At the same time, by encouraging original ideas, respect for intellectual property rights, the establishment of talent program projects and other methods, to stimulate the healthy development of consulting talent team, to provide sustainable talent support for decision-making consultation, enhance the capacity and level of S&T decision-making advisory bodies. Thirdly, it should be pay more attention to cultivating and promoting the professional ethics of decision-making consultation talents. In the selection of advisory members and experts, social responsibility and academic ethics should be the basic standards, and the professionalism of responsible consultation should be actively promoted so that S&T decision-making consultation can truly win the affirmation and trust of the society.

5 Developing multi-channel financing system

A certain amount of financial support is a necessary condition for the normal operation of decision-making advisory bodies. The advisory bodies of developed countries are mainly funded by government grants, corporate grants, private donations and dues. At present, China mainly supports the operation of decision-making advisory bodies through the way of government financial allocation, while the proportion of enterprises and private financial support needs to be further improved. Therefore, the management system of decision-making consultation funds should be reformed, change the homogenization mode of financing, encourage enterprises to invest in the establishment of advisory bodies and promote their market-oriented operation. At the same time, civil and individual donations, etc., should also be given some recognition and support, in order to further enrich the funding sources of decision-making advisory bodies. Of course, whether it is from the public finances or corporate sponsorship and social donations, there should be transparent and open management of financial intervention in order to prevent the possible existence of "undercover operation" through financial support, affecting or shaping the advisory opinions. Then the advisory bodies are not disturbed by some kind of "external" factors and can objectively provide independent advice on a fair attitude.

6 Optimizing the system of public participation in society.

Many decision-making problems in social development are often closely related to the public interest, and actively promoting public participation is of great significance to improve the sound consultation system of S&T decision-making. Firstly, through the systematic formulation of system rules, introducing orderly and effectively public participation in the progress of decision-making advisory activities can help to jointly promote the formation of decision-making solutions, and also can make the decision-making advisory bodies widely accept public supervision, better promote the openness and transparency of the consultation process; Secondly, the Government should strengthen the guiding role of public participation in decision-making, speed up the institutionalization of public participation, create a good institutional environment, make public participation an integral part of the decision-making consultation process, so that the public really enjoy the right to participate in decision-making consultation, and have a practical role and influence in the process of decision-making consultation; Thirdly, a multi-subject decision-making consultation platform including government, S&T decision-making advisory bodies and the public should be further built, so as to smooth out the information communication channels between the government and the society.

7 Strengthening the system of interactive international cooperation

In the context of globalization, international influence is one of the important goals pursued by S&T decision-making advisory bodies, for which most national decision-making advisory bodies adopt open policies and conduct international research, operation and exchange in order to obtain a voice on international issues. In order to meet the requirements of the new era, China should further promote the international development of S&T decision-making consultation, and promote the competitive platform of intellectual products to the international market. Firstly, carry out cooperative research and exchange dialogue with foreign S&T decision-making advisory bodies, draw on their organizational methods, operating models and discourse paradigms, and selectively integrate them into the construction of our own advisory bodies in accordance with the actual situation in China. Secondly, expand the voice of domestic decision-making advisory bodies in the international arena, strive to "lead" in some global issues and China issues that arouse world concern, and build a group of decision-making advisory bodies with international influence. Thirdly, cultivate a team of consulting talents with critical spirit and innovative consciousness, international discourse ability and competitiveness, launch original research achievements with the value of the times and global consciousness, and improve the academic reputation in the international arena. The last is to actively promote the establishment of S&T decision-making advisory branches abroad, as a means of establishing effective international cooperative relations for the exchange platform, and to expand the international recognition and influence of advisory bodies through advisory activities on China's foreign policy.

Acknowledgement

This paper was financially supported by the project of Science and Technology Plan of Xiangxi Autonomous Prefecture, "The Research on the Mechanism of University -affiliated think tanks participating in Local Science and Technology Innovation Decision-making consultation" (No.2018SF5015)

References

1. The Executive Office of the CPC Central Committee and General Office. On strengthening Chinese characteristics Views on the construction of a new think tank. [2016-09-30]. http://www.gov.cn/Xinwen/201501/20/content_2807126.htm
2. The Executive Office of the CPC Central Committee and General Office. Deepening the implementation of scientific and technological system reform case. [2016-09-30]. http://www.gov.cn/guowuyuan/2015/09/24/Content_2938314.htm
3. Xi Jinping. Strive to build a world science and technology power. *People's Daily*, **6**(2016).

Talking about the Application of High-tech Elements in the Innovative Design of Daily-use Ceramics

Fei Yu [a]

The department of art and design, Jingdezhen University, Jingdezhen, Jiangxi, China

Abstract. The relationship between technology and design is an eternal discussion as well as controversial topic. In the innovative design of daily-use ceramics, the advancement of technology has brought a lot of room for development in this field. This article will elaborate some effective combination of high-tech technology in daily-use ceramic design in the following four aspects: the combination of electronic technology and daily-use ceramics; the application of double-layer thermal insulation ceramics in the molding process; the analysis of the application of materials such as temperature-sensitive inks and the intervention of new healthy elements such as biochemical materials in the processing technology and surface treatment. Through these aspects to explore the current breakthrough in the design of daily-use ceramics.

1 The effective combination of electronic technology and innovative design of daily-use ceramics

In terms of molding process, one of the most prominent manifestations in recent years is the combination of various materials and ceramic materials. This will result in a variety of different process molding methods appearing in the design of daily-use ceramics, moreover, it has become a new design highlight that the combinative design of electronic technology and ceramic materials. There are three cases to illustrate the successful application of this aspect. The first one is the design of the ceramic heating cup in Figure 1, which consists of a cup body, a heating device and a bottom case. It is characterized in that: the bottom of the cup body is convex, the heating device is connected by a coil, an electronic temperature controller and a power connector, the electronic temperature controller is fixed at the bottom of the cup body, and the coil enwinds around the cup body protruding at the bottom to form a heating coil, the power connector is fixed on the bottom case, and the bottom case covers the bottom of the cup body and the heating device. The electric heating ceramic cup can be directly connected to the USB interface of computers or the vehicle power supply, as well as can be suitable for use in office and automobile.

Figure 1 USB ceramic heating cup

The successful design of another case is the combinative design of the CD player and the coffee cup in the picture. The coffee cup is as the knob part of the CD player, which has both aesthetic and practical dual effects. It's a blessing to enjoy your favorite concert while enjoying the wonderful taste of coffee! (Figure 2)

Figure 2 CD coffee cup

The cup in Figure 3 is a perfect combination of electronic components and ceramic design. It is a light-emitting cup with an inductive switch design. This cup is illuminated by an energy-saving LED light. If it is not touched for a long time, the light itself goes out. Such a cup is very suitable for using in places where lighting is not sufficient. You can imagine this kind of induction lighting design, using in other varieties of daily-use ceramics can also inspire some new ideas of designers, giving users a sense of freshness and at the same time, it is suitable for modern people to seek the idea of stimulating life!

Figure 3 Untouched effect and Light effect after touch

2 Improvements in the molding process have promoted more innovations in the combination of beauty and function of daily-use ceramics

In the past, the ceramic cup has always maintained its own thin appearance, while now there are some new technological trends in the design of the cup. For example, it is an unique and novel design that the insulated. ceramic cup in Figure 4, which breaking through the traditional ceramic pattern, integrating daily use and functional art. Also, it caters to the aesthetic values of modern people. Its inner tank is filled with new nano ceramic materials, which are fired at high temperature. It is high technology, and has various compound functions, great thermal stability (180 degrees -- 20 degrees heat exchange without cracking). The shell is a fully transparent pc material (commonly known as space glass). It has many functions such as high strength, good toughness, difficult breaking, playing a role in protection, decoration, heat insulation, relative insulation and so forth.

Figure 4 Ceramic cup

The PANTON insulation cup is a premium quality mug with a combination of aesthetics and craftsmanship (Figure 5). One-time compression molding, the double-layered cup body forms a hollow heat-insulating area in the middle, which has the function of heat preservation and anti-scalding. No matter whether it is cold juice or hot tea in the cup, it will not make the hand holding the cup feel too cold or too hot. When using it to fill cold drinks, it is not easy to produce water drops on the outer edge of the cup which always drip wet the tabletop.

The PANTON insulation cup is a premium quality mug with a combination of aesthetics and craftsmanship (Figure 5). One-time compression molding, the double-layered cup body forms a hollow heat-insulating area in the middle, which has the function of heat preservation and anti-scalding. No matter whether it is cold juice or hot tea in the cup, it will not make the hand holding the cup feel too cold or too hot. When using it to fill cold drinks, it is not easy to produce water drops on the outer edge of the cup which always drip wet the tabletop.

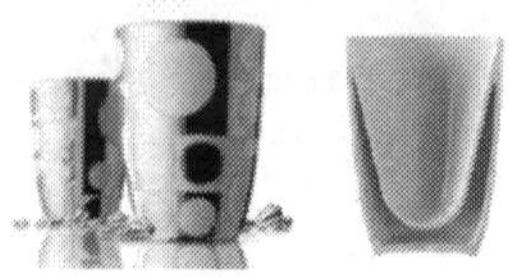

Figure 5 The picture of ceramic molding profile

Beautiful cup pattern from Geometry 1 designed by Verner Panton in 1960. The insulated cup is fired with high-quality porcelain clay at the high temperature of 1320 Celsius. With excellent strength and surface quality, this cup has won the accreditation of the FORM and DESIGN PLUS design awards for its superb design. One of the similar designs is a double-layer insulated green cup with the modern style produced by Starbucks in Figure 6. This double-layer cup also has a concept of environmental protection, which makes these portable double-layer ceramic cups replace the paper cups that were often used before, in order to reduce the pressure of the earth's pollution!

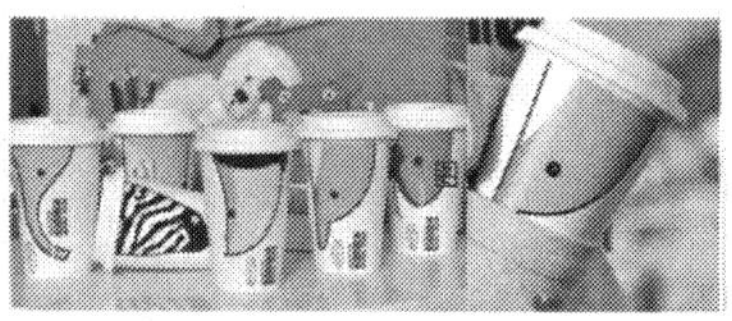

Figure 6 Ceramic cup

3 In terms of external processing technology, the development of external materials has added new elements to the innovative design of daily-use ceramics

3.1 Application of temperature-changing ink materials on the surface decoration of daily-use ceramics

In the past, the exterior decoration of daily-use ceramics' model was mostly based on flower paper design, while the material of flower paper can only show a constant appearance. However, nowadays, the application of temperature-changing ink materials has brought new improving room for the field of flower paper design (Figure 7). Temperature-changing ink, also known as thermochromic ink and changing color after meeting heat, is a special ink that can change color with temperature, because it undergoes physical changes (such as taking off crystal water, crystal structural interconversion, spatial configuration interconversion, etc.) or chemical changes (decomposition, compounding, oxidation, reduction, etc.),

 https://doi.org/10.1051/itmconf/20192503008

leading to changes in molecular structure and molecular morphology. As the result, it has an effect of color changing in appearance, which is classified into reversible achromatism, reversible coloration, reversible changing color, memory type, interval coloration, irreversible coloration and non-reversible color seven series. Anyone who can restore the original color of the pigment after the temperature drops is called the reversible thermochromic effect; otherwise it is called the irreversible thermochromic effect. Generally, a temperature-sensitive pigment can only produce one color, which is called a single thermochromic effect; when two or more temperature-sensitive pigments are used together, two or more colors can be produced during heating, which is called multi thermochromic effect (Figure 8).

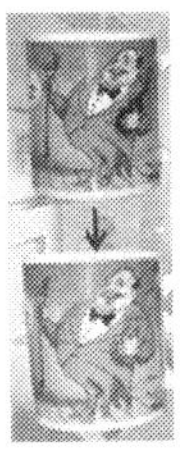

Figure 7 ceramic cup

Figure 8 ceramic cup

3.2 Application of electroplating silver and electroplating gold technology

The application of electroplating technology glazing on the electroplating is bright no glazing, is matte electroplating, is the process of electroplating a thin layer of other metals or alloys on certain metal surfaces by using principle of electrolysis, is the process of attaching a metal film to the surface of metal or other material parts to prevent corrosion, improve wear resistance, electrical conductivity, light reflection, enhance aesthetics and other functions by using electrolysis effect (Figure 9).

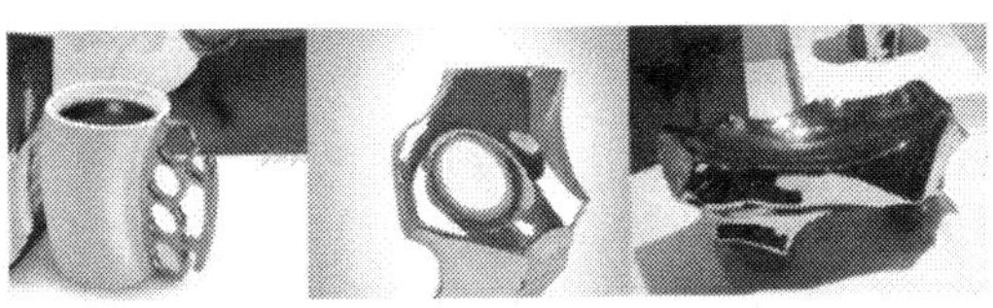

Figure 9 other functions ceramics

4. Application of biochemical elements in the design of daily-use ceramics

The 21st century is a new century in which high-tech advances the world to develop. The world's ceramics and Chinese ceramics in the new century didn't demonstrate the past features. At present, the problem of the amount of heavy metals such as lead and cadmium in daily-use porcelain has been basically solved. Most of the daily-use porcelains like decaling on glazes, coloring on glazes and coloring underglazes have achieved the requirements of non-toxic, durability and beauty. With the development of technology and the improvement of people's living standards, it is increasing that the requirements for improving the living environment, improving the quality of life and cherishing the health of the body. People have raised the basic functions of daily-use ceramics from aesthetics and using to a high requirement. Therefore, developing design and producing daily porcelain with the functions of antibacterial health care have a wide development potential.

Figure 10 ceramic cup

Shows a new product in the past few years. The tourmaline bone china double-layer activated water health cup is a double-layer heat insulation applied by one-time grouting (in the same condition, it is increased 30% than the ordinary tea cup on effect of heat preservation); at the same time, the tourmaline activation ball has the function of health care on the human body. Tourmaline is a natural crystal gemstone with unique piezoelectric effect and thermoelectric effect, which has various promoting effects on human health: it can improve human microcirculation by launching the far-infra red which the wavelength is 4-14 micrometers, called as "light of life" and matching with the far infrared wave of the human body; it can also release negative ions called as "air vitamins." The water is instantly activated by the tourmaline biochemical ceramic bead filter. Then the generated hydroxy anion can eliminate and neutralize oxygen free radicals in the body, play an antioxidant role. After drinking a long period of time, it can enhance immunity, delay aging, prevent cancer, prevent diabetes, cardiovascular and cerebrovascular diseases and other chronic, non-communicable diseases.

Of course, tourmaline is not the only type of biochemical materials, there are many materials such as medical stone and photocatalyst antibacterial agents, rare earth elements, silver antibacterial agents and so forth, which we can apply to the innovative design of daily-use ceramics. These healthy new ceramics will form a new trend in the innovative design of daily-use ceramics.

From the above analysis of the four points, we can see that the innovations of daily-use ceramic design are endless, and the development of all aspects of technology has promoted the pace of daily-use ceramic design. The above four points are just some small parts in this big ocean. The design is to make our life better, and our designers are slowly tasting our wonderful life brought by new technologies and discovering more new creative ideas through after tasting, in order to create a new height point for our China in daily-use ceramic design in international status.

References

1. Yang Yongshan. Ceramic Model Design [M]. Shenyang: Liaoning Science and Technology Press, 1988
2. Wang Xiaomu. Ceramic Technology [M]. Beijing: Light Industry Press, 1995
3. Xu Kaiqiang. Product Semantics - A Beautiful Interpretation of Design [J]. Packaging and Design, 1999, (1): 84 - 86
4. Wang Jianzhong. International Ceramic Design Grand View [M]. Beijing: Beijing Arts and Crafts Press, 1991.

ITM Web of Conferences **25**, 03009 (2019) https://doi.org/10.1051/itmconf/20192503009
ICICCI 2018

Research on the Construction Path of Power Financial Market in China under the New Situation of Power Reform

Menghua Fan[1], Haoyuan Qu[1]

[1]*State Grid Energy Research Institute Co., LTD (SGERI), No. 18 Binhe Road, Future Science Park, Beijing, China*

Abstract. In China, with the deepening of power reform and construction of the electricity spot market, urgent and realistic demands have been put forward for the construction of power financial trading market. In this paper, based on the background of power market construction and current power financial transaction practice, the significance of introducing power financial transaction is analysed and the path for construction of power financial transaction market in China is proposed.

1 Background of power market construction in China

In 1998, China began to build a competitive power market on the power generation side. Pilot projects were carried out in the six provinces (municipalities) electricity market and the northeast, eastern and southern regional electricity market, and combined with the practice of various forms of power trading such as cross-provincial trading, the generation right trading, direct trading between power user and power generating enterprise. It has made a beneficial exploration in the construction of the power market. After the issuance of "Some Opinions on Further Deepening the Power Reform ([2015] No.9)" by the Central Committee of the Communist Party of China and the State Council in 2015 [1], the pace of China's power market construction has been accelerating, the policy system and market rules have been continuously improved, and the market system combining mid-to-long-term and spot has been gradually established. The market size power has reached a certain scale, and the reform dividends have been accelerated release. In 2017, the national electricity market transaction power totalled 1632.4 billion kWh, accounting for 33.5% of the national power sales (i.e. the marketization rate of sales power), accounting for 25.9% of the total social electricity consumption. With the continuous growth of market size trading power and the gradual improvement of various physical trading mechanisms, urgent and realistic demands have been put forward for the construction of electricity and finance trading market of China.

2 The practical significance of introducing power financial transaction

On the one hand, introducing power financial transactions is an inevitable trend to improve China's power market system. In "Some Opinions on Further Deepening the Power Reform ([2015] No.9)", the government demands speeding up the construction of the power market, and proposes to "explore the trading of electricity futures and electricity over-the-counter derivatives when the conditions are ripe, and provide forward price benchmarks and risk management tools for power generation companies, power sellers and users". At present, China is still in the initial stage of power market construction, mainly to carry out the medium and long-term electricity trading and spot power market pilot projects. In the future, transaction varieties should be gradually enriched, and a diversified market system including electricity market, auxiliary service market, financial market, capacity market and green certificate transaction, etc. should be established and perfected as soon as possible. The development experience of the mature power market in the world shows that the power finance market is an important part of the complete power market system, which helps to discover the real price of electricity and enhance the liquidity of the market. Meanwhile, it can provide risk management tools for market participants and guarantee the smooth and orderly operation of the market.

On the other hand, introducing power financial transactions is a realistic requirement for China to deepen the reform of the power market. At present, China's power trading is still dominated by physical contracts. With the proportion of market trading power continues to increase, the physical execution of power trading contracts is subject to greater deviation adjustment pressures in the day before and during the day. At the same time, with the advancement of the power spot market pilot, the market participants face greater operational risks. Therefore, some regions in China have

[a] Menghua Fan: fanmenghua@sgeri.sgcc.com.cn

begun to explore the "medium and long-term Contract for Difference (CFD) + Whole electricity quantity spot competition" centralized market trading model. CFD is a kind of power finance derivative that is widely used in the UK power pool market model, Australia and other power markets. It can be seen that with the launch of the spot market pilot, gradually introducing of power financial trading tools (for example, CFDs) is of great practical significance for exploring the power spot market model suitable for the national conditions, alleviating the pressure on balance of electric power and energy, gradually increasing the market size trading power, and deepening the construction of the power market.

In addition, the development of power finance transactions has a positive effect on enriching and implementing the functions of the trading center and promoting the large-scale optimal allocation of resources. In February 2016, the National Development and Reform Commission and the National Energy Administration issued the "Reply on the Establishment Scheme of Beijing and Guangzhou Power Trading Centers" [2], and approved the "Beijing Power Trading Center Formation Scheme" to clarify the future power finance transactions of the Beijing Power Trading Center. It can be seen that with the deepening of market construction, further enriching the market trading varieties and gradually exploring the power financial transactions is the actual need to enrich and implement the functions of the power trading center. At the same time, due to better market liquidity and flexibility of the power finance market, it can achieve a wider range and more market participants to participate in the market, and to guide medium and long-term power system planning through price signals, which is of great significance for promoting the optimized allocation of nationwide resources.

3 The current status of power financial transaction practice in China

The current domestic power transaction is still dominated by physical contracts, and have not yet formed a mature power finance market. Mainly combined with actual conditions of China and the demand for flexible adjustment of medium and long-term trading contracts, practical exploration of financial transactions has been carried out, such as the generation right trading, contract repurchase, transfer, replacement transactions, etc.

3.1 The generation right trading

The generation rights trading is mainly based on traditional planned electricity management of China, and is a transitional trading method proposed to implement energy conservation and emission reduction policies and balance the interests of all parties. In the foreign power market, the variety of generation rights trading has not been clearly proposed and defined. According to the "Interim Measures for the Supervision of Generation Rights Trading" (Electricity Supervision Market [2008] No.15) [3], which is issued by the former State Electricity Regulatory Commission (SERC), generation rights trading refers to the trading behaviour of realizing the substitution of electricity between generator sets and power plants by means of the market, i.e. the compensated transfer and purchase of scheduled contract energy. According to the transaction mode, the generation rights trading mainly includes centralized bidding trading and bilateral negotiation trading. The transaction price under the bilateral negotiation trading mode is negotiated by both parties of the generation rights trading. The price formation mechanism under the centralized bidding mode mainly includes the high and low matching mechanism and the unified clearing mechanism. According to the trading range, the generation rights trading can be divided into generation rights trading in the province and the inter-provincial generation rights trading. According to the trading cycles, the generation rights trading mainly includes the annual, quarterly, monthly, weekly and over a week medium and short-term trading. In 2017, the scale of the generation rights transfer trading in the national grid operation area totalled 121.4 billion kWh, accounting for about 10% of the market size trading power in 2017, accounting for 3% of the total electricity.

3.2 Contract repurchase, transfer and replacement transactions

The contract adjustment transactions such as contract repurchase, transfer and replacement are in the medium and long-term power market environment in China, through the market size way to realize the compensated transfer and purchase of the contract power, which have been signed between the market participants. The contract repurchase transaction is negotiated by the parties to the original contract, and the seller repurchases the trading volume of some of the trading power. The repurchased electricity and price are determined by the parties to the contract. A contract transfer transaction is a transaction in which all or part of the contract's electricity is transferred to a third party other than the contract. The contract replacement transaction means that the two parties to the transaction will replace their respective power sales (or power purchase) contract execution period, keeping the total contractual power of the two parties unchanged throughout the year. Contract repurchase, transfer and replacement transactions can be divided into medium and long-term transactions such as many years (2 years and above), annual, quarterly, monthly transactions and multiple days of the month according to the power trading period. Generally, it is carried out according to the annual and monthly transaction schedules. If necessary, it can carry out medium and long-term transactions for many days in the month. According to the organization of power trading, it can be divided into bilateral negotiation, centralized bidding, and listing trading.

4 The path for construction of power financial transaction market in China

From the actual situation in China, the establishment of

the power finance market needs to go through a longer period of cultivation, development and evolution process. It needs step by step construction, by stages of expanding trade market behaviour, gradually improving the market microstructure, and carrying out standardized physical trading contracts, and then gradually transition to financial contract transactions, and finally introducing standardized power futures and options contracts in time, and gradually form a power financial trading market with multiple trading varieties, active market participants, and sound trading systems [4].

4.1 Construction objectives and key tasks in the near future

4.1.1 The construction objectives

Recently, it is the initial exploration stage of electric power financial market in China. On the basis of continuously deepening the power market construction of our country medium and long-term and spot trading combination, we will carry out generation rights trading, contract repurchase and transfer transactions, CFD, green certificate transactions, etc. power financial transaction varieties, strengthen the construction of market rules and management systems, regulate the trading behaviour of all parties, cultivate market participants awareness, promote trade openness, standardization of contracts, legalization of management, and gradually improve the physical market foundation needed and microstructural conditions for the construction of power financial market to prepare for the establishment of a mature power finance market.

4.1.2 The key tasks

Firstly, we will further develop electricity utilization plans, improve the spot electricity market and price mechanism, and lay a good foundation for the construction of electricity financial market. To establish a perfect electricity financial markets, we must first have perfect electricity spot market. With the construction development of the spot market, the market main body will face price fluctuations, the problem such as market risk, to gradually introduce futures varieties as risk aversion means to provide a good opportunity.

Secondly, we further regulated the trading of physical forward contracts for electricity, and carried out financial transaction practices such as power generation rights trading, contract transfer and buyback, price difference contracts, and green certificates. We conduct a preliminary exploration on financial transactions mechanism, realize a smooth start in the early market. The physical forward contract is the basic transaction form in the power market, while the futures contract is the highly standardized and financialized forward contract. Therefore, in the early stage of the market, the existing forward contract terms should be further regulated, gradually moving towards standardization. It also allows contract transactions (buybacks, transfers, etc.) to gradually introduce financial attributes. At the same time, combining the current situation of China's planned coexistence with the market and promoting the demand of clean energy consumption, the existing power generation rights trading mechanism is further optimized and improved, and the renewable energy green certificate trading is explored. We will gradually introduce power financial trading instruments (contracts for differences in price differences) to reduce the risks of market members caused by large fluctuations in the spot market price of power.

Thirdly, we will further cultivate market players, gradually establish the concept of financial trading, and accumulate market experience. We will further open up user options, accelerate the development of electricity sellers, encourage more market members to participate in electricity market transactions, and jointly allocate market risks and benefits. In the initial stage, the participants of electric power financial market mainly include power generation enterprises, large power users, power selling enterprises and power grid enterprises. Considering the market main body experience relatively insufficient in our country, this phase will temporarily not ordinary users, power brokers and speculators into the market, to ensure the safety and order of the market. Through the development of electricity financial transactions, the participation awareness of market players and the concept of financial transactions are gradually cultivated, and the market experience is accumulated.

Fourthly, relying on the power trading center, we should organize and manage financial transactions, perfect the technical support system and rule system, and make preparations for the introduction of mature power financial trading varieties. Relying on the existing power trading center to organize and conduct power financial transactions has natural advantages and can fully consider the particularity of power commodities. It is helpful to reduce the operation cost and difficulty and ensure the stable operation of power market. In this stage, based on the existing transaction organization and management, the transaction mechanism and management system can be further improved, and the technical support system and rule system can be improved, ensuring fair, open and standardized operation of transactions.

4.1.3The boundary conditions

Firstly, it has perfect and clear contract terms, specifying quantity and unit, quality and grade, quotation unit, minimum fluctuation price, maximum daily price fluctuation limit, trading time, trading place, default penalty, etc., realizing the standardization of terms of the contract. Secondly, it has a market price, and the contract for the bib contract has to be set up in the spot market. Thirdly, it has a certain number of market participants, with a certain degree of market awareness and credit awareness. Fourthly, it has some policy support, such as green certification deals that need to be implemented alongside renewable energy quotas.

4.2 Construction objectives and key tasks for the long term

4.2.1 The construction objectives

On the basis of the recent market, we will further enrich the trading varieties, activate the trading market, improve the trading system, and introduce trading varieties such as electric power futures, options, financial power transmission rights and virtual bidding. We will attract speculators, power brokers, market makers and other trading entities to participate in the market, improve the trading system, credit and regulatory system, and form a complete power market system that coordinates the operation of the electricity market and the financial trading market and complements each other.

4.2.2 The key tasks

Firstly, on the recent basis, we will continue to enrich trading varieties and timely carry out standardized financial contracts such as power futures and options. The transaction varieties of financial power transmission rights and virtual bidding are introduced to form a complete power market system in which the power market and financial transaction market operate harmoniously and complement each other. Market players can independently choose to sign forward contracts in the physical market for trading, and can also participate in the futures, options and other trading varieties of the electric power financial market. In this way, it can provide market players with means to optimize the cost of power and avoid market risks, improve market liquidity and promote the optimal allocation of power resources.

Secondly, we will further liven up the market, introduce more diverse participants and increase market liquidity. Forward electricity financial market participants in the recent market based on the gradual introduction of speculators, power brokers, becoming the subject of the transaction. Through more diversified market players, market liquidity can be improved, so that hedging can transfer price risk. At the same time, it can better promote the effectiveness of market price positioning, so that information can be timely reflected in the price.

Thirdly, we rely on the power exchange centers to set up power futures, options trading platforms, and strengthen the power financial market system. We will actively communicate with relevant authorities of the state, establish trading platforms for electric power futures and options, and gradually improve trading systems in financial markets. It mainly includes implementation rules of trading business, market access system, trading margin system, risk fund system, daily settlement system, ups and downs stop board system, physical delivery system, information notification and disclosure system, bidding and tendering system, etc.

4.2.3 The boundary conditions

Firstly, it is necessary to obtain the approval and policy support from the relevant government departments, and have a trading place approved by the relevant government departments. Secondly, we need to have a sound market technical support system, which can meet the needs of the registration, management, settlement, information release and other core businesses of electricity financial trading parties. Thirdly we must have enough market players, speculators, power brokers, etc. Fourthly, we should have a sound market credit system, supervision and risk control mechanism.

5 Conclusions

Generally speaking, China is now in the critical period of deepening power market construction. With the deepening of the electricity spot market, the gradual formation of the pattern of multi-purchase and multi-sale market and the gradual maturity of the market environment, a good opportunity is created for the timely introduction of electricity financial transactions. It needs to support and promote the top-level design and trading mechanism research of the electricity financial market synchronously. Through the combination of financial market and the spot market, it provides effective means for avoiding market risk, promoting price discovery and market competition, which promoting our country gradually perfect and stable operation of the electric power market system.

Acknowledgement

This paper is supported by Science and Technology Project of State Grid Corporation of China (Research on Power Financial Transaction Mode and Operation Mechanism in the New Round of Power Reform).

References

1. Central Committee of the Communist Party of China and the State Council. Some Opinions on Further Deepening the Power Reform. (2015).
2. National Development and Reform Commission and the National Energy Administration. Reply on the Establishment Scheme of Beijing and Guangzhou Power Trading Centers. (2016).
3. State Electricity Regulatory Commission (SERC). Interim Measures for the Supervision of Generation Rights Trading. (2008).
4. Huang Renhui, Zhang Lizi, Wu Yaguang, Pang Bo. An Investigation on the Implementation Path of Power Financial Market in China. Automatin of Electic Power System. Vol 34(11), (2010).

Study on the Definition of College Students' Employability

Hongjie Li[1], Zhenjia Sun[2,a]

[1] *School of Chemistry, Beihang University, Beijing, China*
[2] *School of Aeronautic Science and Engineering, Beihang University, Beijing, China*

Abstract. With the further exploration of high-level talent cultivation in universities and the improvement of the demand for talents by employers, researches on college students' employability have been valued by scholars and universities. Cultivation of excellent employability has been a shared concern and objective for both college students and universities. The concept of employability has evolved over time. Scholars at home and abroad have different definitions on college students' employability from different perspectives.
Keywords. Employability, college students, definition

Studies on employability have long focused on the needs of the labor market. The concept of employability has evolved with the progress of the times. Scholars at home and abroad have different definitions on college students' employability from different perspectives. This thesis centers on the development process and trends of both employability and college students' employability research, intending to lay a theoretical foundation for the future development and study of college students' employability.

1 Development process of employability

The concept of employability was first proposed by British Beveridg at the beginning of the 20th century [1]. It was initially proposed from the perspective of the labor capacity of workers and focused on the availability of mature workers, so as to distinguish workers with more labor capacity in the market. The concept of employability has evolved with the development of the times, closely linked to the employment priorities of the time, and assumed different functions.

Gazier et al. summarize the development process of employability and divide them into seven stages according to its connotation. The first is the dichotomic employability at the beginning of the 20th century, focusing on the opposite poles of employability and un-employability. The second is the social-medical employability in the 1950s. The third is the manpower policy employability in the 1960s. The fourth is the flow employability in the 1960s. The fifth is the labor market performance employability in the late 1970s. The sixth is the initiative employability in the 1980s when the employability research, as a human resource management tool, began to be used at the corporate or organization level. The seventh is the interactive employability in the early 1990s.

2 Definition of employability

Studies on employability have emerged very early, but there has been no uniform definition on relative concepts yet. The Canadian Labor Force Development Board (CLFDB) defines employability as "the ability of individuals to gain valuable employment in the interaction with the labor market". Paying more attention on the employability at work, the International Labor Organization (ILO), defines employability as "the ability to make progress at work and to react to changes in work".

With the trend towards new types of relationships between employers and employees, individuals have assumed more and more subject responsibility in their career development, and the definition of employability based on individual perspective has received extensive attention. For example, definition of employability proposed by Fugate et al. has received much attention in recent years. They clearly state that employability, which reveals itself as a form of individual adaptation at work, is essentially a psycho-social construct, including individual traits that help to form active cognition and action and to promote individual-work interaction. They even propose that employability is (pro)active adaptability specific to work and careers [2]. Hillage and Pollard define employability as having the capability to gain initial employment, maintain employment and obtain new employment if required. Individuals can realize their potential through sustainable employment. For the individual, employability depends on the knowledge, skills and attitudes they possess, the way they use those assets and present them to employers and the context within which they seek work [3]. Their definition of the

[a] Corresponding author: szj@buaa.edu.cn

structure, measurement and intervention ability of the employability of college students who seek employment influenced by psychological capital is one of the most frequently cited definitions in the study of employability.

3 Definition of college students' employability

Foreign scholars in different groups have different perspectives on the definition of college students' employability. From the perspective of supply and demand in the labour market, college students' employability refers to the ability of college students to acquire and maintain their careers in the labour market. It also includes the prediction and perception of individuals' external environment and job changes [4]. From the perspective of the knowledge and skills required by college students to acquire and maintain employment relationships, it can be defined as the sum of a series of abilities college students hold to obtain initial employment opportunity and continuous employment. These abilities are mostly related to talent fostering. However, even from the perspective of college students, differences exist in college students' employability because of various definitions.

The definition of college students' employability in China is mainly concentrated on career exploration. Relative studies focus on college graduates' employability, emphasizing the education, training and ability improvement required by employment. Most notably is the view held by Zheng Xiaoming. He defines college students' employability earlier as a kind of skill acquired by students during their school years from studying basic and professional knowledge, practicing, and developing various comprehensive qualities. This skill can help graduates achieve their employment ideals and realize their own value in social life, and also meet social needs. It consists of intelligence (IQ) and non-intellectual factors (EQ).

4 Conclusions

From the literature review, we find that in defining employability the concept definition and structure are different under different development stages of society. The definition of college students' employability could be generally divided into two types. One centers on the ability structure of the characteristics owned by college students. The other pays more attention to features presented by college students when they acquire and maintain a job.

References

1. Beveridge, William Henry. Unemployment A Problem of Industry [M]. London: Longmans, Green and Co., 1909.
2. Fugate M., Kinicki A. J. A Dispositional Approach to Employability: Development of a Measure and Test of implications for Employee Reactions to Organizational Change [J]. Journal of Occupational and Organizational Psychology, 2008, 81(3): 503
3. Hillage, J, Pollard, E. 1998, Employability: Developing a Framework for Policy Analysis. Research Brief 85, Department for Education and Employment.
4. Andries de Gri P, Jas Per van Loo, Jos Sanders. The Industry Employability Index: Taking account of supply and demand characteristics [J]. International Labor Review, 2004, 143(3): 211-230.

 https://doi.org/10.1051/itmconf/20192504002

Exploration of Building "the Second Learning Space" Education Mode

Zhongbao Chen

Jilin Institute of Chemical Technology

Abstract. The realization of "the second learning space" mainly includes two aspects: one is to "pave the road and build the bridge" by technology; and the other is to provide professional and systematic high-quality teaching resources with the help of the professional teachers.

The research content mainly includes five parts: the connection of broadband network, the functional services provided by the system, the acquisition of high-quality resources, the storage of resource data, and the construction of security system.

The fundamental purpose of the research and development of the "second learning space" is to break through the limitations of time, space and region, to form a new educational model of learners' autonomous learning and mutual learning under the network environment, to mobilize students' initiative and enthusiasm in learning, to exercise students' creative thinking, to cultivate students' innovative ability and to improve education and teaching quality, and to promote education and teaching reform.

1 Explore the background

According to the "12th Five-Year Plan" of the Ministry of Education, it is the general trend to strengthen the construction of high-quality educational and teaching resources, to explore the guiding principles for the formation of the road of educational informatization with Chinese characteristics, and to closely focus on the strategic goal of "strengthening provinces in Colleges and universities". The construction of digital campus is the trend and its quality, level and utilization rate of a university education is the realization of comprehensive strength such as the level of education and teaching in a university.

Combining with the actual situation of information construction in our university, it lays a material foundation for the development of "the second learning space". Efforts should be made to integrate high-quality teachers' resources, cultivate high-quality talents of compound type, break through the existing teaching mode, and research and develop the "second learning space", in order to make it possible for the diversity of knowledge acquisition channels, the autonomy of content selection and the flexibility of learning time.

Therefore, the research and development of "the second learning space" is conducive to improving the quality and efficiency of education and teaching, and has a positive practical significance and long-term historical significance for building a learning society and promoting the in-depth development of education and teaching reform in our school.

2 Similar research level and development trend at home and abroad

With the rapid development of science and technology, global education is showing great changes. China is also carrying out education reform in an all-round way and vigorously innovating Education. In recent years, with the rapid development of information technology and penetration into every sphere of life, all aspects of our lives have been greatly impacted, and also injected new life for the modernization of education.

The combination of modern education concept and new computer technology provides a wider development space for education, and meanwhile also provides a new stage for people's lifelong education and sustainable development. The study of learning space started late in China.

In 1994, the State Education Commission chaired the construction of "China Education and Scientific Research Computer Network". On the basis of this computer network environment, in 1996, Dazhong Wang, President of Tsinghua University, took the lead in proposing that colleges and universities should develop modern distance education.

Since then, some colleges and universities in China have set up a network education platform. However, these platforms are mostly based on school enterprise cooperation mode of joint development, and will serve as an independent form of learning network teaching, mainly to provide training of higher education to the society.

In the national teleconference on education

informatization in 2012, Vice Premier Yandong Liu pointed out that "innovative education mode and learning mode must be innovated, high-quality education resources should be shared, information-based learning environment should be accelerated, network learning space should be accessible to all, and sustainable operation and maintenance mechanism should be explored". In March 2012, the Ministry of Education issued the Ten-Year Development Plan of Education Informatization (2011-2020). On the basis of in-depth research, the Ministry of Education condensed the development goals and tasks of the Ten-Year Development Plan of Education Informatization.

In the period of the 12th Five-Year Plan, three key objectives and tasks are put forward: strengthening the construction of broadband network in schools, strengthening the construction and sharing of high-quality digital educational resources and the construction of real-name network learning space environment, as well as two key projects: the construction of educational management information system and the construction of public service platform for educational resources.

The Deputy Minister of education emphasized that "E-learning space is the future development direction of education informationization, the innovation and exploration of new models of students' learning, teacher-student interaction and teacher-student interaction in the network era" and summarized it as "three links and two platforms".

Individualized education in foreign countries has developed earlier and studied more. It is in the leading position both in theory and in practice. The second learning space is widely used in foreign countries, especially in vocational education and the training of professional and technical personnel.

In the new situation, combined with the development trend of education informatization, "the second learning space" will inevitably become an effective driving force to promote education and teaching reform and improve personnel training, and will be accepted by more people.

3 Technical analysis

The program is to solve the technical difficulties and key points and expect goals and major technical and economic indicators.

The construction of "Second Learning Space" project utilizes the mature network technology to achieve knowledge imparting. In this environment, students can get the guidance of famous teachers in a professional or a certain learning field, so that students can learn the knowledge they need easily, freely and actively.

In the process of the project construction, the first step is to build the learning space platform, which mainly includes: system development architecture selection analysis, related technology principle analysis, system functional module demand analysis, system overall design analysis, etc.; Secondly, according to the requirement of learner autonomy, high-quality educational and teaching resources are produced. Through online learning and assessment, learners complete the completion of a certain subject. In the process of project construction, the process design and function realization of system research and development are solved by means of school-enterprise cooperation and multi-party participation.

The key issues of this project construction are the choice of the learning space platform system architecture, data processing process, especially the development and construction of high-quality education and teaching resources, which is the key link and one of the weakest links of current education informatization. In order to solve this problem, we should fully mobilize the relevant teachers to participate actively in the production of resources, and give them corresponding subsidies. "The Second Learning Space" uses network transmission technologies such as audio and video transmission and data collaboration to simulate real classroom environment and provide effective learning environment for students through the network. Students directly use browsers on communication devices connected to the Internet, sign up for the "second learning space" and become spatial trainees.

The "second learning space" project is expected to be completed in two years and divided into three steps, First of all, to achieve the publication of elective course information, students can log into the space to select courses online, through time learning, complete homework, participate in online assessment, to meet the credit requirements, in this way to complete the whole management process of elective courses in school; Secondly, in this space to complete the training of students' second degree, through online registration, payment, learning professional courses, qualified assessment, application for graduation certificate to complete the continuing education degree; Finally, when the system runs steadily and maturely, we will carry out the "Classroom for Famous Teachers", take learning space as the supporting platform, expand and extend the functions of the system, provide services to other brotherly institutions and people in need in all walks of life, and give full play to the role of demonstration and promotion of Famous Teachers.

4 The research methods (or technological process, implementation plan) that the project intends to adopt and its feasibility analysis

The objective reason for building the "second learning space" is that teachers face too many students, and that teachers are too demanding and that teachers lack teaching means, tools and carriers. There are only "five ones", that is, "a mouth, a chalk, a blackboard, a textbook, a classroom". Doctors can make use of detection equipment, laboratory tests and surgical equipment and facilities to carry out medical treatment; The actors perform with the help of props, stage, lighting, sound and electronic background. Set up the network teaching implementation platform of each course, solidify many teaching requirements of the new curriculum standard in the network teaching implementation platform, according to certain inquiry route and operation process, provide teachers with teaching assistants and tools, provide students with inquiry platform, let teachers have "three heads and six arms", and let teachers do what they should do. "What", "can do" and "must do".

The realization of "the second learning space" mainly includes two aspects: one is to "pave the road and build the bridge" by technology; and the other is to provide professional and systematic high-quality teaching resources with the help of the professional teachers.

The project construction plan should include seven parts: project construction background, project construction significance, project construction feasibility analysis, project construction content, project construction progress, project construction guarantee and project construction expected effect.

According to the "Twelfth Five-Year Plan" put forward by the Ministry of Education, we should strengthen the construction of high-quality educational and teaching resources, explore the way to develop educational informatization with Chinese characteristics, closely focus on the strategic goal of "strengthening provinces in Colleges and universities", and combine with the actual situation of informatization construction in our university, develop the "second learning space" and form the network environment. Next, the new educational model of learners' self-learning and mutual-aid learning breaks through the limitations of time and space and learning methods of the existing educational model, promotes educational equity, improves the quality of education, establishes a learning society and promotes the development of educational and teaching reform, which is of great significance to the construction of continuing education, lifelong education and learning society. Righteousness.

Using the existing network communication technology and closely surrounding the construction of the "Second Learning Space" project, it can be divided into the following links, Firstly, using the existing network technology to achieve full coverage of the campus network, to ensure the security and stability of the entire campus network; secondly, targeted research and development of learning environment, breaking through the time and space constraints, to create new learning opportunities for learners; Finally, the study of the multi-source, optional, accessibility and timely accessibility of information resources provided by the "second learning space" will essentially change the distribution pattern of information resources and the way people own them, so as to realize the reconstruction of educational relations.

Through the existing mature data access strategy, data encryption technology, user control, system and information backup and system log technology, to ensure the safe and stable operation of hardware and software systems.

In order to enable the project to proceed smoothly and gradually, a project team of experts has been set up to review the implementation of the project from time to time, to give theoretical and methodological guidance, and to train the personnel of the project research team on an ad hoc basis, Cultivate a group of professionals with higher information literacy and engaged in network teaching research and development.

Utilize the informatization environment of the school reasonably and effectively, raise funds in many ways for the research of the project and the study and training of teachers.

Research on the Participation of University-affiliated Think Tanks in Local Economic Development

Zijun Tang[1,a]

[1]Office of Scientific Research Management Jishou University Jishou Hunan China

Abstract. The basic function of modern university is to train talents, produce and disseminate scientific knowledge, and promote technological progress. As an important birthplace of high technology, universities are the natural matrix of good think tanks. Compared with the government-affiliated think-tanks and the social think tanks, the university-affiliated think tanks have some unique advantages, such as the concentrated embodiment of the university resources, the role of the third party of non-profit, more advanced and standardized operational model, and the strong scientific research foundation and ability. Therefore, in the current period of important strategic opportunities for local economic and social development, the construction of university-affiliated think tanks should be strengthened, giving full play to the role of university-affiliated think tanks, so as to promote local economic development.

1 Introduction

With the accelerated evolution of new scientific and technological revolution and industrial transformation, the innovation of science and technologe has become the leading factor of industrial upgrading, high-tech industry has become the main driving force of local economic development. The rapid development of science and technology brings the complexity and specialization to the decision-making of scientific and technological affairs. This situation puts forward realistic requirements and challenges to the local governments. The basic function of modern university is to train talents, produce and disseminate scientific knowledge, promote technological progress, and be the institutional guarantee of free scholarship [1]. It can be said that universities are the embodiment of science and technology, is the natural matrix of think tanks. Compared with other types of think tanks, university-affiliated think tanks have a strong foundation of scientific research in the field of emerging technology, innate disciplinary advantages in support of advanced ideas, methods and means, and abundant intellectual resources in terms of experts and scholars. Therefore, in the face of the diversified, professional needs of science and technology for the current local social and economic development, how to take advantage of the university-affiliated think tanks then deeply participate in local economic development, will become a new mission for universities in the new period.

2 Advantages of university-affiliated think tanks participating in local economic development

2.1 University-affiliated think tanks are the concentrated embodiment of superior resources owned by the universities

Universities are an important part of China's science and technology innovation system, and the main force of theoretical, basic and frontier research, which have a lot of advantages such as complete discipline system, talent density, strong knowledge reserve, solid foundation of innovation research and so on [2]. Relying on the high quality resources and strong ability of universities, the university-affiliated think tanks has the strong backing of human resources, scientific research foundation, theoretical and policy reserve, ideological innovation and so on. They are the concentrated display of the comprehensive strength or the resources of the universities, as well as the important channel of the transformation and dissemination of intellectual resources from the universities to the government and society, and the spillover effect is very obvious, which can provide strong support for the local economic development.

2.2 University-affiliated think tanks play the role of the third party of non-profit

At present, there are a large number of government think

a Corresponding author: zijuntang@163.com

tanks and social think tanks in China. Government think tanks are closely linked to relevant government departments and are even an important part of the system and chain of government decision-making. Therefore, they have an important impact on government decision-making, but it is also difficult to get rid of issues such as official colors within the system and complex relationships with the government. As far as the social think tanks are concerned, in view of the current situation, it is not enough and there is still a lot of room for them to participate in and influence on government decision-making. Compared with these two think tanks, the university-affiliated think tanks have a relatively independent and moderate position and relationship with the government, representing the objective scientific justice and the general interests of the public. Whether plays as an advisory board or publicity group, the role of the university-affiliated think tanks make them have a stronger credibility. Moreover, the characteristics of independent, nonprofit third part which the university-affiliated think tanks have, may also make them be the preferred ones for government policy makers.

2.3 University-affiliated think tanks have advanced and standardized operational model

Constrained by the institutional mechanism, it is difficult for the government think tanks to fully apply advanced ideas and methods to improve its governance structure and operation model. Social think tanks have advantages in management mechanism, governance structure, influence of public opinion, etc., but there may also be problems such as chaotic capital background and loose management. Universities are a relatively complex but flexible system, can accommodate the coexistence and development of different types of institutions, and create a more suitable and powerful policy environment and institutional environment for the growth of new think tanks. With the advantages of resources, standardized management and advanced ideas, the university-affiliated think tanks often take the initiative to seek innovative operation mechanism, governance structure, talent team, technological platform and other innovations, but at the same time also subject to the guidance and constraints of universities. This flexible system which owned by the university-affiliated think tanks, both advanced and normative, can bring new ideas to the development of local economy.

2.4 University-affiliated think tanks have excellent genes for the consultation of decision-making

The work of scientific research has always been the core competence of the universities, and is also an important focus of their construction and development. Meanwhile the work of scientific research itself contains a lot of think-tank work. Engaged in the work of scientific research, especially innovative one, needs to fully investigate the current situation of domestic and abroad, master the latest progress in the field, and form a judgment on specific issues through comparison, analysis, induction and thinking progress. This process has a high degree of overlap with the main process of research and consulting by think tanks. Moreover, in practice there are many important suggestions for scientific and technological decisions come from the early preparation works of large-scale scientific research activities. On the premise that the mechanism of the two processes is more consistent, universities with the high maturity of the scientific research system play the role of think tanks, which not only takes the advantages of universities, but also reduces the construction cost of think tanks. The advantages are obvious.

2.5 University-affiliated think tanks have the foundation and ability of scientific research

Local economic development is an open and complex system work, which needs the vision of cross-integration in multi-disciplinary fields, the research methods and means of combining qualitative and quantitative, and the technological innovation and transformation channels that need to be combined with basic research and applied research. Historically, universities themselves have been the main players in many major scientific projects, with strong capabilities and research base of scientific research. At present, with the traditional advantages of advanced technology research, the university-affiliated think tanks not only have the conditions and foundation to carry out traditional scientific research, but also constantly strengthen the cutting-edge scientific research based on big data technology and intelligent technology, such as data analysis, model reasoning, policy deduction, etc. This large, cutting-edge scientific research is hard to conduct by other types of think tanks. With these advantages, the university-affiliated think tanks can form three spiral curves: the knowledge transformation curve, the technological innovation curve and the talent rotation curve. These three curves of knowledge, technology and talents are closely coupled and influenced by each other, which is the intrinsic characteristic embodied in the unique natural advantages of the university-affiliated think tanks.

3 Suggestions on the participation of the university-affiliated think tanks in local economic development

3.1 University-affiliated think tanks explore channels and platforms for participating in the development of local economic development

Firstly, the university-affiliated think tanks should take the initiative to participate in various consultation activities of decision-making organized by local government, actively undertake research projects, and invite the personnel of local government departments or research institutions so as to strengthen the connection between the think tanks and the government. Secondly, the university-affiliated think tanks should monitor the world's major technology trends, follow up the study of major national projects, timely formation of research reports for the reference for the policy-making of government departments. Thirdly, the university-affiliated think tanks, as a third party, should participate in the evaluation of local economic projects, conduct independent assessment on local economic development strategies and policies, etc. [3]. Currently, a lot of information websites of local governments release information regularly on scientific and technological needs, which deserves sustained attention.

3.2 University-affiliated think tanks improve the analysis and research ability on economic development policy

The university-affiliated think tanks should constantly strengthen their analysis and research capabilities on economic development strategies and policy. Firstly, according to the functional orientation, the universities should scientifically plan the overall construction of think tanks, innovatie organizational forms and governance methods, highlight their own characteristics and advantages. Secondly, the university-affiliated think tanks should strengthen the communication with local government, emphasize the demand, problem and application orientation, so as to enhance the ability of research and evaluation on practical issues, then provide scientific, targeted and professional research results for government decision-making. Thirdly, the university-affiliated think tanks should strengthen the efficiency of decision-making, not for profit, but to introduce market-oriented operation into the local consulting markets on economic development and to become the "unicorn" of the think-tank industry;

3.3 University-affiliated think tanks gather related academic research resources and social resources

For the complex system of local economic development, a single think tank or the combination of multiple think tanks are unable to meet its needs. However, it needs to share resources, joint research to build a system. Firstly, the university-affiliated think tanks should strengthen exchanges and cooperation with other decision-making bodies and scientific research institutes, and jointly set up professional think tanks or joint research groups ; Secondly, the university-affiliated think tanks should participate in relevant collaborative organizations, expert organizations or academic groups, take advantage of the collaborative platforms to expand impact; Thirdly, according to the subject advantage and cross-integration situation, the university should explore the establishment of university-affiliated think tanks alliance, sharing data, technology, platform, facilities, talent and other resources [4].

3.4 University-affiliated think tanks develop the intelligent data-based research tools

At present, the Internet plus, big Data, artificial intelligence and other disruptive technologies have risen. The university-affiliated think tanks can no longer stay in the original mode of work should develop the application of new intelligent research tools, open up new ways of working. Firstly, the university-affiliated think tanks should develop intelligent big data analysis and research tools that meet the actual work needs, and fulfil the collaboration of consulting work with modern tools; Secondly, the university-affiliated think tanks should cooperate deeply with data software companies, etc., and carry out research with the help of advanced tools and abundant resources; Thirdly, the university-affiliated think tanks should strengthen empirical investigation and research, establish new methods, new means and tools based on data and intelligent technology, and put forward policy suggestions and problem solutions based on facts and data basis; Fourthly, with the combination of qualitative and quantitative research methods to become the mainstream, the university-affiliated think tanks should develop integrated platform to realize the automatic and intelligent decision system which combines human, machine and network as early as possible [5].

3.5 University-affiliated think tanks strengthen the transformation and application of research achievements to local economic development

The science of information has the concept of "Sleeping Beauty Literature", the field of think tank also has the same problems that a lot of good research achievements are frozen or forgotten, mainly because the channel of transformation is not smooth, or do not meet the needs of the practice, or academic properties are too strong, or the incentive mechanism of transformation and application is missing and so on. Therefore, the university-affiliated think tanks should resolve the issue of the "last mile" of the transformation and application of the research achievements. Firstly, the university-affiliated think tanks should figure out the specific or potential needs of local economic development, regularly produce the latest brief of achievements for the reference of decision-making departments of government. Secondly, the university-affiliated think tanks should use the opportunities of conference exchanges, as well as local information network of science and technology needs and other platforms, to publicize and promote research achievements and demonstrate scientific research ability. Thirdly, the university-affiliated think tanks should establish rules and regulations suitable for the application and transformation of the research achievements, encourage faculty to provide research achievements for the think tanks to adopt; Fourthly, the university-affiliated think tanks should change the style of the theoretical research, and attach importance to providing targeted, empirical and feasible suggestions for practical problems.

3.6 University-affiliated think tanks attach importance to all-media publicity and brand building

The universities have always been regarded as "ivory towers" and not to seek fame and fortune, which is a good style of study for academic research. However, for the university-affiliated think tanks, in order to better serve the local economic construction and development, they must actively participate in the social practice, solve the actual problems in the development of local economy. Therefore, the university-affiliated think tanks should promote themselves, cultivate brands and gain the trust of government departments and society, then open up the channel through which the university-affiliated think tanks can serve the local economic development better. Therefore, the university-affiliated think tanks should use all-media to promote their own consulting products and well-known experts to establish a good brand image in the public.

Acknowledgement

This paper was financially supported by the project of Science and Technology Plan of Xiangxi Autonomous Prefecture, "The Research on the Mechanism of University -affiliated think tanks participating in Local Science and Technology Innovation Decision-making consultation" (No.2018SF5015).

References

1. Wu Guosheng. What is science [M]. Guangzhou: Guangdong People's Press, **115-129**(2016).
2. Xu Qingsen. Three relationships should be handled well in the construction of the university-affiliated think tanks [J]. *Theory and practice of think tank*, **8-9** (2017).
3. Li gang. " University and think tank ":" South Great think-tank "general sequence idea of the broker: think tank and the rise of the new policy elite [M]. Nanjing: Nanjing University Press, **1-9** (2016).
4. Zhouyang, Lu Shengjun. Some thoughts on the construction of National defense science and Technology think tank under the new situation [J]. *Theory and practice of think tank*, **61-67**(2016).
5. Lu Shengjun, Wang Yang, jamming and so on. Preliminary thoughts on the construction of new national defense decision-making consulting system in China [J]. *Theory and practice of think tank*, **42-47**(2016).

Research for Development Path of Vocational Education of Ceramic Art under Economic New Normal

Fei Yu [a]

The Department of Art and Design, Jingdezhen University, Jingdezhen, Jiangxi, China

Abstract. The economic new normal formed in recent years has significant impact on the ceramic art industry and further influences the development of vocational education of ceramic art so that the vocational education of ceramic art is facing the new requirements and new challenges. Therefore, the vocational education of ceramic art under the economic new normal shall be developed from macroscopic and microcosmic idea, the target shall be established to build the modern vocational education system through concept update, system reform, self-management, reasonable assessment and other methods.

Foreword

In the past two years, the economic new normal has become the hottest and most active research topic involving many aspects of national economy. There is no that the ceramic art industry is contained in these aspects. Superficially, the new normal of ceramic art industry trends to develop at low and middle speed from high speed. In essence, the ceramic art industry transforms the traditional development model into the modern model and pursues the quality and innovation instead of pursuing the scale and speed. And the vocational education of ceramic art is an education type which attaches to the development of ceramic art industry, so, the vocational education of ceramic art must actively and positively know the new normal of ceramic art industry and effective measures and strategies shall be made to adapt the economic new normal. Under the economic new normal, many economic areas are comprehensively developing along with the development path under the economic new normal. However, the research about how to develop the ceramic art industry is just started. Moreover, the research about how the vocational education of ceramic art achieves the transformation development to adapt the economic new normal is scarcely developed. For this reason, the author attempts to make comprehensive research about this topic and expects to offer some references for the promotion of the development of vocational education vocational education under the economic new normal.

1 Impact of economic new normal on development of vocational education of ceramic art

Chinese economic new normal is just formed, but with its continuous development, the economic new normal produces greater and greater impact on the vocational education in which the vocational education of ceramic art is included. Since the Reform and Opening-up Policy, Chinese ceramic art industry has gradually entered into the fast lane of development, especially, after entering the 21st century, its development trend advances by rushes, the industry scale continuously expands, the number of ceramic art enterprises and individual workshops and studios sharply increases and ceramic workers are more and more. However, the ceramic art industry which ever experienced the high-speed growth suddenly enters into the middle- and low-speed growth period and transforms the economic normal with high-speed growth into the economic new normal. The performance of the economic new normal in the ceramic art field not only influences the development of ceramic art, but also produces great influences on the vocational education of ceramic art, so it puts forward to the new times requirement for the development of vocational education of ceramic art.

The new requirements of the economic new normal on the vocational education of ceramic art are mainly reflected on that: the vocational education of ceramic art must pay more attention to the cultivation of middle and high end ceramic art talents and reverse the development mode which cares more about the quantity of talents into the development mode which lays more emphasis on quality cultivation; the employment promotion is taken as the important educational guidance to conduct the diversified education. This kind of requirement is expressed in both the foundation of educational and teaching modes and methods and the reform of whole vocational education system of ceramic art. The vocational education of ceramic art in many aspects, such as talent structure, education level and innovation, shall

[a] Feiyu: 653104053@qq.com

be comprehensively reformed to adapt the requirement of economic new normal. Otherwise, it will enter into the arrested development period, and even get into trouble.

The new requirements proposed by the economic new normal on the vocational education of ceramic art are both the great opportunities and the great challenges for the development of the vocational education of ceramic art so that the vocational education of ceramic art in colleges and universities also suffers a large amount of problems and difficulties. And the biggest trouble brought by the economic new normal to the vocational education of ceramic art is the educational input problem. By reason that the growth rate of economy slows down, the growth rate of the educational input must slow down so that the fund necessary for the vocational education of ceramic art is difficult to be gained. Moreover, the employment problem becomes the second trouble. Because the growth rate of ceramic art economy obviously slows down under the economic new normal, the demands of ceramic art enterprises and individual workshops for talents increasingly decline but the number of ceramic art talents trained by colleges and universities rapidly increases annually to bring a huge difficulty for the employment of ceramic art talents.

The difficulties on the educational input and the employment brought by the economic new normal to the vocational education of ceramic art cause that the vocational education of ceramic art suffers the development bottleneck from the source and flow and faces the challenge of the reform of whole educational system. Therefore, the vocational education of ceramic art must be deeply reformed, reintegrate the educational resources, have complementary advantages and strengthen the professional construction. However, those need more workers and relevant departments of the vocational education of ceramic art put in more efforts to solve the problems appeared under the economic new normal and guarantee the vocational education of ceramic art can still healthily and continuously moves forward.

The huge impact of economic new normal on the vocational education of ceramic art enables that the vocational education of ceramic art must also enter into the new normal accordingly and strive to take the characteristic education, vitality improvement, reduction of student sources, quality-oriented education, cooperative development and so on as the new normal of the vocational education of ceramic art. As a result, the matter how to build a new normal of the vocational education of ceramic art under the economic new normal also is the huge challenge for the vocational educators of ceramic art, but the vocational educators of ceramic art must show their new attitudes towards the new normal, would rather actively struggle than positively and sluggishly face difficulties and attempt to explore and achieve the new development under the new normal.

2 Thoughts and targets of development of vocational education of ceramic art under economic new normal

The confirmation of new development thoughts is the basis to develop the vocational education of ceramic art under the new normal, where new thoughts can be divided into two parts: macroscopic thoughts and microscopic thoughts. From the macroscopic thoughts, administrators of administrative department in charge in the vocational education of ceramic art shall look far ahead and aim high, lead to change their thoughts and attach importance to and deeply develop the transformation of the vocational education of ceramic art under the new normal. Firstly, administrators of the vocational education of ceramic art shall get a clear understanding of challenges and opportunities brought by the economic new normal to the vocational education of ceramic art and promote the comprehensively reform of the vocational education of ceramic art; secondly, administrators see clearly that the core of talent training of the vocational education of ceramic art is the quality-oriented education and promote the mode transformation of the vocational education of ceramic art from traditional mode to the quality-oriented education mode. From the view of microscopic thoughts, both the middle and low administrators and a lot of teachers occupied in the vocational education of ceramic art should deeply realize that new developmental strategies must be developed on the vocational education of ceramic art under the economic new normal to change the educational thoughts and adjust the work emphasis to the educational reform under the economic new normal. In the first place, they must adapt the impact and transformation which have occurred in the vocational education of ceramic art under the economic new normal; in the second place, they need to accelerate to build the teaching mode to match with the economic new normal and actively train talents to fit with the economic new normal.

In addition that thoughts should be actively changed to adapt the economic new normal, the new development target of the vocational education of ceramic art should be confirmed, which is the key in the development. The first step to confirm the new development target is to determine the new position of the vocational education of ceramic art which confirms to the development orientation of the ceramic art industry under the economic new normal. The development orientation of the ceramic art industry under the economic new normal should transform the growth method, adjust the industry structure and promote the high-end update, and the vocational education of ceramic art under the economic new normal should adapt and service the development method of the ceramic art industry under the economic new normal to promote the new development of the ceramic art industry, which shall be its mission and duty, become the assistor to adjust and update the industry structure of ceramic art and solve the adjustment of its own system and the employment conflict.

Chinese ceramic art industry has ever experienced a high-speed growth period before the new normal appears so that the vocational education of ceramic art has ever pursued the scale and speed, which obviously falls behind the development of the times under the current economic new normal. In order to adapt the economic new normal, the new target of the vocational education of ceramic art should be to build a set of modern vocational education system. This set of modern vocational education system will break the old vocational education system, conform to the Decision of State Council of People's Republic of China About Speeding up Development of Modern Professional Education issued in 2014 and transform to become the important components of significant strategic adjustment to comprehensively service the innovative development of ceramic art industry through reform. And the modern vocational education system for ceramic art with Chinese characteristics and world level should try to be built within a short period. The modern vocational education system built for the vocational education of ceramic art contains the relevant regulation and law system, institutional structure system, teaching system, administration system and so on, all of which should form a new harmony relation with the economic new normal.

3 Development path of vocational education of ceramic art under economic new normal

The economic new normal has been formed and has produce a significant impact on the development of the vocational education of ceramic art, but most vocational educators of ceramic art still don't care about and recognize the urgency of this important topic and still follow the old teaching system. Therefore, there is a long way to go about how to build a perfect and scientific vocational education system of modern ceramic art and the progressive development path need be adopted for the final success.

For the development of the vocational education of ceramic art under the economic new normal, firstly, the concept should be updated and the thought should be emancipated. However, the economic new normal is ignored and even contradicted, so the development is impossible. Therefore, the competent department, school leaders and teachers of the vocational education of ceramic art, and even students, parents and whole society should actively face and attach importance to the economic new normal and form a clear ideological understanding in that thee vocational education of ceramic art must adapt the economic new normal for the modern transformation. Only do these can the obstacles which impede the development of the vocational education of ceramic art under the new normal are removed and can various educational and teaching reform measures be fully implemented and mutually coordinated.

On the basis of concept update, the vocational education of ceramic art under the economic new normal need further establish the corresponding system. Currently, the vocational education of ceramic art has had relatively perfect law and regulation system and educational and teaching administration system. However, on the whole, their contents are still relatively old so as not to adapt the new trend formed under the economic new normal. Therefore, a set of vocational education system of ceramic art is urgent to be built to adapt the economic new normal. These systems contain not only the vocational education policy of ceramic art and articles enacted by various colleges and universities but also the specific, feasible and operable implementation system, mainly the rules and regulation for daily education and teaching. These rules and regulations should accord with the reform and development under the economic new normal and should be optimized and perfected targeting the establishment of the vocational education system of modern ceramic art.

In order to guarantee various regulations can be smoothly implemented and achieve the development of the vocational education of ceramic art under the economic new normal, a whole set of efficient and scientific administration system and mechanism also should be established. Schools should have more independent administration power and all levels of administration departments of schools also should have relatively high independent administration power. On one hand, the independent administration is good for the improvement of enthusiasm of administrators; on the other hand, the rigid implementation of rules and regulation can be avoided. Schools should also advocate and encourage ceramic art teachers participating in the administration, because the development of the vocational education of ceramic art under the economic new normal is still a new thing so that the administrators also face many difficulties and problem and teachers who fight bravely in the teaching site should continuously feed the information back and put forward to the valuable practice experiences and lessons.

The reasonable evaluation is also a key measure to achieve the progressive development of the vocational education of ceramic art under the economic new normal, so a set of scientific evaluation system should be established. The vocational educators of ceramic art under the new normal always lack of experiences when they develop the educational and teaching reform work and need do a large amount of trials. Therefore, if the evaluation is excessively rigorous and unreasonable, it is inevitable that reformers don't dare to reform, and even their enthusiasm will be reduced. Therefore, a reasonable evaluation system relates to the success of the vocational education of ceramic art under the economic new normal. And the reasonable evaluation system should correspond to the development of economic new normal, make integrated evaluation and should not deny all due to the local imperfection. Meanwhile, it should be flexible to consider the difference and also be open so that teachers, students and the ceramic art industry will participate in the evaluation.

References

1. Wang Huan. Analysis for Development Trend of Chinese Ceramic Art Under New Normal [J]. Arts Criticism, 2016 (04).
2. Ai Jun, Sun Chuanhao and Zhen Jingying. Startup Problems of College Students Majoring in Ceramics Under New Normal and its Countermeasure Study. [J] Journal of Ceramics, 2015 (02).

3. Wang Qun and Wang Jungang. Study for Employment Problem of Graduates Majoring in Ceramic Art Under Economic New Normal - set the Ceramic Institutes of Jingdezhen School of Technology and Art as an example [J]. Travel Together, 2016, (07).
4. Zhang Xinjin. Chinese Economic New Normal and New Opportunities of Ceramic Industry [J]. Ceramic Studies Journal, 2016 (01).

Application of Big Data Technology in College Information Construction

Wei Deng

Shanxi Normal University

Abstract. As a new technological means, big data plays an important role in the construction of intelligent campus in Colleges and universities. Taking Shaanxi Normal University as an example, this paper introduces the development of college information construction, and elaborates on the typical application scenarios of big data in colleges.

1 Background

With the rapid development of information construction in colleges and universities, the application system of various business departments in colleges and universities has accumulated a great deal of data. This lays the foundation for the application of big data technology. Big data [1] not only refers to massive data itself, but also includes a series of technical methods for data storage, processing, analysis and visualization. It is an effective means to explore its hidden value from massive data.

The information construction of colleges and universities generally goes through three stages: infrastructure construction [2], digital campus construction [3] and intelligent campus construction [4]. In the stage of infrastructure construction, hardware is the main construction content. It includes network equipment, one-card system, access control system. It has accumulated plenty of students online authentication data, campus card consumption, access control card data. In the stage of digital campus construction, software is the main construction content. It mainly includes business management systems such as scientific research, educational affairs, assets, and personnel. Its purpose is to support the daily operation of various business in colleges and universities, transform offline work into online services, improve working efficiency, and improve users' experience. Smart campus is the construction goal of colleges and universities at present. It integrates advanced technologies such as Internet of Things, big data and artificial intelligence to improve service quality, enrich teaching means and improve decision-making methods.

2 Present situation of construction

The network information center of Shaanxi Normal University began to explore and try the construction of big data in colleges and universities in the second half of 2014. The construction content includes two parts: big data platform and analysis modeling system of business data. The construction ideas mainly focus on the collection, storage, analysis and visualization of structured and semi-structured data generated by various business systems throughout the school. The purpose of the construction is to provide objective data support for the school's scientific research, teaching, management, and services.

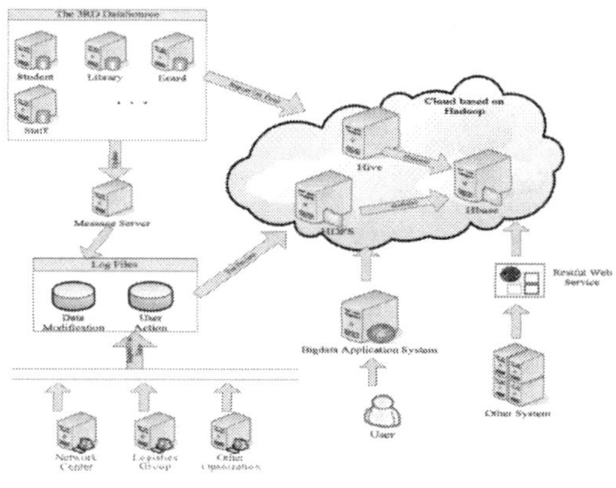

Figure 1. Platform Architecture

In the construction of big data platform, a big data management platform is built with Cloudera 5.9 (open source system) on 20 physical servers, with a total storage capacity of 300TB (Figure 1). On this basis, Sqoop and Linux script are used to collect data and HDFS and Hbase are used to store data. Besides, Mpp cluster and Redis cluster are used to store real-time data and hotspot data. MapReduce and Spark are used to analyze data while Spring MVC and Echarts provide a visual representation of the data. The big data platform has access to data for a total of 12 business systems. This includes personnel system, scientific research system, educational administration system, graduate management system, employment system, one-card system, book lending system, library access control system, dormitory access control system, wireless network management system, network authentication system, online behavior management system. At present, the platform supports the division of authority according to five roles: system administrator, school administrator, department/college administrator, instructor, teacher and student. The data and statistical analysis results stored in the platform can be used for external data sharing services in the form of API.

3 Typical application

The analysis modeling system of business data realizes decision support module for business departments and personal data center for teachers and students of the whole school. Moreover, it realizes the early warning module for student management and the heat map of campus wireless network for network management.

1. Decision support module establishes models by setting analysis indexes for different business systems. It uses a variety of statistical reports to visualize the model. The most commonly used report components are bar charts, line charts, and scatter charts. The bar chart is mainly used for the horizontal comparison of indexes in the model between different colleges. The line chart is mainly used as a vertical comparison of the indexes in the model at different time points (ie, showing the trend of development). The scatter chart is mainly used to analyze the correlation between the two indexes when modeling across business systems. Currently, the established models mainly include:

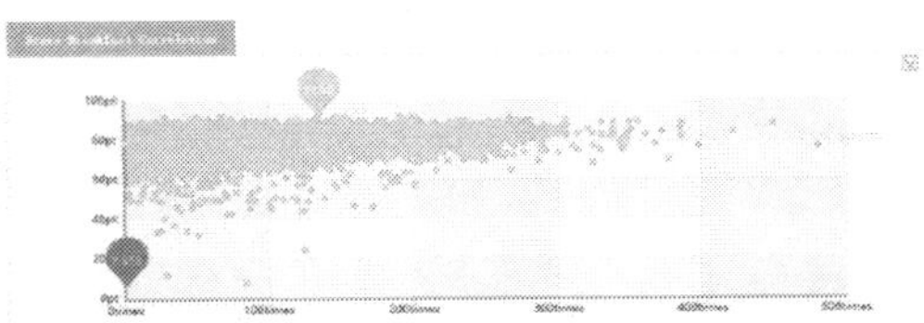

Figure 2. Breakfast frequency-score

Correlation analysis of students' breakfast frequency and test scores (Figure 2);

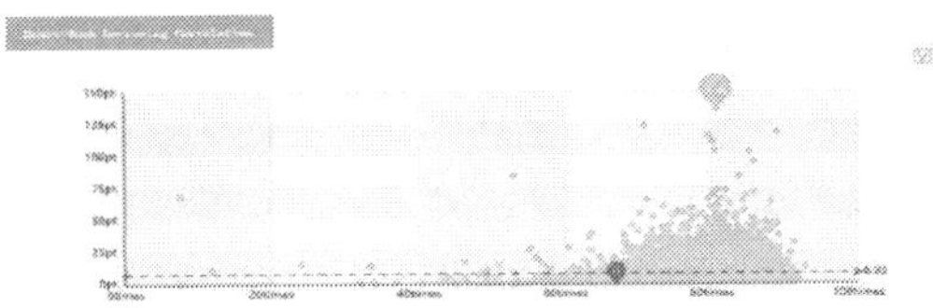

Figure 3. Book borrowing-score

Correlation analysis of the times of student's book borrowing and test scores (Figure 3);

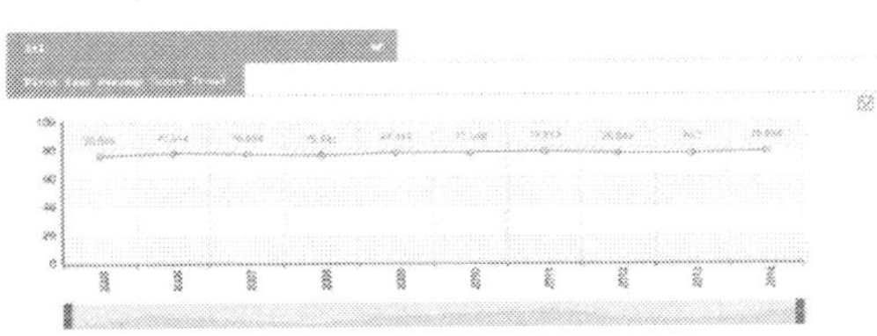

Figure 4. Freshmen average score trend

Quality analysis of undergraduate freshmen (Figure 4);

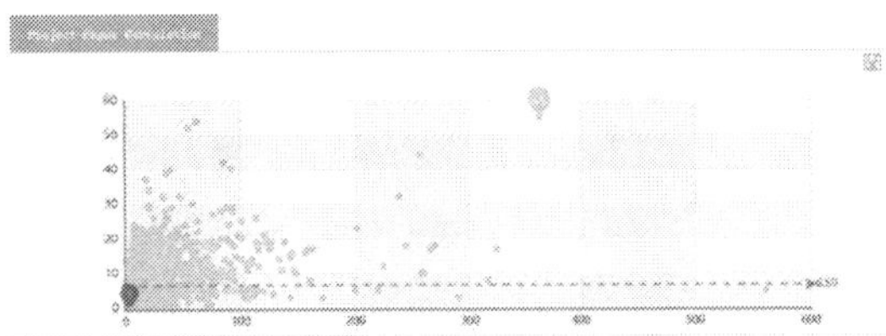

Figure 5. Project-paper

Correlation analysis of the number of teachers' projects and papers (Figure 5);

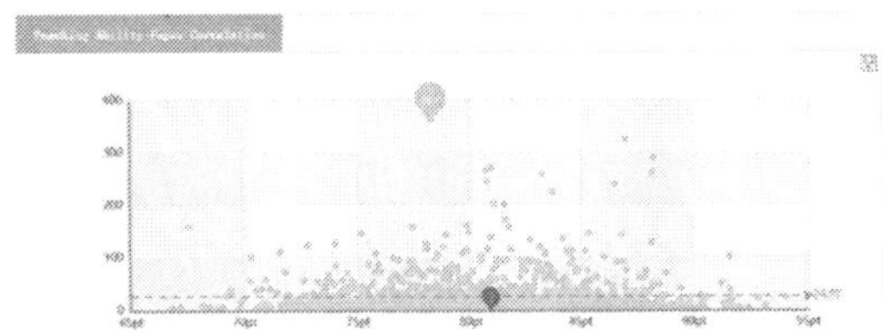

Figure 6. Teaching ability-paper

Correlation analysis of teachers' teaching ability and the number of papers (Figure 6);

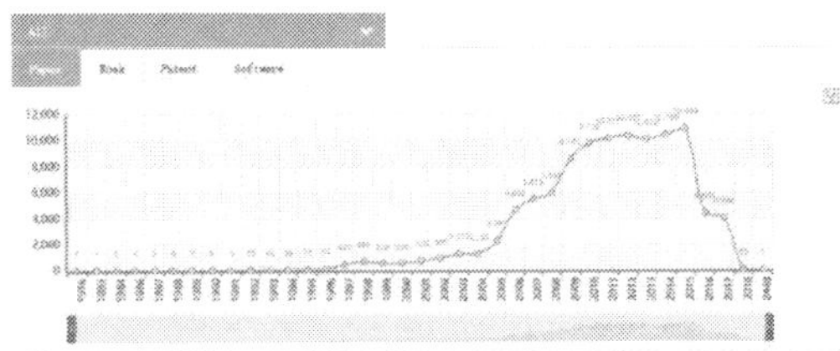

Figure 7. Scientific research trend

Development trend analysis of scientific research achievements of the whole university and various colleges (Figure 7);

Comparison of the number of scientific research achievements between different colleges;

Automatic generation of quality analysis report of the annual employment;

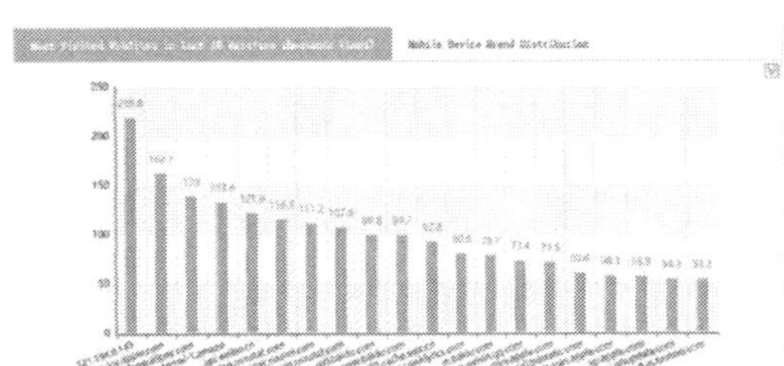

Figure 8. Popular website

Analysis of popular website of on-campus visits (Figure 8);

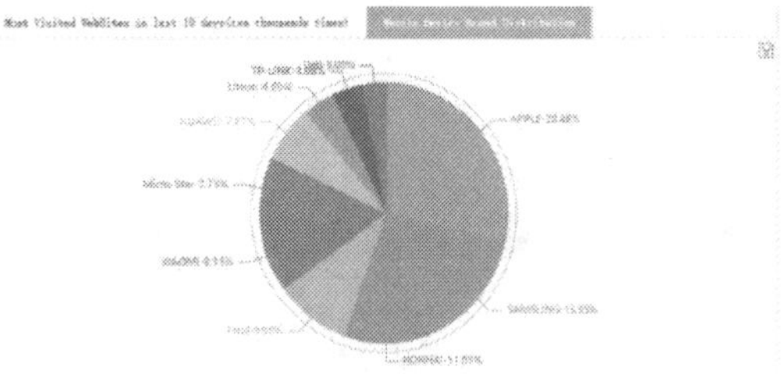

Figure 9. Brand distribution

Distribution of mobile devices' brand used by staffs and students (Figure 9).

Combined statistical analysis of the attributes of basic information of teachers (Basic information attributes of teachers include: Native place, college, gender, professional title, education background, age, category, time of admission);

Combined statistical analysis of the attributes of basic information of students (Basic information attributes of students include: Native place, college, gender, nationality, enrollment time);

2. The personal data center is a page that aggregates the basic information of the teacher or student and various types of school data and displays the portraits. Teachers and students do not need to log in to each business system separately to view separately.

After logging in, teachers can see their personal basic information, course setting, scientific research results, one-card consumption, device online behavior and other data. In addition, teachers can also see portraits based on their teaching ability, scientific research ability, consumption ability and awards.

After logging in, students can see their personal basic information, course arrangement, test results, one-card consumption, online behavior of devices, library borrowing and other data. Moreover, they can also see portraits according to their learning ability, consumption ability, time spent online, social activity ability and award.

3. Early warning of students is an attempt in student management. At present, it mainly makes early warning for poor students and suspected non-return early warning, which can provide a basis for the grant and student safety management.

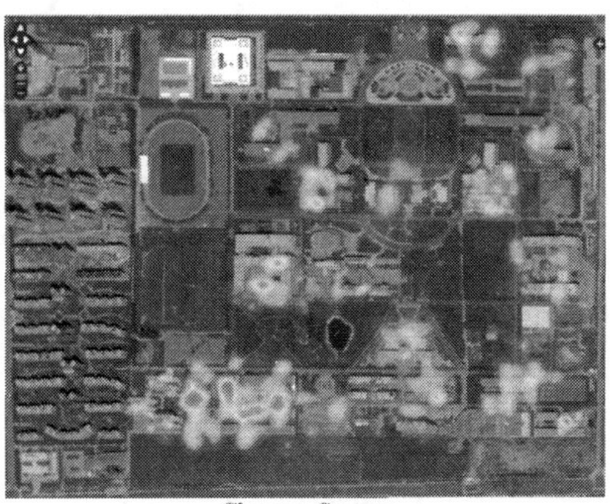

Changan Campus

Yanta Campus

Figure 10. Wireless network heatmap

4. Campus wireless network heat map (Figure 10) is a real-time heat map of campus mobile devices distributed by correlating the data of wireless network management system and authentication system. It can show in real time the degree of people's density distributed in the school, and what equipment is available in every building, floor and room on the Internet. Through further analysis of the heat map, it is possible to diagnose whether the distribution of wireless hot-spots in schools is reasonable, to grasp the trajectory of each student and the places that they often go, for monitoring the safety of students who are focused on.

4 Conclusion

Big data technology can effectively integrate the data generated by the existing business systems of colleges and universities within the scope of the whole university. Through data correlation analysis, we can mine the core value of data, provide deep information value-added services for college teachers and students, and provide data support for scientific management and decision-making in colleges and universities. Finally, we will transform the data into school benefits, improve management efficiency, promote the quality of scientific research, teaching and service, and enhance the comprehensive competitiveness of schools.

References

1. Wu Yakun, Guo Haixu, Wang Xiaoming. Research Overview on Big Data Technology I [J]. Journal of Liaoning University (Natural Sciences Edition), 2015, 03 (8): 236-242.
2. CAO Chuang. The Present Situation and Countermeasures of the Development of Management Information System in Colleges and Universities [J]. Education Teaching Forum, 2018, 47 (4): 12-13.
3. Tand Kailin. A Brief Analysis of Digital Campus Construction and Application [J]. China Computer & Communication, 2018, 20 (4): 237-238.
4. Yang Long. Research on university informationization service based on big data and artificial intelligence [J]. Experimental Technology and Management, 2018, 35 (11): 153-156.

AUTHOR INDEX